FRANK SWIFT

MANCHESTER CITY AND ENGLAND LEGEND

FRANK SWIFT

MANCHESTER CITY AND ENGLAND LEGEND

MARK METCALF

DB
PUBLISHING

First published in Great Britain in 2013 by DB Publishing, an imprint of JMD Meida Ltd

ISBN 978-1-78091-200-4

Printed and bound by Copytech (UK) Ltd, Peterborough.

Contents

Introduction   7

Chapter 1   Growing up in Blackpool   9

Chapter 2   Signing for Fleetwood   14

Chapter 3   The Maine Road to fame   19

Chapter 4   A regular first-team place   26

Chapter 5   FA Cup Final success   37

Chapter 6   First full League season and getting married   45

Chapter 7   Building a title challenging team and winning a first
             representative honour   53

Chapter 8   Champions   63

Chapter 9   Charity Shield success and relegation   77

Chapter 10   No quick return   88

Chapter 11   Wartime football   90

Chapter 12   Playing for England   115

Chapter 13   Touring with England in post-war Europe   128

Chapter 14   The return of competitive football   133

Chapter 15   Promotion at the second attempt   138

Chapter 16   Full England honours and captaining his country   144

Chapter 17   Back in the big time   160

Chapter 18   The final hurrah   168

Chapter 19   Brief return before new career dawns   173

Chapter 20   Munich 1958   177

Frank Swift statistics   186

Bibliography   187

Acknowledgements   189

Introduction

Frank Swift is one of the greatest English goalkeepers of all time. A First and Second Division, FA Cup and Charity Shield winner with Manchester City, his only League club, he represented his country on 33 occasions between 1941 and 1949.

At 6ft 2in, and with massive hands, Swift, who began his career with Fleetwood Town, made it his business to dominate the penalty area in a constant battle with some of the game's most feared forwards such as Dixie Dean, Tommy Lawton, Trevor Ford and Billy Liddell.

Although often injured, and on many occasions knocked unconscious, Blackpool born Swift was fearless and unmoveable in the City goal, playing all but one of over 200 games from the day of his debut, 25 December 1933, up to the start of World War Two.

By then he had won the League in 1936-37, three years after fainting at the end of the 1934 FA Cup Final victory against Portsmouth, 2-1. Revived, the emotionally drained youngster then marched up the Wembley steps to be congratulated by King George V who told him 'well done, you played well'.

Debuting for England during the war he was a member of the XI that thrashed Scotland 8-0 at Maine Road in 1943, a side, containing Matthews, Carter, Mercer and Cullis that Swift rated as the finest he ever played with.

When competitive football resumed, Swift was a regular between the posts for England, and in 1948 was honoured by becoming the first 'keeper to captain his country in the professional era when he played brilliantly in one of the country's greatest ever performances, a 4-0 success against Italy in Turin. By then he had refined his throwing and kicking skills to a fine art, helping to turn defence into attack in an instant. No wonder the likes of Tom Finney rate him as England's greatest 'keeper.

Fans too also adored Swift for his sportsmanship, broad smile and constant banter with spectators behind his goal. Autograph hunters and star-struck youngsters were guaranteed to be charmed by a man who enjoyed his football and the stardom it brought with it.

After helping Manchester City to regain their place in the top flight by winning Division Two in 1946-47, Swift retired two seasons later after playing over 500 games for the club, a figure which would have been exceeded if not for the war. In his absence City slipped back into Division Two.

Successful on the pitch, 'big Frank', always cheerful away from it, became a big success off it with a career in journalism at the *News of the World*. Flying home, with ex-teammate Matt Busby, after covering the Red Star Belgrade –

Manchester United European Cup tie he was one of eight journalists tragically killed at Munich in February 1958.

Forty years later in 1998, Swift was one of four City legends named in the Football League 100 legends selected to celebrate 100 seasons of League football. Long gone – but never forgotten – it was a wonderful honour for a great man and a great goalkeeper. Now in the first biography to be written on him, find out more about the 'keeper and his exploits.

Chapter 1
Growing up in Blackpool

The man who became one of the world's greatest goalkeepers started life in humble surroundings. Frank Victor Swift was born at 33 Ibbison Street, Blackpool on Friday 26 December 1913 to labourer Frederick Swift and Jane Cornall.

World War One storm clouds were approaching and this probably explains why his parents were married in Preston on 5 December 1914, as it meant the newly appointed corporal in the Seaforth Highlanders would be entitled to an allowance as a married soldier. This was increased on 15 March 1915 to 21s (£1.05) for a wife and two children, with an extra 2s (10p) for each additional child. This was at a time when average male earnings were around 31s (£1.55) a week, bacon cost 1s (5p) a lb, a loaf of bread 6d (2.5p) and a lb of potatoes 4d (2p).

At number 37 Ibbison Street lived grandfather Cuthbert Cornall and uncle Frank Victor Cornall, after whom the newborn was named. The boy was the unmarried couple's fourth child with Fred [born in Oldham] the first to arrive in 1907, Elizabeth in 1910 and John in 1912. Sadly, Frank's sister died in 1911 and he would have grown up with no knowledge of his youngest brother as he died on 14 June 1914. His half brother Cuthbert Cornall, born in 1904 and also living at number 33 did, though, play a big part in Frank's life.

In later years further tragedy was to strike when Fred Swift senior died aged 49 on 21 August 1921. Then followed the birth in 1921 of twins Alice and Arnold, the latter failing to survive into his second year. Six years later Frank's mother [better known as Jinnie] gave birth to Frank's half-brother Alfred H. Swift, who grew up never knowing his father.

Fred Swift senior was buried in Layton Cemetery on Talbot Road in Blackpool, where his son Arnold and Jinnie [who died in December 1944 aged 58] later joined him.

Frank's mother came from a Blackpool family stretching back to at least the start of the 19th century and in 1871 40-year-old Cuthbert Cornall, a boatman, was living with his wife Eliza at 33 Bonny Street. Their son, also named Cuthbert was born in 1862 and after marrying Elizabeth Ellen the couple became parents to Jinnie in 1884.

The Swift family originated from Grimsargh near Preston and Frank Swift's grandfather, a fire wood hawker, lived at 8 Skiffington Road North, Fishwick, Preston in 1881. Their third son, Fred was born in 1872 and married in 1900 only for his wife to die shortly afterwards.

Frank Swift's home just off the busy Central Drive was almost equal distance between Blackpool's world famous 518ft tall Tower and Bloomfield Road, home to Blackpool FC, then of Division Two. By the time he was a strapping youngster the future England 'keeper could probably have run to both in under five minutes, although only if he avoided the passing trams; these incidentally, would eventually take him to Fleetwood, where he was, for a brief period, to play reserve team football.

The stables that were used to house donkeys from the nearby beach meant Ibbison Street was known as 'the Donkey Men's Street'. It was a rough, working-class road in the Revoe district of Blackpool. Nearby streets might have had cake shops, fish parlours and restaurants, chemists, hairdressers, sweet and Blackpool rock shops but Revoe's attractions for those who lived there were its low rents.

Development of the area only began in the late 1860s when, because it was outside the Local Corporation's jurisdiction, developers were attracted because they could ignore building and sanitary regulations and not pay rates.

The Corporation was to eventually annex the land and by the early 1890s large property magnates James Ward and the brothers Thomas and Henry Brown collectively owned close to 250 properties between them. In 1901 the district had the largest population density in Blackpool at 131 per acre, a figure that rose considerably during the busy summer months when overcrowding would have meant increasing levels of squalor and deprivation.

Revoe was close enough to the gas works, first established in 1852, that the smell permeated the whole atmosphere. As a trading concern it passed to the Corporation in 1869 and under the management of three generations of the Chew family – John, William and John – it proved to be one of their most successful trading concerns with £538,767 taken in profits to relieve rates between 1869 and 1939.

The gas was mainly for domestic use as Blackpool was almost entirely residential with only a few light industries such as biscuit, sweet and toffee making. Frank Swift was to work at the gasworks when he left school, running out also for/the local works team.

Revoe, and especially Ibbison Street, were what might be described as rowdy. During World War One neighbour Margaret Eleanor Ogden summonsed Frank's mother, and another neighbour Bessie Wilkinson, to the Police Court alleging assault. The complainant alleged that Jinnie had dragged her from her house and after passing Ogden's baby daughter to a little girl had then allowed Mrs Wilkinson to strike her on the face. Two children backed up the complainant before the defendants called rebutting evidence. The case was dismissed by the magistrates when Police Constable

Potter said he had seen the complainant using abusive language and reported: 'she suffers from delusions, and is very hysterical'.

Local lad, the late Alan Stott, who became the first from the area to go to Cambridge University wrote that 'after one brawl a man had to send for a doctor. He shouted through the letterbox "Quick, a gentleman from Ibbison Street has been injured." Back came the reply "There are no gentlemen in Ibbison Street."'

Before the NHS, local doctors were only called for in a real emergency. Consequently, Jinnie Swift delivered the new born and laid out the dead before the arrival of the undertaker.

There was though a strong community spirit. Women ensured the front steps were kept scrupulously clean, while small flagged back yards were a haven where on an evening dads could be found mending shoes and in which most families kept a few hens as an extra egg or two was always welcome. A coal shed and outside toilet completed the layout.

Monday was washday and bread making on coal-fired ovens was a daily necessity. For those who missed there was Sam Womack's bakery. This was owned by the uncle of City fan Geoff Ireland, who recalls being told how 'Swift as a lad came into the shop for a loaf and his hands were so big you couldn't see the bread when he picked it up'.

Local clothing clubs to rig kids out for school were popular, while the Police Chief Constable also had a fund that would supply vouchers for applicants for school uniforms.

Every May Day the Maypole was carried round the streets by youngsters from Revoe School, where Frank Swift became a pupil after the end of World War One.

As Bloomfield Road is visible from the school it's perhaps no surprise that some local youngsters fancied playing there! Blackpool first did so in 1899 and took up permanent residence two years later. Yaggie 'Harry' Read lived at 45 Ibbison Street and scored on his League debut in a 2-2 draw with Grimsby Town on 26 October 1907. He played 31 League and FA Cup games for Blackpool and scored three goals.

More than two decades later Frank Swift's elder brother, Fred made his League debut for Blackpool as an amateur in a 2-1 defeat at Millwall on 6 April 1929. Fred signed as a professional for the 1929-30 season but remained just one year before moving on to Dick Kerr's of Preston, Chorley, Oldham Athletic, Bolton Wanderers, Shrewsbury Town and Swansea Town. It was reported Blackpool were keen on signing Frank during Fred's time at the club but that their mother did not want the two to be in direct competition.

Football too also ran in the Eastham family blood. Three brothers from the Revoe district, Billy, Harry and George, all played for Blackpool with the latter, the father of George junior who went on to play for Arsenal and to represent England, being the most famous although he originally joined Bolton Wanderers and only returned to Blackpool in 1938 after playing for England against the Netherlands in 1935.

Blackpool's record appearance holder and most capped England international, former captain Jimmy Armfield, also went to Revoe school, where during World War Two he played little football as there were no balls to play with. Jimmy won 43 England caps and was voted the best right-back in the world at the 1962 World Cup Finals.

Sadly, the details of Frank's time at Revoe School are not well recorded. The 1918 Education Act raised the school leaving age from 12 to 14 and abolished all fees in state elementary schools, the cost for this being born by central government as it sought to foster increased professionalism among teachers by improving pay and pensions. Major cuts in public expenditure during the economic depression of the 1920s were to prevent further radical changes until after World War Two. Frank Swift's education would have been basic with a strong concentration on the four R's – reading, writing, arithmetic and religion.

He had, at a very early age, decided he liked playing in goal when any game was organised, be it with jumpers for goalposts or wooden posts. Naturally right-footed, he turned to using his left when he broke it 'in a goalmouth tussle', and this may explain why when he was photographed as part of a Revoe School team that won an (unidentified) Shield in 1924-25 he was playing at left-half with Moss Parker, who later owned a rock (confectionery) shop in Blackpool, in goal.

It is known that at school Frank enjoyed physical education – he got involved in most sports really – and at a relatively young age he was often seen practising his goalkeeping technique with a heavy medicine ball of around 14in in diameter and weighing 5-6lb. Using one of these certainly built up the muscles in his arms and shoulders, and already blessed with huge hands, he could quite easily hold one of these balls in one palm as well as throwing it out a fair distance.

Towards the end of his time at school Frank was playing at weekends for his school and also for a local junior club. He often turned out in two games on the Saturday, one in the morning, one in the afternoon. Years later he recalled that one weekend he saved three penalties and also scored a goal – with one almighty punt down field on a very bumpy, bouncy pitch.

On leaving school at aged 14, he had a number of odd jobs before signing on at Blackpool Gasworks as a coke-keeper. In his 1948 autobiography *Football in the Goalmouth* the 'keeper recalled: 'that occupied five days of the week. On the sixth day I played football for the Gasworks team, and on the seventh talked about it.' When time allowed the 'keeper also represented Revoe Young Men's Christian Association. (YMCA)

Meanwhile during the summer weekends and evenings he began assisting his brother Fred, and other relations, with the sail boat *The Skylark* that they ran from Blackpool beach between the North and South piers. It was here he met his wife, Doris, one of many romances on sands that stretch for over seven miles, and which drew thousands of working class tourists following the building of the first rail link to the town in 1846.

A family day out with bucket and spade, or a relaxing stroll was a welcome relief from a day in the factory or down the pit. When in autumn the weather became less hospitable there was the added attraction of the Illuminations that were introduced in 1879 to decorate the promenade. Seventeen years later, Blackpool Pleasure Beach was opened, an amusement park that drew visitors like a magnet especially when in 1904 the Flying Machines were added. Still operating today, this stunning piece of engineering must have amazed visitors of the early 20th century.

Frank Swift's birthplace was a place of fun, and his outgoing personality was a clear reflection of everything good about it. If the 'keeper had been around today the advertising world would select him as one of Blackpool's figureheads.

Chapter 2
Signing for Fleetwood

His confidence high from playing well for the Gasworks side Frank Swift 'wrote to Fleetwood FC asking for a trial'. (*Football from the Goalmouth*) The following Saturday he was delighted to receive a letter inviting him for a trial. The only problem was that it was that afternoon. Dashing home he mistakenly took his brother Fred's boots, which he never returned.

Watching the trial was the Fleetwood club chairman, Eddie Johnston, and he signed the 17-year-old as an amateur in time to play in the 1931-32 season. Frank's new club was just seven miles from home. Formed in 1908, the club had won the Lancashire Combination League in 1923-24, which is where the first team continued to play their matches when he joined the Trawlermen.

The small coastal town of 25,000 people had, at the time, a thriving fishing industry with around 9,000 employed. The 1930s were to see the town's golf course, Model Yacht Pond and Marine Hall entertainment complex all open as its sea front was developed to encourage visitors who found Blackpool's brashness a little too daunting. In 1927 a huge flood that put 90 per cent of it under water had hit the town.

Too scared to play
Swift was selected to make his debut for Fleetwood reserves in a West Lancashire League (formed in 1904) match at home to Westhoughton on 29 August 1931.

There is no record of the attendance that day at Fleetwood's North Euston ground – located directly behind the North Euston Hotel that is still standing today. It was certainly a lot less than many of the crowds the Blackpool lad subsequently played in front of during his football career. In the event though, it was still too big for the nervous frightened teenager. He was feeling 'indisposed', reported the *Fleetwood Chronicle*, and he took fright. With usual right-back Mark Fawley taking over, and playing well in goal, the home side lost 3-1 with Cookson scoring for Fleetwood. The result set up Westhoughton for a fine season, as they were to finish as League Champions at the end of it.

Debut
It was not for another three weeks before the 'not so big' Frank Swift made his debut. This was on Wednesday 23 September 1931 when he lined up for Fleetwood Reserves in a West Lancashire Cup round one tie against Blackburn Rovers A (third) side. The away XI included former Fleetwood reserve 'keeper

Bill Gormlie, who after the war coached Anderlecht and Belgium. The match took place at the North Euston Ground.

Fleetwood reserves: Swift, Kirkpatrick, Wright, Atkinson, unknown, unknown, Walsh, Yeardley, Dell, Butcher, Tyler.

The home side were ahead after 15 minutes when Tyler, formerly of Fleetwood Corinthians, raced down the wing and, when he centred, Yeardley headed home.

The Fleetwood 'keeper – perhaps he was still a little anxious – then made a mistake by carrying the ball for too long in his box. From Bob Morris's indirect free-kick, Swift appeared to have secured the ball only for it to slip away to leave Cort with a simple equalising opportunity.

The game though was to finish in success, Tyler crossing for Dell to make it 2-1 before Yeardley made it 3-1 after Gormlie saved Butcher's hard shot. The Rovers 'keeper then made a great save when Walsh almost converted a free-kick but 'not that the Blackburn goalkeeper absorbed all the limelight for at the other end Swift made a really wonderful save in the second half.' (*Fleetwood Chronicle*)

Three days later Swift finally made his West Lancashire League debut, playing against Barnoldswick Park Villa on the North Euston ground.

Fleetwood Reserves: Swift, Kirkpatrick, Wright, Atkinson, Dickinson, Thompson, Shannon, Haydock, Butcher, Tyler.

Barnoldswick Park Villa: Botrill, Upley, Connelley, Wylie, Miller, Broughton, Stanworth, Reed, Smith, Melling, Ainsworth.

Referee: H. Hartley of Bolton

Fleetwood reserves were to go down to defeat by five goals to three. Swift was kept busy throughout the entire 90 minutes and had no chance with the first goal when an unmarked Ainsworth headed home at the far post. The 'keeper though was at fault for the second when his attempts to reach a centre were unsuccessful and left Ainsworth with a simple header. As half-time approached Swift made a scrambling save from Smith and although Fleetwood rallied to make it 3-4 a late hat-trick goal for Ainsworth deservedly gave the visitors both points.

After his mistakes in the first two games, the youngster had to wait till his 18th birthday before being selected for his third match in the reserves who, prior to the Boxing Day game at home to Nelson reserves, had won six and lost six of their 15 League matches. The 'keeper was beaten just once when Bernasconi equalised an early Howorth goal. He had little to do after this as Fleetwood won easily, 8-1.

It was another two months before he was back between the posts as Fleetwood reserves narrowly beat Prescot Cables reserves 2-1 at home in the Richardson Cup second round. Swift earned deserved applause when he made a neat save to push away Boult's point-blank shot and the *Fleetwood Chronicle* match report also makes mention of two further fine saves; he also enjoyed a touch of fortune when twice Boult hit shots against the crossbar.

This time there was to be a much shorter wait for a next appearance. On 12 March 1932 Swift played in a 1-1 draw at home to Darwen reserves whose side included Welsh schoolboy internationals Sullivan and Robinson, who only weeks earlier had played in the Darwen side beaten by Arsenal in the FA Cup.

Swift resisted a challenge by Cuthbert on him and then close to the interval he 'cleverly held a high shot from Smith'. Penalised for carrying the ball he was grateful when his defenders blocked Cuthbert's shot and a fine game ended level.

The following Saturday he played his sixth game – all at home – against Preston North End A in the Richardson Cup semi-final. The away side included Simmons, who had played in the Preston first team, and who opened the scoring and then later missed an open goal before Haydock equalised to make it 1-1 at the break.

When play resumed Swift 'was fortunate to block Nixon's close-range shot with his body' but 'then twice within a minute Swift saved dangerous shots' (*Fleetwood Chronicle*) and when Butcher headed a fine goal the match ended amid great enthusiasm with the home side having won 2-1.

Best player

The following weekend, Swift retained his place as the reserves travelled to face Barnoldswick Park Villa. The away side took a point in a 2-2 draw in which the young 'keeper was the outstanding player on the pitch with the *Fleetwood Chronicle* headlining his 'brilliant work in goal' and highlighting his fine play in the few minutes before half-time.

Fleetwood reserves also scored twice in the following game at Calderstones but they were routed 8-2. It would have been many more but Swift turned Mayo's shot round the post, prevented Robertson from scoring when the home forward was sent clear and made two other fine saves, including a brave sprawling dive to block Hayton's shot from close to the goalline. 2-1 down at the interval Fleetwood collapsed in the second period.

Without a league fixture the following weekend, Swift played in a 5-2 home friendly success against Hinsford before Fleetwood reserves beat Lancaster Town reserves 2-1 at home in the West Lancs League. Although Fleetwood were behind at the interval goals by Yates and Butcher gave them both points at the end of the match, denying their opponents a place at the top of the table. Swift, reported *the Chronicle*, was 'cool in goal'.

Playing away to Burnley A, Swift played competently, twice diving at Lawson's feet to prevent a goal, before the Burnley centre-forward scored twice as Fleetwood reserves went down 2-0.

Losing Cup finalist

On 7 May 1932 he was selected to play for Fleetwood reserves against Darwen reserves in the Richardson Cup Final. The game was played at Chorley FC, where his brother Fred has just completed his first season – of two – with the Lancashire Combination side.

Fred's younger brother's side were given a great chance to take the lead but Almond missed a penalty. Then on 35 minutes Frank Swift did well to block an advancing Shaw. However, when the ball ran loose the Darwen centre-forward was quickest to it and scored what ultimately proved to be the winning goal. That was harsh on the losing side that, especially in the second period, were the better side and only desperate Darwen defending prevented an equaliser.

At the end of the game Mr F. Hargreaves of host club Chorley handed the Cup to Darwen and congratulated the winners. If Frank Swift was disappointed he had the consolation of knowing that in his first season he had played 12 times for Fleetwood reserves. The standard of football was a good one and this was a fine record for someone so young. What is also apparent from the match reports is that his form was improving as the season progressed.

With Clitheroe Reserves, Whittingham and Leyland Motors having joined over the summer, then the West Lancs League would provide a heavier and more attractive fixture list for Frank Swift in 1932-33. In the opening fixture at Atherton against the Bolton Wanderers A side only Swift and Winstanley of the previous season's Fleetwood side were included.

The Fleetwood 'keeper was quickly called into action. He did well to punch away a Hudson shot, before being powerless to prevent the Bolton inside-right making it 1-0 after 10 minutes. Two second half goals added to the home side's advantage as Fleetwood went down 3-0.

On August Bank Holiday Monday Fleetwood Reserves easily beat new boys Whittingham 6-2 at home. They then beat Preston North End A 5-3 in a fine match in which a first half mistake by Swift gave the away side a 2-1 lead at the interval. Having made fine saves from Mann and Kerr the Fleetwood 'keeper needed treatment after suffering a second half injury in a game where home centre-forward Taylor scored a hat-trick. Fleetwood recovered from going behind three times to grab both points.

The following weekend Fleetwood Reserves rose to third in the League with a comfortable 2-0 victory at Nelson Reserves and then won for the fourth consecutive match as Darwen Reserves were beaten 2-1 in the West Lancashire Cup first round. The home 'keeper made a diving save to deny an unmarked Dewhurst and later in the game 'saved well' as a Pye goal took Fleetwood through.

Back in the League a 2-1 success at Westhoughton made it eight points from 10. In a free-flowing game Swift was kept busy, especially after the home side reduced the arrears with 15 minutes remaining.

After such a good win there was disappointment when on 1 October 1932, Calderstones took home a point in a 2-2 draw at North Euston. It might have been worse for the home side but Swift made a number of good saves – 'scrambling the ball away in a remarkable fashion two or three times when Calderstones appeared likely to score'. (*Fleetwood Chronicle*) Mayho finally beat him on 82 minutes for what ultimately proved to be the final goal he conceded for Fleetwood.

As to the exact circumstances in which Frank Swift came to be playing for the Manchester City A [or thirds] the following weekend we shall never know. It was reported years later that he had been approached by a stranger impressed at his displays for Fleetwood. In his autobiography the 'keeper wrote 'Mr Jimmy Haslam, who is now a director of Blackpool, heard that Manchester City were interested in goalkeepers, and took me through to Maine Road'. What is certain is Fleetwood had no idea he was unavailable to play for them on 8 October 1932 – a game they lost 3-2 to Barnoldswick with N. Greenwood, previously of Blackpool North End in goal – because on 11 October 1932 club secretary Harold Colley wrote City a complaint letter.

In his reply, dated the following day City manager Wilf Wild wrote 'I am very sorry to hear of the trouble you were put to in order to find a substitute for him. The question of being reimbursed for the cost of the taxi (for Greenwood) I will have to mention to my Board. We have again selected Swift to play in our A team for Saturday and you may rest assured that if the lad makes good, your club will not be forgotten.'

In fact the last word proved to be exactly what did happen when Frank Swift signed for City as the Division One side sent Fleetwood just £10 10s. Even then it was only posted after he had already played more than half a dozen first team games.

Swift departed having made the following appearances for Fleetwood reserves: West Lancs League 13, West Lancs Cup 2, Richardson Cup 3 and 1 friendly. Total – 19.

Despite the circumstances in which he departed Fleetwood Frank Swift was grateful to the club and at the time of his death in February 1958 the *Blackpool Gazette* reported that: 'Former club secretary Mr Harold Colley recalls the time when Fleetwood signed his brother Fred in the first season after the war, and then replaced him with another young goalkeeper. Frank brought one of his international jerseys along to Fleetwood for the youngster to wear in his first match.'

Chapter 3
The Maine Road to fame

The headline in the *Manchester Evening News* of 8 October 1932 said simply 'SWIFT DEATH'. Nineteen miners at Plank Lane Colliery, Leigh, had died when the cage carrying them underground had crashed through the girders at the bottom and into the sump hole. One man, Robert Kilshaw of Golborne had survived after hauling himself through the cage doors and jumping free. Kilshaw had led a charmed life having already been buried under a heavy coal fall, wounded in World War One and been at the point of death from pneumonia. Working-class life in the 1930s was harsh, could Frank Swift make a better life for himself by becoming a top-class professional footballer?

His debut that afternoon for City's third team against Stockport County thirds took place on a bitterly cold, dark, dank afternoon when hardly anybody turned up to watch. The game was the second of the season between the sides after City won an opening day fixture 6-2. Before kick-off the away side lay mid-table in the 14-team Manchester League that was to be won by Droylsden at the end of the season. City was to finish sixth.

Reporting on a 6-1 success, the *Manchester Evening Chronicle* reported the A's had made the best display of the season so far with two goals each from Percival and Crawshaw. Bird had scored for County in a rare breakaway.

Brilliant save sets seal on deal
Swift had little opportunity to show his skills but on 70 minutes County broke away and their inside-right Harry Watson fired in a real ripsnorter. The 'keeper, positioning himself splendidly, went up with insolent, lazy grace and caught the ball as if his mother had thrown him the tea-cloth to wipe up the cups and saucers! It was on that one save alone that Manchester City made up their minds about 'Swifty'.

That didn't mean though that they were going to pay him a great deal. Ten shillings (50p) a week as a part-time professional footballer was the offer and as this was less than he was getting at the coke works his mother was unimpressed. Mr Hughes junior, the son of the City chairman, was sent to Blackpool and only after some persuasion was it agreed that her son could sign for Manchester City. Frank Swift was registered as a professional footballer on 16 November 1932. The new man was confident of doing well as he had already gained a commitment that he would get 20s (£1) if he made the first team. Within two seasons he was on top wages, where he remained throughout his career.

Swift's new club had been formed in 1880 as St Mark's (West Gorton) and as Ardwick AFC entered the Football League as founding members of the Second Division in 1892.

Financial troubles two seasons later led to a reorganisation and a new name, Manchester City Football Club. After gaining promotion in 1899, City went on to claim their first major honour when they beat Bolton Wanderers 1-0 in the 1904 FA Cup Final played at the Crystal Palace, London. Billy Meredith, one of the finest footballers ever, scored the winning goal before a crowd of 61,374.

The winners, though, were to lose Meredith, and three of his colleagues, transferred to Manchester United in 1906 after the club were found guilty of making 'under the counter' payments that breached the maximum wage regulations of the day and for which 17 players were suspended. This was to tip the balance of power in Manchester, with United going on to win the League in 1907-08 and 1910-11 and matching City's Cup achievement by beating Bristol City 1-0, courtesy of a goal from transferred City forward Sandy Turnbull, in the 1909 FA Cup Final.

Neither Manchester side, though, were to rival Huddersfield Town in the 1920s, the Terriers winning the League three years running from 1924-26. In 1926, though, City did again reach the FA Cup Final, which by this time had moved to Wembley Stadium. Again they faced Bolton Wanderers, but this time the roles were reversed as the Trotters won 1-0. To make matters worse, the losing finalists lost their final League game of the season, away to Newcastle United, and were relegated.

Despite this misfortune Manchester City were a club on the rise. In 1923 they had moved from a cramped Hyde Road to a new ground, Maine Road, with a capacity of 80,000. Larger crowds meant more money and after a narrow miss in 1926-27, when Portsmouth squeezed up in second place with a 0.005 superior goal average, City returned to the top-flight after finishing Champions of the Second Division in 1927-28.

Manager Peter Hodge had strengthened the side with some important signings in Eric Brook, Fred Tilson and Bobby Marshall, players with whom Frank Swift was to enjoy success in the mid 1930s.

Hodge himself had left the club by then, moving back to his former club Leicester City in 1932. This saw Wilf Wild, the assistant at Manchester City since 1920; reluctantly take full control of team matters. If present day football managers think they have it tough it was whole lot more difficult back in the 1930s, when a manager was responsible for virtually every aspect of the day-to-day running of the club including the stadium. Wild was known on match days to rush from giving the brief team-talk to the tannoy system microphone to ask fans to move along in order to allow others to enter the terraces.

Wild would leave the training regime to a trainer, with training concentrated on keeping the players fit and away from the ball, the belief being that if they didn't see it during the week they'd be hungry for it at weekends.

In his first season, Wild did well and City returned to Wembley for a second time only to be fairly easily beaten 3-0 by Everton. Afterwards the manager attracted criticism over his decision to leave out Tilson, who had failed to convince club director and medic, Dr Bowling Holmes that he was fully fit to withstand the rigours of the heavy Wembley turf. Marshall deputised.

At the start of the 1933-34 season Frank Swift, aged 19, was offered much better terms by Wild and taken on as a full-time professional. Playing for the thirds he again performed with distinction. City were in mid-table and had, with the exception of eventual champions ICI, conceded the least amount of goals when only weeks before he was to end his teenage years he took over as goalkeeper to the second team, which was then playing in the Central League.

The first team had been doing well. Half-back Jimmy McMullan, who had captained Scotland when the 'Wembley Wizards' had crushed England 5-1 in 1928, had been allowed to move on after the Cup Final defeat to become Oldham Athletic's player-manager. That aside, Wilf Wild was confident that his side had it in them to challenge for greater honours and was prepared to largely stick by those who had done so well.

Regular 'keeper Len Langford, who had been signed from Nottingham Forest in June 1930, had missed the first match of the season but had enjoyed a 19-match run and when City beat Liverpool 2-1 in the 20th League game of the season they had taken 26 from a possible 40 points. A knee injury to Langford in the match saw Jimmy Nicholls return, for his second game of the season, in the away fixture at Molineux. It proved a difficult afternoon for him and after arriving just minutes before kick-off the away side were thrashed 8-0 with Wolves' Cuthbert Phillips scoring a hat-trick.

First team debut

City's next game was two days later, a Christmas Day fixture away to Derby County. Having just played his third Central League match (against Sheffield United in a 3-0 win), Swift was aware of the newspaper rumours of major changes to the City side, although few speculated on a new 'keeper and even on 30 December the *Manchester Evening News* ran a special profile piece on Nicholls, a former guardsman. A phone call from the manager on Christmas Eve confirmed Frank Swift was one of three changes from the Wolves match and that he was to get his first team chance just a day before he became 20.

The change happened so quickly that the 'keepers' name was listed in the reserve programme as playing against Birmingham City reserves on 25

December at Maine Road and it was to be missing from the following day's first-team match programme costing 2d (1p) for the return with Derby County.

Writing in his autobiography Swift recalls the excitement, 'What a Christmas Day it was. I really began to believe in Santa Claus when I reported to the Exchange Station to join the party for Derby. Everybody was very helpful and understanding at my nervous excitement, and I listened intently to all the advice this great bunch of lads handed out.'

Derby were one of the best sides of the 1930s and possessed a fine attack – it later being argued that an emphasis on scoring goals cost the Rams a first major trophy – and Swift was set for a baptism of fire.

    Derby County: Kirby, Cooper, Collin, Nicholas, Jessop, Keen, Crooks, Groves, Bowers, Ramage, Duncan

    City: Swift, Barnett, Corbett V., Busby, Marshall, Bray, Toseland, Herd, Gregory, Tilson, Brook

    Referee: Mr R. Bowie (Newcastle)

City, backed by a good number of fans, were to lose their second consecutive match, beaten 4-1. Derby's centre-forward Jack Bowers had finished as Division One's top scorer the previous season with 35 goals and he was to repeat the feat in 1933-34 with 34 goals. A powerful player he possessed two good feet and was a constant aerial threat.

Swift was unable to prevent Bowers from scoring and blamed himself for the opening two goals saying 'I did not keep my eye on the ball, because I was looking for Jack'. The 'keeper appears to have been a little too self-critical, as the first on four minutes saw the County attack rip apart the defence in front of him to leave 'the unmarked (Peter) Ramage with little difficulty in beating Swift'. (*Derby Evening Telegraph* 27 Dec 1933)

With the Rams wingers, England international Sammy Crookes and Scottish international Dally Duncan, a constant threat the away defence was given a torrid time and it was no surprise when Bowers made it 2-0. City's new 'keeper then made a fine save to deny the goal predator a second from a long-range effort. There was little Swift could do, though, when on the stroke of half-time Bowers made it 3-0 in a game watched by a then record Baseball Ground attendance of 32,786.

Bravery

On the restart a powerful shot by Ramage made it 4-0, but clearly determined to keep the score down Swift was in bravely at the feet of Bowers to prevent a fifth. For his sins he was knocked out, something that was to become a regular feature of the 'keeper's career over the next 15-16 years.

Leather football boots in the 1930s were much heavier than today, had metal studs or tacks hammered into the sole and contained a steel front toecap. A 'keeper kicked – accidentally or not – by a forward's boot was much more likely to be badly injured and/or knocked out. Only the bravest could expect to make it to the top of their profession.

The crowd waited several minutes before the rudimentary treatment of applying a cold sponge to the youngster's face paid dividends and he staggered to his feet. At 4-0 down a lesser – some might say more sensible – man might have decided to recuperate in the more relaxed surroundings of the dressing room. Swift played on. As a result he witnessed Ernie Toseland scoring Manchester City's consolation effort.

Swift's first-team colleagues included Jack Bray, who a few weeks earlier had unknowingly met Swift as they both journeyed to Maine Road for a reserve match in which the 'keeper was making his debut.

The Blackpool youngster believed he had enough time to walk from the city centre to Maine Road. He became concerned after seeing fans jump on the trams, which were an important part of Manchester's transport system until the development of the motor car led to a decision to faze them out in 1937. The formal closure date of February 1939 was however missed due to petrol problems for buses and it was not till January 1949 that the 'last' tram ran, by which time many lines were unusable due to the bombing Manchester sustained during the war. Trams eventually returned to Manchester in 1992.

Asking an immaculately dressed stranger Swift was relieved to be re-assured that he had plenty of time, but after continuing walking for a while his fears returned. Jumping on a tram he found himself sitting next to the same stranger. A blushing Swift offered his apologies before the pair alighted outside Maine Road and went their separate ways.

Well, not quite because when Swift entered the dressing room he found himself being asked, 'What on earth are you doing here?' He replied 'I'm the goalkeeper, Sir' and after a few seconds in shock left-half Bray introduced himself.

Bray cost City £1,000 when they signed him in October 1929 from Manchester Central, a club formed by former City director John Ayrton in disgust at the move from Hyde Road to Maine Road. Bray was to play consistently for City in over 430 first team appearances and was good enough to play for England, winning six caps and playing three times for the Football League.

Journeying home from the Baseball Ground, Swift arrived in Blackpool for a belated Christmas dinner, where he was joined by his brother Fred, by now a 'keeper with Oldham, as he told the whole family about 'what I had done right, and wrong, at Derby'. Fearing he might not be playing on Boxing Day he left home at 7.15am for the 2.15pm kick-off at Maine Road. With his family 'as scared as I was' his offer for them to accompany him was declined.

Swift's home debut was a success as Derby were beaten 2-0 with early goals from Fred Gregory and Eric Brook. Unlike the previous day Crooks and Duncan rarely had the master of City's full-backs Laurie Barnett and Fred Corbett and it wasn't until just before the interval that Swift, on his 20th birthday, was first called into action when he fisted away a Duncan effort. He had a lot more to do in the second period, and 'Ramage, Hutchison and Crooks had shots well saved' reported the *Derby Evening Telegraph*.

At 57,218 the match had been watched by easily the largest crowd the 'keeper had ever played in front of 'But that welcome ('the crowd rose to Swift' reported the *Manchester Evening News*) and some of the remarks, good natured and rough in typical northern fashion, helped to settle me.' Returning to Blackpool that night he got a great reception from all the family.

Swift's daring save from Dewar's feet

Four days later he played his third first-team match, a 1-1 draw at Hillsborough. Swift was beaten after a minute but Jack Percival cleared from the goalline. It was a temporary reprieve as within minutes Ronnie Starling had scored for Sheffield Wednesday, selling Corbett a dummy before beating Swift with a shot that 'keeper got his hands to but couldn't hold.

Alec Herd and Gregory then both hit the Wednesday woodwork before 'Rimmer got away and centred for Starling's head but Swift made a capital save right on the post'. (*MEN*) Minutes later came the save of the match when 'Dewar had his first real chase when Hooper slipped the ball through but Swift made the most daring save imaginable with a headlong dive'. (*MEN*) In his first away game at Derby, Swift had been knocked out towards the end and it was clear this was not going to prevent him playing his normal game. This was a sign of intent, a way of showing he was here to stay and that only a very good 'keeper would be taking his place in the City goal.

City's equalising goal came from Matt Busby. The Scot – who as a miner participated in the nine-day 1926 General Strike in which miners, railwaymen, transport workers, printers, dockers, iron and steelworkers took action in defence of the miners' pay and conditions – had signed for City in February 1928 only days before the then 17-year-old was set to emigrate to Canada with his widowed mother. Unemployment meant that emigration from Lanarkshire mining villages such as Bellshill was a fact of life in the 20s and 30s, but thanks to Peter Hodge, a rare footballing talent had been rescued from obscurity.

Busby was to give Manchester City a series of outstandingly classy performances at wing-half, playing 226 times and scoring 14 goals before being transferred to Liverpool in 1936. Early in Swift's debut season the later Manchester United manager played his only match for his country, a 3-2 defeat against Wales. His 'exile' in England and the fact he was a Catholic living in a period when anti-Catholic feeling was entrenched in many of Scotland's most basic institutions could well account for the lack of more caps.

Chapter 4
A regular first-team place

On New Year's Day 1934, Swift made his fourth League appearance. He did so with the backing of the club, the programme for the match with West Bromwich Albion stating 'at Derby we were very well pleased with the work of Swift who strengthened our confidence in him in the return fixture with the County in Boxing Day. We consider we have in him a young goalkeeper of great promise...he has been developed in our A team under the care of Mr H. Hughes, junior, and Mr A. Alexander, junior, the sons of our directors, who have charge of the side.'

The Albion arrived one place below their opponents in sixth place. The Throstles, so-called because of the Black Country word for the thrush that inhabited the local hawthorn buses at the Hawthorns Ground, had won the FA Cup in 1931, beating neighbours Birmingham City 2-1 in the Final. They possessed a powerful attack, and all five forwards – Glidden, Carter, W.G. Richardson, Sandford and Wood – who had played at Wembley faced Swift.

Centre-forward Ginger (W.G.) Richardson had scored his side's goals at Wembley. In his day, Richardson had only a few equals and not too many superiors at snapping up half-chances, especially those inside the penalty area.

Things looked bright for City when they took a 2-0 lead. But when Bray was carried off injured the remaining nine outfield players simply didn't have the legs – for their fifth match in nine days – to compete on a heavy waterlogged pitch. West Brom were to win 7-2, thus recording the biggest away win in Division One during the season. It was the only time in his League career that Swift conceded seven.

Interviewed in 1952 Frank Swift admitted that as a youngster he used to get nightmares.

He said: 'All night long fierce shots would be rained at me from all angles and I would lunge about in vain attempts to stop them. Occasionally I would wake up from a dream, startled at times, as the face of a centre-forward came charging towards me.'

Once he bedded in with Manchester City those nightmares quickly disappeared – but it is likely that Richardson was one of those who featured in them as he notched three of the Baggies goals in January 1934.

Swift said, 'He was sharp, nippy, clever and cunning. I always felt ill at ease when he was around – such a fine goal-poacher who could shoot with both feet and use his head when he had to.

When the ball was out wide you could always see his mop of ginger hair hovering around the penalty spot. He was certainly a fine finisher who I believe scored well over 200 League goals for the Baggies.' As to why West Brom are known as the Baggies it appears no one knows!

After such a heavy defeat Swift was, quite naturally, a little scared of going home that evening. With his brother Fred waiting up to welcome him the pair stayed up discussing the match in order to try and spot the 'mistakes I had obviously made'.

Swift, from the very beginning of his footballing career, analysed all the goals he conceded in order to iron out any faults in his game. It was a painful experience, but a necessary one if he was to go on to great things.

The young 'keeper expected to make way in the next match, at home to Leicester City. Langford though was still injured and if a change was being considered Nicholls was also unavailable due to an injury. Swift stayed in the side. The programme for the game reaffirmed City's confidence in him saying 'the 12 goals conceded have been an unhappy experience for him, but we think he has shown great promise, and he has the confidence of the team. He may have made mistakes, but we think he has shown ability, courage and confidence, and we feel sure that he will develop with experience'. The match finished 1-1 with inside-forward Alec Herd scoring for Manchester City.

Herd had made his City debut a year earlier; when after signing from Hamilton Academical he played against Blackpool in February 1933. His career at Maine Road was to last beyond World War Two and he had made 380 first team appearances (90 during the war) by the time he moved on in 1948 to Stockport County, where he later appeared in the same team as son, David, who afterwards went on to win honours with Manchester United. A wonderful passer of the ball, Herd was also a regular scorer with 124 League and FA Cup goals for Manchester City.

FA Cup action
On Saturday 13 January 1934 Frank Swift played in his first FA Cup match, a home tie against Blackburn Rovers. With seat tickets costing three and four shillings [15p–20p], around 4–6 per cent of the average wage of £4 a week at the time, a crowd of 54,336 assembled at Maine Road. Blackburn had won the FA Cup a record six times – equal with Aston Villa – the last time in 1928 when they beat Huddersfield Town 3-1 in the Final.

City's Cup record was nowhere near as good but captain Sam Cowan was determined to lead his side back to Wembley and win the Trophy last captured in 1904.

Swift had been at Wembley for the previous year's Cup Final, journeying down as a sidecar passenger on his workmate, Harry Murrow's, motorbike. Harry only had one eye and an hour into the trip at 4am he hit the kerb at half-light throwing the fast asleep passenger out onto the grass. Fortunately no lasting damage to either men resulted and the pair travelled on to see the match with Everton.

Armed with 2s 6d standing tickets [12.5p] the gasworks workers had been thrilled at their first glimpse of Wembley Stadium, the beautiful green pitch and the sight of the Duke and Duchess of Kent.

Standing behind the goal Swift had told his good friend only half jokingly that he would be between the posts the next time City were at Wembley. This was their first chance to retrace their steps and in preparation the City first-team players were taken for 'special training to Southport'.

Swift enjoyed the short break at the seaside and in his autobiography recalled how he 'really learned of the magnificent team spirit, coupled with the school-boyish sense of humour, which had helped to take City to Wembley in 1933'. Golf and cowboys and Indians were all part of the general fun, which 'helped me more than ever to knit into the happy comradeship which made up this great team'.

Blackburn was the first team to know that when the fun ended the City team were intent on winning the 1934 FA Cup. The away side were accompanied by 5,000 of their own fans. The match was to be won by City's wingers, Toseland and Eric Brook, whose penetrative raiding and deadly shooting saw the home side through 3-1. Rovers' full-backs Bill Gorman and Crawford Whyte were unable to stop the pair from wreaking havoc and they scored all three of the City goals.

Toseland, signed from Coventry City in March 1929, was a Manchester City regular for over a decade and it was a surprise he was never capped for England. Toseland scored 75 goals in 409 first team appearances for City.

After Brook opened the scoring, Rovers made it 1-1 on 32 minutes through a wonderful picture book header that flashed into the top corner of the net from England international winger Jack Bruton – who had signed for Burnley in 1925 as he emerged from the coal mine where he was working. Three minutes later though came another goal of real quality when from Brook's cross, Fred Tilson deceived Whyte by allowing the ball to pass beyond him for Toseland to beat Cliff Binns in the Rovers goal.

With the away side's dangerous centre-forward Ted Harper – Division One top scorer in 1925-26 with 43 goals – thereafter rarely given a chance, when Toseland made it 3-1 on 66 minutes the game as a contest was over. Things might have been different if early in the game the City 'keeper had not enjoyed a touch of fortune, when at 0-0 'Harper broke through the light blue line in front of me. In my nervousness I anticipated too soon and dived before he kicked the ball. To my amazement and delight, the ball hit my right hand – and stuck. The roar of the crowd, as much as the save, helped give me confidence.'

Armed with this, Swift then played a fine game and after\ complimented his Blackburn counterpart Binns saying: 'No one could ...ve kept a better goal.' This praise of an opponent – especially goalkeepers – was typical of Swift during his long career. It was one of many aspects of his character that helped make him so popular among players and supporters of all clubs. As he developed as a professional he was also happy to pass on his experiences and skills to up and coming young players.

When the fourth round draw was made Manchester City were pitched against another Second Division side, Hull City. Four seasons earlier the Tigers had almost made it to Wembley, being pegged back to 2-2 after leading by two goals in their semi-final match with Arsenal, losing the replay 1-0 after having Arthur Childs sent off.

Buoyed by their Cup success, City now hoped to make a charge up the table. Reigning Champions Arsenal arrived at the head of the League and plenty of fans wanted to see if they could repeat their success with 60,401 inside Maine Road. Fifth place City were seven points off top spot.

The same weekend *Daily Mail* owner Viscount Rothermere was giving his support to the British Union of Fascists, a political party formed by Sir Oswald Moseley in 1932 to follow in the footsteps of Hitler and Mussolini in Germany and Italy.

In defence of these dictatorial regimes, Rothermere said, 'Nazi atrocities in Germany consist merely of a few isolated acts of violence... (which critics use) to give the impression that Nazi rule is a bloodthirsty tyranny' and 'the BUF is a well organised party of the right ready to take over responsibility for national affairs with the same directness of purpose and energy of method as Hitler and Mussolini have displayed.'

Swift's performance against the champions didn't attract as much attention as the Honourable Gentleman's rant, but it was still good enough to have Monday's *Daily Mirror* suggest he was 'CITY'S NEW CAP?', with reporter T. Preston writing 'a special word must be reserved for Swift, who was in the third team until a few weeks ago and would not have played on Saturday if Langford had been fit. On this form, Swift, who has played finely on previous occasions, is an international in the making.' At just 20 this was some praise.

City fans, though, had become accustomed to watching fine 'keepers. Jack Hillman, the man between the posts when the FA Cup was captured in 1904, would have won more than one cap for England except for the fine form of Jack Robinson, while between 1911 and 1927 Jim 'Naughty Boy' Goodchild was a fine stopper of shots, brave in the air and a good organiser of the men in front of him. It is arguable whether any club has ever had so many good 'keepers as Manchester City.

The home side beat Arsenal 2-1. Bobby Marshall scored the first, but it was the second that was the pick of the three with Alex Herd beating Frank Moss from all of 25 yards. Pat Beasley, Arsenal's best forward on the day, scored a late goal as City cut the deficit on the leaders.

The away side was still coming to terms with the sudden loss of manager Herbert Chapman, who had died of pneumonia on 6 January 1934. Chapman has strong claims to be British Football's greatest ever manager as, after assuming control of Huddersfield Town in 1921, he took the Terriers to success in the FA Cup in 1922 and consecutive League successes in 1923-24 and 1924-25. The Leeds Road side then went on to win a third title the following season, by which time Chapman had become manager at Highbury.

Utilising the 1925 changes in the offside rule – whereby attacking players now only needed two defenders, rather than three, between them and the goal to be onside – Chapman pioneered the development of a stopper centre-half that ended the previous roving role of such players. With inside-forwards being brought back to assist in midfield it meant team formations changed to what became known as the WM formation, so called after the shape of teams spelled out in letters.

Armed with a five-year plan, Chapman – after taking his side to the 1927 FA Cup Final where they lost 1-0 to Cardiff City – succeeded in taking Arsenal to their first major success when the Gunners beat his former side, Huddersfield Town, 2-0 in the 1930 FA Cup Final. Back at Wembley in 1932, Arsenal, that season's League runner's up, lost to Newcastle in the FA Cup Final but in 1932-33 stormed to a first Championship success. Chapman was en route to his fourth League title as a manager when he died.

Such was his respect in the world of football that Hendon Parish Church was packed for his funeral, with mourners travelling from as far as France, Austria, Denmark and Sweden.

With Chapman's passing, coach Joe Shaw assumed charge of the team and was to do the job with great success, handing over the reins to new man George Allison during the summer of 1934 with Arsenal still champions.

Manchester City's fourth round FA cup opponents Hull had knocked them out in 1930 and were now intent on a double. With many having travelled from Manchester to Boothferry Park there was a great atmosphere for players of both sides to enjoy.

Both teams were quickly on the attack with Herd shooting just over before Bill McNaughton, scorer of 42 goals for the Tigers the previous season, did the same for the home side. On 15 minutes Hull enjoyed a touch of good fortune when Melville headed against his own bar but on 29 minutes 'Swift distinguished himself by making a glorious one-handed save from Duncan's header'. (*MEN* 27-01-34)

Then from 'yet another corner Melville headed well, but Swift made a neat save and cleared in the face of a concerted rush' (*MEN*) and after which City profited from the 'keeper's heroics by scoring twice before half-time. First some wonderful passing saw the ball fed out to Brook who crashed home a beautiful shot from a tight angle.

Then on 42 minutes Toseland fastened on to a loose ball before beating three or four defenders and finding Herd for a simple finish.

Hull were back in the match with an early second half goal when Jack Hill, capped 11 times for England, headed a fine goal. Soon after an equaliser seemed certain only for 'Swift to play a hero's part, especially when he gathered a shot which was almost diverted past him by a defender'.

Hull equalised on 70 minutes when Billy Dale – a former Manchester United man who played 269 times for Manchester City – beat his own 'keeper with a back header. The home side should then have won the match but after bursting through Duncan hit his shot high and wide as City survived to take the tie to a second match.

When this took place a small number of Hull fans were in great voice before kick-off. The home side were unchanged with the Tigers replacing Melville at left-half with Stanley Denby. And it was the away side who should have scored first, only a 'first-class save from Swift, turning the ball over the bar with his left hand' preventing McNaughton from doing any damage.

The Hull centre-forward did eventually get his reward when, after goals from Toseland and Tilson had put City two up, he reduced the arrears on 70 minutes. That at least had the bonus of rousing a lethargic Manchester City side into action and after Tilson had raced half the length of the field to make it 3-1, the City centre-forward repeated the trick before setting up Bobby Marshall to make it 4-1.

Tilson had joined Manchester City as part of a double signing with left-sided forward partner Eric Brook from Barnsley in March 1928, the Tykes receiving a fee of £6,000 for both. An early injury meant it wasn't until the 1931-32 season that he established himself in the first-team. Tilson's success in the 1933-34 Cup run helped him secure a first of four England appearances in the summer of 1934.

With Sheffield Wednesday having beaten Oldham Athletic 6-1 in their replayed tie it meant Manchester City would be back in Yorkshire for the fifth round of the FA Cup. It was going to be tough as Wednesday were on a long unbeaten run.

Meanwhile, having disposed of a Yorkshire side in the Cup, City followed it up by beating another in the League, Middlesbrough losing 5-2 at Maine Road with Busby, Tilson (2) and Brook (2) scoring the goals. Brook's efforts were two of 177 League and FA Cup goals that he bagged during his 12 years with Manchester

City, a record that puts him top of the all-time goalscorers' list for the club. The outside-left was never content to hug the touchline and his fierce shot and deadly finishing from the penalty spot made him a tough opponent for defenders and 'keepers alike.

Brook won 18 caps for England, and against Italy in November 1934 he scored twice as England beat the World Champions in a match that earned the infamous title of the Battle of Highbury. The City man was one of the victims, sustaining a broken arm. Brook would have won more caps, but found himself in competition against his friend, Arsenal's Cliff Bastin, one of the greatest players ever to play for the Gunners. Brook's career came to a premature end when he was involved in a car crash with Sam Barkas en route to a wartime international against Scotland at St James' Park. A fractured skull ruled him out of heading the ball and he retired aged 32.

After beating Boro there was disappointment when in a midweek game City played poorly to lose 2-0 against Everton. As it was a working day only 17,134 were inside Goodison Park.

In goal, Everton had 24-year-old Ted Sagar, who had signed in March 1929 and remained for 24 years during which time he made 497 first-team appearances. In 1935-36 he played four times for England.

Early on, Sagar was kept busy and made two fine saves from Toseland. Everton though should have scored first when they were awarded a penalty after a Jimmy McLuckie handball. England right-half Cliff Britton beat Swift from the spot but the ball rebounded from the upright. The midfielder directed the ball into the net only for the effort to be disallowed as no other player had first touched it.

Norman Higham then hit a hard shot from 30 yards that Swift saved confidently, before the big 'keeper touched over Ted Critchley's shot. On the stroke of half-time, Jimmy Stein, a scorer in the 1933 Cup Final, slotted Charlie Gee's free-kick beyond Swift and when former City favourite Tosh Johnson scored in the second half the game as a contest ended.

On 10 February 1934 the crowd at Ewood Park for the game with City was a disappointing 14,076. The continuing crisis that had gripped the World economy following the 1929 Wall Street Crash was throwing millions out of work and with money extremely tight attendances at football matches fell. Rovers were doing well and were to finish eighth with 43 points, two of which came in a 3-0 beating of City.

Death at the football

The following weekend, the largest crowd that has ever watched a football match in Sheffield – 72,841 – packed out Hillsborough.

Many years later the ground was the scene of great carnage when 96 Liverpool fans lost their lives on the Leppings Lane terraces, that with fences at the front offered no escape from the overcrowded, badly stewarded terraces. In 1934 the large crowd was more fortunate, but ambulance men tending groaning casualties who had been crushed on the Spion Kop blocked the players from running down the entrance tunnel.

Swift later recalled that 'after forcing my way through with other players, I had to stand aside to let pass a stretcher bearing a man crushed to death against the Spion Kop railings'. This being the 1930s the game continued.

At the start it was clear that events off the pitch had affected those on it, especially among the City players and following a Sam Cowan miss-kick the Owls Neil Dewar nipped in to find England international winger Ellis Rimmer to make it 1-0.

It took the away side until the 30th minute to draw level with a goal of stunning quality. Receiving the ball from a free-kick, Herd threw off the nearest players, Ted Catlin and Tommy Walker, feinted to send the ball out wide before driving towards goal and then unleashing a 25 yard rocket that smashed home.

City fell behind at the start of the second period when Dewar scored but again Herd came to their rescue; equalising in a scramble following a Toseland corner. A replay would be needed to decide the tie. 'This I think was our toughest match of all on the path to Wembley' wrote Swift later.

There were 66,614 people at the replay. They saw City give a glorious performance that suggested that their skill, courage and determination would return them to Wembley at the season's end.

In the first match Wednesday centre-half Walter Millership had exerted a stranglehold on Tilson, but the City centre-forward was too good a player to allow that to happen a second time. Tilson's performance though was overshadowed by that of City captain Sam Cowan, who brilliantly supported his full-backs and produced a series of accurate forward passes.

Cowan; whose career spanned the change in the offside law, had once scored a hat-trick of headers for first club, Doncaster Rovers. Now in his 10th season with Manchester City his experience must have been an invaluable aid for the young City 'keeper behind him.

Wednesday did have some chances and Rimmer's effort from 40 yards almost caught out Swift, while Dewar shot narrowly wide and Millership nearly headed home from a corner. In general though the away side were outplayed and the 2-0 scoreline would have been considerably higher if not for some remarkable heroic saves by England international 'keeper Jack Brown.

The home side went ahead on 63 minutes when Tilson nipped between the Wednesday backs to net. Soon after, Bobby Marshall powered home a header from a Billy Dale free-kick. Wednesday, suffering their first defeat in 19 matches, would have to wait till the following season to win the FA Cup at Wembley for the first time – they beat WBA 4-2 in the final.

Record crowd

City's quarter-final opponents were Stoke City. The Potters had won promotion the previous season and had beaten Bradford Park Avenue, Blackpool and First Division Chelsea 3-1 to make it to the last eight. Nineteen-year-old winger Stanley Matthews had scored two of his side's goals against the Londoners and was clearly set for a fine career.

As City were at home Swift was in a confident mood prior to the game. Not that the away side would lack for support and the Stoke *Sentinel* reported how the 'Cup tie is the sole topic of conversation on any bus going into town'.

'You're on the Sentinel.' Where can I get couple of five-bob [25p] tickets for the match?' What an optimist! There will be some empty North Staffordshire stomachs, and many sets of working clothes, judging by the hundreds who say they are 'going to make a dash for it straight from work'. Starting out at 7am, 18 special trains carrying 17,000 people made the short journey to Manchester. In the event an estimated 25,000 Stoke fans were packed inside Maine Road at kick-off time, with many more locked out when the gates were closed with a record attendance for any game in England outside of London at 84,568.

The match was played in glorious weather and despite the away fans enthusiasm there was little doubt that the City fans expected their side to win. With McLuckie injured, Bray was at right-half.

It was Stoke who started quickest and Matthews should possibly have beaten Swift after just two minutes. The only goal came after just 15 minutes. Brook floated over a cross that the wind took high into the air and when Stoke 'keeper Roy John moved to grab it the ball slipped from his grasp and bounced over the line. There was a delay as the crowd realised a goal had been scored and then the City fans let rip a roar that could be heard miles away.

Fans of both sides were divided as to whether the scorer had aimed to score, some rating it as the finest they ever witnessed and others viewing it as a bit of a fluke. No one seems to have asked Brook his intentions and so we shall never know.

Three minutes later Stoke might have equalised but Matthews was just too slow to a loose ball and his half-hit shot allowed Swift time to make a vital save. With Busby in fine form that appeared to have ended the away side's chances but in the last minute they forced a corner. Coming up from defence Arthur Turner rose to powerfully head the ball 'and with me standing helpless – and with 84,000 hearts in similar number of mouths, the ball curled slowly over the bar' wrote Swift.

Seconds later the referee's final whistle meant Manchester City were in their third consecutive semi-final of the FA Cup – Arsenal having beaten them in 1932.

Their opponents were Aston Villa, who had last won the FA Cup in 1920 when they had beaten Huddersfield Town in the Final played at Stamford Bridge.

The game was played at Leeds Road, Huddersfield. Ten days beforehand the sides drew 0-0 at Villa Park, a match in which Swift made some outstanding saves. Despite the pre-match predictions of a tight affair it was to be as one-sided a semi-final as there has been in the FA Cup. Dai Astley had scored seven times in the earlier rounds but his eighth was to be mere consolation as the victors scored six.

The Birmingham side started quickly and Swift had to be alert to prevent Joe Beresford and Eric Houghton from scoring. Then Astley was only inches away. Seconds later though City were ahead when Toseland, receiving a Brook long pass easily beat Thomas 'Smokey' Wood and tried a speculative effort that Harold Morton clearly felt presented no problems as he attempted to knock the ball down to his feet. The 'keeper's confidence soon evaporated when the greasy ball passed over his hands and into the net.

On 33 minutes the scorer again beat Wood and Scottish international full-back Joe Nibloe before producing a wonderful cross that Tilson headed through to make it 2-0. Swift's prediction at the 1933 Cup final about returning to play at Wembley for City was looking a pretty good bet. Especially as three minutes later Herd banged in a third and soon after Tilson headed his second of the match to make it 4-0 at half-time. Tilson scored his hat-trick on 70 minutes and his fourth two minutes later and long before the end the Villa fans were streaming home and thus missed their late consolation effort.

City had played magnificently and with Portsmouth having thumped Leicester City 4-1 in the other semi then it was going to be a case of North versus South in the Cup Final.

There were still eight League games to play before the big match. Back at Leeds Road, the away side lost 1-0 and then lost 4-0 at the Hawthorns to make it Manchester City 2 WBA 11 in the season. Three weeks before the big day City beat Portsmouth 2-1 in a League match at Maine Road. The same score at Wembley would do nicely.

Four days later fewer than 10,000 were inside Roker Park for a midweek fixture that kicked off during the working day. There were plenty of idle workers who would have appreciated the chance to watch the action. Thousands of shipyard workers had been thrown out of work and unemployment peaked in Sunderland in 1934 at 29,000, around half the working population. None had the money to get into a football match.

Not that they would have seen anything too exciting on this particular day. The home side started swiftly, and when the ball was crossed into the box Swift was charged by Sandy McNab and strong appeals were made for a goal, which the referee refused. The 'keeper then saved a good shot by Bob Gurney, who with 228 goals remains Sunderland's record goalscorer, and 'later made a miraculous save from one of his headers' reported the *Northern Mail*. 'Swift for City kept a good goal' reported the *Newcastle Journal* in a game that ended goalless. City's confidence in Swift over Christmas and the New Year was being fully repaid.

Four days later however the giant 'keeper was beaten five times as Spurs beat their opponents 5-1 at White Hart Lane. To compound matters McLuckie twisted his knee in falling after a tackle by Jimmy McCormick. A brilliant ball-artist, McLuckie had signed for City from Hamilton Academical in February 1933 but had missed out on a Cup Final place against Everton.

The injury was to cost him a place in the Cup Final side on 28 April 1934, by which time in an attempt to kick start the economy the Chancellor, Neville Chamberlain, had cut income tax by 6d in the £ and rescinded a proposed cut in unemployment benefit. It was a 'prosperity' budget remarked the newspapers.

Chapter 5
FA Cup Final success

Despite enjoying an unbroken run of 27 League and FA Cup matches in his first season Frank Swift was worried he might miss out on a place in the Manchester City side for the FA Cup Final with Portsmouth on 28 April 1934.

Former first-team regular Len Langford had now fully recovered from his knee injury and when the City players went to their usual resting spot at the Palace Hotel, Southport the youngster couldn't help but note that the former number one was among a number of reserves to accompany the League XI. Langford though hadn't played in the first team in 1934 and had also played poorly at the 1933 Final, when his mistakes contributed to Everton's two opening goals.

On the Tuesday before the match Swift's fears were put aside when the team for the big day was announced and he was in it! His prediction the previous year had proved accurate. Early in 1934 British Pathe News, one of the oldest names in motion pictures, had visited a number of football clubs as part of its 'Famous Football Clubs' series. Frank Swift was the last City player – 'last but not least' said the commentator – to be shown on the short newsreel. Cinemagoers in the days before the Cup Final got the chance to see it again, this time accompanied by coverage of Portsmouth.

Pathe, who had introduced sound in 1928, had also covered the semi-final defeat of Aston Villa and over the next few years Frank Swift was to be a regular on the big screen. Particularly popular was coverage of FA Cup matches and in addition to the 1934 Final City were also shown playing Spurs in 1934-35 and Millwall twice in 1936-37 and 1937-38. Other coverage was of the first League game of the 1934-35 season away to West Brom and Rangers 1-0 defeat of City in a specially arranged match between the two Cup winners held soon after Wembley.

Towards the end of the war Swift was to be one of the first footballers shown in action on the Big Screen, playing in a specially arranged match at the Stade Oscar Bossaert Stadium in Paris.

Travelling down the night before the 1934 Cup Final, City stayed in a hotel on the edge of Epping Forest and Swift, set to become the youngest 'keeper to play in a Wembley final, was paired off with skipper Sam Cowan.

This was clearly an attempt to calm the 'keeper's nerves. With, unknowing to the management, Cowan nursing blood poisoning of the right big toe, it meant that as the centre-half sat with his throbbing foot in a bowl of scalding hot water the pair chatted away till 3am before both men went to sleep exhausted.

They woke at 11am. It meant Swift had little time to get anxious as, suitably refreshed, he dashed downstairs to get breakfast, before going for a walk and then jumping on the bus to Wembley. He promptly dozed off, only to be rudely awakened and ordered off the bus to buy the rest of the players some chewing gum, a regular City ritual that meant the youngest team member paid for the rest.

Approaching Wembley, Swift observed the 'hustling, hurrying excited masses' who 'suddenly burst into cheering as some of the more observant recognised us' and 'then the giant sweep up to the imposing stadium, surely the greatest sight in the world to a young footballer'.

City's opponents had never won the FA Cup. The nearest Pompey had come was in 1929 when they lost to Bolton Wanderers 2-0 in the final. Only two of the side – 'keeper John Gilfillan, who had played for East Fife against Celtic in the 1927 Scottish Cup Final, and full-back Alec Mackie – were in the 11 that faced Manchester City five years later.

City had seven of their 1933 losing side on display at the 1934 FA Cup Final, with just four playing in their first Final – Swift, Laurie Barnett, Billy Dale and Fred Tilson.

Manchester City: Swift, Barnett, Dale, Busby, Cowan, Bray, Toseland, Marshall, Tilson, Herd, Brook

Portsmouth: John Gilfillan, Alex Mackie, Billy Smith, Jimmy Nichol, Jim Allen – captain, David Thackeray, Fred Worrall, Jack Smith, Jack Weddle, Jim Easson, Sep Rutherford

Sitting in the dressing room Swift could hear the faint hum of an expectant crowd. Then the team were allowed to examine the surface of the pitch, but not practise on it, with some players expressing their disappointment at it being 'rough'.

Having done his best to settle his nerves, Swift was then thrown into confusion when one of his teammates, too nervous to do so himself, asked the unfortunate McLuckie to tie his boots.

Trainer Alec Bell swiftly came to the rescue, hauling the big 'keeper into the washroom, slapping his face and giving him a tot of whisky. If Swift was in a state of confusion that was certainly not something Alec Herd could have been accused of. Sitting quietly reading a book he even managed to miss his teammates filing out of the dressing room to make their way on to the pitch for the game to start. Bell scurried back to remind him there was a game on and he was playing in it!

As City's players steadied themselves just along the corridor the team from the south coast were being entertained by the famous comedy duo, Bud Flanagan and George Doonan.

Maintaining a tradition started in 1926 City players' maroon strips carried a badge of the City of Manchester, a symbol of pride in representing the northern city at a major event.

Portsmouth in white shirts and black shorts were pinning their hopes on a tight defence that had conceded just three goals in their earlier Cup games with Manchester United, Grimsby Town, Swansea Town, Bolton Wanderers and Leicester City. In comparison City would attack. The game was set to be a keen tussle that some pundits believed would need a replay to decide who took home the most famous trophy in the world.

Marching out at Wembley the sides were greeted with a huge roar and this intensified when King George V appeared to meet all the officials and players, starting with Portsmouth's. Swift was delighted to shake the King's hand before the teams broke to get a chance for a quick pre-match kick about.

For the referee Stanley Rous this was his penultimate game in charge and he was to use it as an experiment for what he was certain would revolutionise football. A diagonal system of scientific positioning refereeing had yet to win FA approval. After seeing Belgium referees use it in late 20s and 30s the man who was set to get the post of FA secretary wasn't going to pass up this opportunity to shows its worth. It was destined to become the blueprint for all refereeing.

After the match, Rous submitted a Memorandum for discussion with the Association, and after the pros and cons had been carefully considered, the FA approved the use of the 'Diagonal System'. The Football League followed suit and in 1948 foreign delegates at the International Conference of Referees in London approved the adoption of the system; which has since been used throughout the footballing world.

With Cowan and Portsmouth skipper Jimmy Allen quickly getting the toss of the coin out of the way then the scene was set for the kick-off. Keen to give his young 'keeper a comforting confidence boosting first-touch of the ball, Matt Busby slipped the ball back to him in the first few minutes.

Busby had spotted Swift's talent within days of his arrival at Maine Road in 1932 and had encouraged the 'keeper to eat and train properly. His tips on keeping goal were a big help and the pair would regularly continue their ball training after the rest of the players had departed. Busby constantly had Swift trying to save his penalties, something that was to count against the Scot at Hampden Park many years later.

With the 1934 Cup Final being played in a downpour, Swift had been unsure whether to use gloves. As Jock Gilfillan wasn't doing so, the City 'keeper chose to keep his in the corner of the net. This was to prove a mistake.

Because after an uneventful first 30 minutes, in which the only winner was the heavy ground, 'Sep Rutherford, the Pompey outside-right, came coasting in and fired a ball across the goal to my right hand. I dived and the ball slithered through into the net off my fingers. I was desolate as I picked the ball out of the net.' Swift, forever the professional, the 'keeper who always analysed each goal to see if he could have prevented it may have been a little harsh on himself with the *Daily Mirror's* Barry Thomas believing that after tricking Barnett, the Portsmouth outside-left was too close to goal to have his shot saved.

Nevertheless it was Manchester City 0 Portsmouth 1 and it stayed that way to half-time as Portsmouth, managed by Jack Tinn, fell back on their noted defence. City's anxiety to quickly draw level saw a number of passes go astray.

Sitting in the dressing room at half-time the young 'keeper was disconsolate. Having missed the previous season's Final through injury, Fred Tilson was keen to have him forget what had gone before and promised to 'plonk home two next half'. The centre-forward, who the previous weekend had scored a hat-trick in a 4-2 defeat of Chelsea, was to prove as good as his words, although not initially as he ballooned over the bar two good chances. With the City backs pushing up the field Portsmouth began to retreat deeper and deeper but when Brook beat Gilfillan the roar of the crowd was chilled when the ball hit the upright.

When Portsmouth did attack Swift did well to deny a close-in effort from Jack Weddle, whose hat-trick in the semi-final had taken his side to Wembley. However, with 17 minutes remaining the Fratton Park side seemed set to pick up the famous Trophy as they continued to lead 1-0.

However, when England international Allen, from a corner-kick, was left injured during a collision with Cowan the loss of their centre-half for a few short minutes was enough to unsettle the Portsmouth defence.

Within a couple of minutes Tilson, soon after Herd had smacked a shot against the crossbar, took the ball off Brook 'coasted over the penalty line, moved the ball to his left foot – and hit it across the goal past Gilfillan inside the far post. We were level!'

Portsmouth 1 Manchester City 1. Suddenly the pundit's predictions of a draw seemed about to be fulfilled, especially as a disappointed Allen came back on to the field to make it 11 v 11.

The match should, however, have been won soon after, but Brook, twice in quick succession failed to beat Gilfillan from only yards out. If Portsmouth felt they had escaped to fight another day they were to have their hopes cruelly dashed.

With Herd, Toseland and Tilson piling forward and Alec Mackie – who when he signed for Arsenal in 1922 demanded, and got, a pet-monkey as a signing-on fee – and Billy Smith coming to meet them it was Tilson, running away from the desperate defenders, who kept his half-time promise by smashing his side ahead on 86 minutes.

—

From the kick-off Portsmouth poured forward and when Freddy Worrall, who was the only Portsmouth player still with the club when they won the Cup in 1939, met Rutherford's cross Swift 'just managed to go full length and save the shot on the ground'. (*Daily Mirror*) In the event it was to prove the last chance for a side that had led for so long during the match. The young 'keeper though feared there was much more to come and as the seconds began to tick away one or two photographers counting down the minutes roused his excitement even further.

The game was all in the Portsmouth half but he was terrified. 'Three minutes to go', 'only two minutes left, Frank', 'one minute to go', 'only 50-seconds, you're nearly there lad', '40-seconds, you've done them now', '30-seconds, it's your Cup son' – even writing the words you can feel the tension. Later in his career Swift was to use it to improve his game, but this was then the biggest day in his short life.

'There's the whistle, it's all over' and as the big 'keeper grabbed his cap and gloves and moved to shake hands with his captain, Sam Cowan, whose pre-match injury had failed to prevent him playing a great game, nothing.

Swift had fainted and only the intervention of the ambulance men and others ensured he recovered sufficiently to walk to the dais to receive his coveted medal from the King who asked him 'how are you feeling now, my boy?'

'Fine sir.'

'That's good. You played well. Here is your medal, and good luck.' Having not got one for being a member of the losing Fleetwood reserve side in the Final of the West Lancashire Cup in 1932 it was his first senior medal.

Watching on proudly was the youngster's mother who had got so excited that she had also fainted and had been brought round after receiving a small shot of whisky from the flask of Mrs Bell, the wife of the City trainer.

After the game Swift's mother preferred to travel back home to Blackpool rather than 'intrude' on his big day. Ibbison-street was festooned with bunting and flags and she told local reporters: 'Saturday was the most exciting day of my life. Frank had seen that I had a ticket months ago, and I went down with a lot of others.

My seat was right opposite to that of the King. It was a great game and every minute was packed with thrills. It makes my heart beat to think of it now.

When Frank collapsed, I stood up and then went over myself in a faint!

I saw Frank afterwards on the balcony of the dressing room – and what a big hug we had for each other! He's been a grand lad all along! Nothing but football has been talked of in this house for years. I ought to know everything about it.'

As she spoke there were a regular stream of visitors knocking at the door to offer their congratulations.

'I do wish I could thank everyone, but it's impossible because of the numbers. I hope you will do it through the papers' said Mrs Swift from her 'little living-room in which pride of place was a photograph of her late husband, Mr Fred Swift, who was in the Seaforth Highlanders, shaking hands with the Prince of Wales when the Prince came to Blackpool in 1921.'

Following the after-match celebratory function attended by the players' wives, the City team went down to Brighton the following day where they drank a glass of champagne with Sir Harry Preston, the man who did much to turn the seaside town into a popular resort at the beginning of the 19th century.

Back in Manchester on May Day Tuesday the players were welcomed by a huge crowd – reported by British Pathe at over one million – and were cheered to the rafters, as sitting with their legs dangling outside the open roof of their coach they moved slowly through the City, displaying the FA Cup en route. A feature of the May Day celebrations had been the number of horses and vehicles lavishly dressed in City colours. The celebrations continued when the Lord Mayor entertained the players in a Civic Reception at the Town Hall, where Swift was delighted to find that via the Lord Lieutenant of the County of Lancashire the King had enquired if he was 'alright'.

Given a lift home to Blackpool by the City chairman Mr Hughes, Swift was welcomed at one in the morning by a huge 'Welcome home again, Frank' banner and cheering crowds outside the little house from which he travelled daily to Manchester.

'Such amazing scenes as attended his return have not been approached in this narrow, cobbled street off Central-drive since the day when the Armistice was signed more than 15 years ago' reported the *West Lancashire Evening Gazette*.

Crowds had started assembling after his mother had returned from Manchester with the news that her son was to follow her by road as soon as he could be released from the celebrations.

With nobody dreaming of going to bed, boys and girls, old men and women who had known the City 'keeper since the days when he practised his skills with a tennis ball, waited at open doors or assembled in the street beneath the drooping flags.

When the car turned the corner a huge cheer went up and confetti began falling from every window and streamers were cast from roofs. The noise was loud enough to rouse sleeping residents in nearby streets who raced to join in the joyous occasion. Unable to make its way through the crowd, the car engine was turned off and it was pushed to the front door where the FA Cup winner waved to the crowds before going inside.

No one though was in a rush to go home. The chant of 'We want Frank' went up and opening a bedroom window the beaming Blackpool lad held aloft his Cup winner's medal and shouted 'Thank you! Thank you! You're all so kind – and I can't say any more.'

'I felt like a film star when I was called upon to speak to all those good people from my bedroom window. Naturally, mother had a little weep, as perhaps she was entitled to.' (Swift's autobiography)

The following morning 33 Ibbison Street continued to have a regular stream of visitors, all desperate to see the medal, which had been lain on its velvet bed on the sideboard, awaiting inspection. Next to it was his dad's wartime King's Medal that on the back listed his Lance Corporal's rank at the end of the conflict.

Frank Swift himself then left Blackpool to play in goal at Anfield where City lost 3-2.

Many of the crowd had come to see their own 'keeper, Elisha Scott, who was making his final appearance for the club, bringing to an end a first team career that had started on New Year's Day 1913. Scott and Everton's Dixie Dean were keen opponents and their rivalry was legendary. Scott made 468 appearances for Liverpool, winning two League Championship winner's medals, and also amassing 31 international caps for Ireland and Northern Ireland. Such was Scott's aura that Liverpool took the unusual step of allowing him to address the crowd before the game.

City's season ended with a 4-0 beating of Wolves to leave the Cup winners fifth in the League. Before the match City staff carried the FA Cup round Maine Road on a wooden board, delighting the crowd. Just to make sure that no one felt like taking it home themselves two police officers accompanied it everywhere – after all an earlier version had been pinched from a Birmingham shop window in 1895 and never recovered

Swift's appearance against Wolves meant he completed the season having played 22 League and eight FA Cup matches.

To top off a great six months in which fame had come quickly to him, Frank Swift left on a 21 day playing tour of France and Italy. City were in demand and played Racing Club de Paris before a sight-seeing trip to Milan, Florence – where they played the local side in a match that ended 3-3 – and Genoa took the team into a tournament in Nice. At this they lost 5-0 in a very rough match against AC Milan, beat Admira Wein 5-3 and topped things off with a 4-4 draw with Marseilles. It proved a great end to a great first season for Frank Swift in the Manchester City goal.

Shortly afterwards the 1934 *Topical Times Sporting Annual* said he was one of the 12 best discoveries of the season and wrote: 'few players can have risen to the heights so quickly. His own ability and courage helped put him there, he was but a raw kid from junior football when he came into the City team, but the improvement was noticeable in every game he played, until at the end of the season he was the cool and finished 'keeper one associates with a first division club. He is very tall and strong, he is daring to a degree, he times a dive to a nicety, has saved many a bad situation by this. He is keen-eyed, alert and agile and now that he has cured a tendency to run out there seems to be a bright future for this lad.'

Chapter 6
First full League season and getting married

The 1934-35 season opened with Manchester City visiting West Bromwich Albion. Swift was soon in action, Pathe News showing him wearing his cloth cap as he made an early save before clearing quickly with his left foot. The coverage later shows him beaten tumbling to his left.

The Manchester City side contained only one change from the FA Cup Final, Sam Barkas replacing Barnett, with Dale switching to right-back.

The Bradford City player cost £5,000 when he signed just before the Cup Final. He was to make close to 200 League and Cup appearances in a career spanning the World War, scoring his only goal in the 1-1 draw with Albion.

Barkas was capped five times for England; a figure that would have been higher except for the presence of the Arsenal legend Eddie Hapgood.

Swift rated the stylish left-back and selected him in his best ever eleven. According to the 'keeper Barkas based his style on the former South Shields, Sunderland, Everton and England full-back Warney Cresswell, who was widely known as the Prince of all full-backs for his jockeying of opponents and fine passing of the ball.

Keeper and full-back were constantly communicating with one another. Geoff Ireland recalls "the late forties, and hearing Swift shouting to Barkas, 'Mine, Sam' in response to Sam's 'Yours Swifty'. It was music to my young ears." According to the City custodian, Barkas also wasn't beyond a practical joke or two as well, often threatening to give away a penalty during games in which Swift had little to do.

Ireland's admiration of Frank Swift later saw him pluck up the courage to visit his house and ask for his autograph. The giant 'keeper duly obliged, as he did for many more youngsters who knocked on his door.

City made it three points from four when they beat Liverpool in the first Maine Road game of the season. The home side were in brilliant form, battling back after falling behind to a goal from Gordon Hodgson [who with 287 goals is the fourth highest in the list of all time top scorers in the top flight] to win with ease. City's forwards, constantly interchanging their positions, ripped apart the Liverpool defence. Marshall brought the scores level and, just before half-time, Bradshaw had the misfortune to turn a Busby centre into his own net. Only fine goalkeeping from Arthur Riley kept the score down, but he was powerless to prevent a third from Brook.

South African born Hodgson played three times for England and was again on the scoresheet when the sides met the following week at Anfield. City, fresh from beating Sheffield Wednesday 4-1, went down to a first defeat of the season by losing 2-1.

At St Andrews the away side maintained their decent start by winning 3-1 and then with three goals from Tilson the same score was recorded at Maine Road against Stoke City. Nine points from 12 became 13 from 16 as successive away victories at Leicester City and Middlesbrough were recorded.

On 6 October 1934 a crowd of just over 35,000 passed through the Maine Road turnstiles keen to see if the League leaders could maintain top spot. City had never won the League but after a first Wembley success there were genuine hopes of further silverware. Blackburn Rovers had six points from their first eight matches and the scene was set for a home victory.

With only one side of the ground under cover, most of the crowd were soaked long before kick-off. Five minutes later City were ahead, Jimmy Heale, signed from Bristol City for £3,500 in January 1934, opening the scoring.

It was the start of a goal rush as by the 23rd minute four had entered the nets, with Blackburn roaring into a two goal lead. First from Tom Turner's smart cross, Jack Bruton brought the ball down on his thigh and with Swift advancing the Rovers forward smartly knocked the ball round him for a goal of genuine class.

The second away goal was also extra special. When challenged by Cowan, Ernie Thompson held off the defender before lobbing the ball over Swift. The 'keeper then made a great diving save from a Bruton shot but was let down by his defence as the Blackburn forward was quickest to the loose ball and made it 3-1.

On 27 minutes City were given a lifeline when Brook scored a penalty and after Tommy McLean was harshly dismissed on 55 minutes, for interfering with City's taking of free-kicks, the match became one way traffic with little for Swift to do.

A point was snatched when, with virtually the last kick of the match, Brook's attempted cross was caught by the wind and drifted beyond Binns and into the net.

City then faced their stiffest test so far when they travelled to face League Champions, Arsenal. Over 68,000 watched the action with thousands locked out. The sides adopted their own distinctive styles, with Arsenal employing centre-half Herbie Roberts purely as a stopper and City allowing Cowan to advance with the ball.

Swift was beaten on 18 minutes when Ray Bowden powered home a header from Wilf Copping's free-kick. Swift was to become a big fan of Copping, who he described as 'the man who never knew when he was beaten and perhaps one of the strongest players who has ever worn an England jersey. He would literally terrify many opponents by his grim tackles, which were always scrupulously fair. I did not see the match, but I am told Wilf played Italy almost on his own in that infamous match against England in 1934, which has gone down in history as the Battle of Highbury'.

Swift went on to have a fine match with F. Stacey Lintott in the *Daily Mirror* reporting 'Swift made a good impression…he saved several really fine efforts in grand style'. However on 75 and 77 minutes Bowden and Bastin made full use of Beasley's crosses to push the Gunners into an unassailable lead.

There had been some fine play in the game. Swift had been his side's man-of-the-match but Barkas had also impressed with his ability to link-up with his half-backs, tackle strongly and even open up an attack himself. The result, though, showed City still lacked the quality that would be needed to challenge Arsenal for the title. Two consecutive defeats, at home to Derby County – a game watched by the Duke of York (future King George VI) – and at Aston Villa, dropped City off the top.

There was therefore relief when City beat Spurs 3-1 at Maine Road, where the away 'keeper Jack Nicholls kept the crowd spellbound with a series of marvellous saves.

City travelled to Roker Park on 10 November to play second-placed Sunderland. The Wearsiders were assembling a fine side and had risen to sixth in 1933-34. The game gave Swift his first chance to see a player who later became an England colleague. Raich Carter was born five days before Swift. The inside-forward had already played for England, against Scotland at Wembley on 14 April 1934, some eight months before his 21st birthday.

It was another England international, though, who started this match in particularly fine fashion, Brooks scoring twice during a first half when Sunderland's half-back line up of Charlie Thomson, Bert Johnston and Alex Hastings had been overrun. Even worse for the home side a rough challenge on Carter had left the little man lamed.

Leading 2-0 with just three minutes of the first half remaining City were rocked when Patsy Gallacher and then Bobby Gurney, looking suspiciously offside, drew the home side level before the break. Things then got even worse when Gurney grabbed a second goal early in the second half. It was then almost 4-2 when, despite a heavy ball, Bert Davis struck a powerful shot that beat Swift but cannoned back into play off the crossbar. With Gurney here, there and everywhere the City defence simply couldn't cope and they had Swift – who kept a 'sound goal although beaten three times' [*Northern Mail*] – to thank for preventing further goals. It had been a fine game, one of many between the sides over the following seasons.

City also scored two in their next away match and it was sufficient to earn both points at Goodison Park, where Everton had won every game so far that season. It was Heale and Tilson who grabbed the goals. The equalising goal at 1-1 would have been one the City 'keeper would have analysed later, his decision to come for an anticipated cross having been ruthlessly exposed when the Everton winger John Coulter changed tack to lob the ball beautifully over and round him. Swift, impeccable in collecting earlier crosses, had been beaten by a cheeky bit of skill.

Charity Shield defeat

Four days after playing Everton, Manchester City travelled back to Highbury to face Arsenal in the Charity Shield, a competition City had never previously won. Being a midweek afternoon match the crowd was just 10,888.

Despite missing key players in Alex James, Bowden, Roberts and Jack Crayston the Gunners were worthy winners. They were though gifted the opening goal when Swift and Barnett, playing the penultimate match of his City career, got in a tangle and James Marshall, a doctor signed from Rangers in July 1934, pounced to make it 1-0 after three minutes. The lead was doubled within seven minutes when Ralph Birkett scored from inside the box. The 'keeper then, in part, atoned for his earlier mistake with a number of confident saves and at the interval the score remained 2-0.

With the away side pushing forward there was always a chance of a counter-attack and when Arsenal broke and the ball made its way to Bastin, he hit a magnificent shot that Swift had no chance of saving. Then Ted Drake, who Arsenal had signed from Southampton for £6,500 in March 1934, neatly headed home a Birkett cross and Arsenal cruised to victory.

Swift rated Drake as the toughest centre-forward he faced during his career saying in 1952: 'Straight from the kick-off, I knew there would be no quarter given or asked, but it was a delight to play against him. There was never a wrong word between us, never a suspicion of a foul and when Ted put in a good old-fashioned English shoulder charge, I never appealed to the referee. Whatever the outcome, at the final whistle, the result being irrelevant, Ted always ran up to me to shake my hand. He was a wonderful player.'

City's disappointment at losing out on more silverware was soon forgotten as in the next three League games all six points on offer were gratefully snapped up. In the third match, a 2-0 win at home to Chelsea, there were welcome signs that the good early season form was returning. Swift's performances had firmly established himself as the City 'keeper and on Saturday December 22nd the following report appeared in the *Manchester Evening News* early edition.

City have League's luckiest and pluckiest goalkeeper

SWIFT'S FULL YEAR OF GREAT SERVICE

He got, and took, his chance quickly, and his play is still improving.

It is given to few footballers to make such an impressive start on their careers as Frank Swift, the Manchester City goalkeeper, has done. He is about to complete his first year of service with the senior team, and during all that time has not missed a match…

Swift must count himself a very lucky player in that he got his chance so quickly and in a side capable of such distinguished feats. At the same time he deserves full credit for the manner in which he jumped at the chance when it came, and has set himself about the task of improving his play.

He had done so enormously, and he is today one of the most promising goalkeepers in the game. He has all the necessary physical advantages, his pluck is undoubted, and his judgement is improving in every game. In Swift City should have a servant who will relieve them of goalkeeping worries for many seasons.

All true no doubt. However, down at Molineux, City, with Swift between the posts, conceded five without reply. The 'keeper had a wretched game, not helped by poor displays by his full-backs, Dale and Barkas. For Wolves, Bill Wrigglesworth, signed from Chesterfield, was almost unplayable, scoring twice and creating a host of chances for his fellow forwards.

Over Christmas Manchester City showed better form by capturing all four points in their fixtures with Leeds United. It meant that with Sunderland collecting just two points from their back-to-back fixtures with Everton, losing 6-2 at Goodison Park before beating the Toffees 7-0 the next day, that City moved level with the Wearsiders at the top.

At Elland Road Swift was in good form and twice he denied Tom Cochrane with great saves and although Jack Milburn did manage a goal for the Peacocks, efforts from Toseland and Heale took both points back over the Pennines. In the return Swift had to be constantly alert in the first half. In the second 45 minutes Manchester City played considerably better and two goals from Heale and one from Brook made it a Happy Christmas.

City maintained their challenge by beating West Brom 3-2 on 29 December. A disappointing 1-0 defeat at Sheffield Wednesday the following weekend was then followed by an early exit from the FA Cup. Facing an injury weakened Spurs side, the FA Cup holders slumped out of the competition at the first hurdle with Willie Evans grabbing the only goal of the game. Swift had little to do but the result was no fluke. January proved to be a poor time for Swift's team, as after drawing 0-0 at home to Birmingham, City then lost 2-0 at Stoke.

Back home, City completed the double for the season over Leicester City and Middlesbrough, scoring 12 times in 6-3 and 6-2 victories. City were now firmly back in the title race and prior to the big match with Arsenal the table was as follows:

Arsenal	28	37
Sunderland	28	36
Manchester City	28	36

The official attendance for the match with the Gunners was 79,491, a then record League gate.

City's hopes of overtaking the League champions in the table floundered on a lack of subtlety, and when Arsenal took a half-time lead through Bowden it was probably deserved as Swift had been the busier of the two 'keepers.

The second period saw the City 'keeper a virtual spectator as his team poured forward in search of an equaliser. However, poor passing meant this rarely looked likely until on 75 minutes, Tilson beat Roberts for the first time and when his shot was pushed out by Moss, Brook came roaring in to crash the ball home. Nevertheless it was Arsenal, missing James and Hapgood, who would have been happier with the result.

Having sneaked a 2-1 win at Derby it was vital for Manchester City to get something from their Monday afternoon match at Ewood Park that was watched by only 11,328.

Victory would have taken the away side back to the top and they enjoyed the majority of possession but missed opportunities meant they left without a point following a Thompson goal. Considering Rovers had taken eight hours to travel back from their weekend match at Roker Park they did well to snatch both points.

Swift had no chance of preventing the goal when Jackie Milne's great run took him clear and when his shot bounced back off the far post, Thompson was on hand to put the ball home. Having created few chances the away side left the field knowing their title chances were receding, although a 4-1 home success against Aston Villa again raised hopes.

These were to largely disappear in the next three matches when only two points were taken. At White Hart Lane, Swift could have been beaten at least twice by Willie Evans. The 'keeper constantly used his long arms to fist over the bar all Spurs' shots. He also amused the crowd by stretching out to reach a long ball by knocking it over George Hunt's shoulders and then running round to collect the ball with a broad smile on his face.

Eleven days after facing Spurs, Frank Swift's fine form was recognised when he was picked to play against England for *The Rest* in a trial match in which the proposal to employ a two referee system was employed for the first time in a professional game. Eric Brook was selected to play alongside him and the game was to finish 2-2. The City 'keeper was beaten twice by Ted Drake, but nevertheless the *Daily Mirror* reported that his 'keeping was sound and he made some outstanding saves'.

The big 'keeper didn't do so well in the next home match, a 2-2 draw at Everton. He was at fault with the first goal when he preferred to push away a Dean header rather than catch it and Charlie Leyfield followed up to net the rebound, his first of two.

City then kept their slim chances of snatching the title from Arsenal – and dented second placed Sunderland's – by winning a tough encounter. The home side had their 'keeper to thank for the victory, Swift playing a blinder and ensuring that when Heale scored a real beauty with just three minutes remaining it was the winner rather than mere consolation. Sunderland did hit the post twice but if that was unlucky what wasn't were 'two remarkable saves' (*Manchester Evening News*) that prevented James Connor scoring.

City now needed a good run to the end of the season to snatch the title, and prevent Arsenal from becoming the second side to win it three seasons in a row. Portsmouth had stood in City's way at Wembley, and now the south coast side took revenge for the disappointment of losing in the FA Cup Final as they beat their opponents home and away over Easter. There was going to be no first title for Manchester City.

Consequently, a crowd of just under 15,000 were at Maine Road for the final match of the season in which City took revenge for a 5-0 drubbing at Molineux in December. The result though was harsh on a Wolves side that, especially in the first half, were thwarted by some fine saves by Swift. Heale put the home side ahead after 20 minutes and doubled the lead 10 minutes later, before Toseland made it 3-0 on 40 minutes. Shortly after this Swift made a great, one-handed save from a terrific Harthill drive.

In the second period, Swift did well to hold a low Tom Galley shot. Then when Brook made it 4-0, Swift performed heroics to keep out another Harthill header before Marshall made no mistake with a well placed right-foot to make it 5-0. It had been a fine end to Swift's first full season in which he had played in all 42 League matches. It would not be the first time!

On 27 July 1935 Frank Swift had further reason to celebrate when he married Doris Potter at All Saints Church, Blackpool. The pair had met when the goalkeeper was working on the boats at Blackpool. Soon after Doris appeared for another trip round the bay and soon became a regular when Frank stopped charging her. The pair, wrote Frank Swift in his autobiography, 'both had a sense of humour' and the following year the newly-weds had a daughter to dote over with Jean Francis born on 10 August 1936. According to Frank his daughter as she grew up overtook his wife as my 'number one critic'. Both regularly attended matches at Maine Road.

Chapter 7

Building a title challenging team and winning a first representative honour

Having finished in fourth place in 1934-35, Manchester City was keen to make a challenge for the title in 1935-36. The side selected for the opening day's fixture at home to West Bromwich Albion was: Swift, Dale, Barkas, Busby, Donnelly, Bray, Toseland, Herd, Heale, Tilson, Brook.

After 11 seasons – and 369 first team appearances as City's regular centre-back, Sam Cowan, had made way for Partick Thistle's Robert Donnelly, and in October 1935 Cowan was to cost Bradford City £2,000 when he moved across the Pennines.

West Bromwich had lost 4-2 to Sheffield Wednesday in the 1935 FA Cup Final and they had their 'keeper from that day, Harold Pearson, to thank for keeping the score down at Maine Road. He was beaten just the once when Herd, dangerous throughout, hit a beautiful fast low drive taken on the run.

Debutant Donnelly – 'who is not one of your modern 'stay-at-home' centre-halves', reported the *Daily Mirror* – did well at centre-half and showed good understanding with Barkas and Dale. Behind them Swift was capable 'and made one great save from Tommy Green, who was Albion's most dangerous forward'.

A crowd of 39,826 had watched the action inside Maine Road. The close season had brought significant ground improvements. In 1923 when it had opened, only the Main Stand, 270ft long, 140ft wide and 56ft high and with 9,700 seats, was covered. For all other fans, stood on the open terraces, a flat cap was essential in a city known for its rain.

In 1931 the corner between Platt Lane and the Main Stand had been redeveloped with space for 6,830 standing and 950 seated. Entrance to this covered area was extra, payable once a spectator had entered the ground. In 1935 covering was extended to the rest of Platt Lane, with the main terracing recreated with wooden floorboards. It now meant around 35,000 people could choose to watch the match under cover.

Ian Niven – a City director between 1973 and 1996 – and a regular attender at both home and away games today, was already attending matches at Maine Road in 1935. It was perhaps inevitable he would be a City fan, as his dad was a close friend of former manager Peter Hodge, a fellow Scot. Initially accompanied by his father, the young Ian, born 1924, was 10 when he started attending matches with his mates.

He recalls Brook beating John in the Stoke goal in the 1934 FA Cup quarter-final match. He still can't make up his mind whether the scorer meant it or not saying 'if he did then it was a goal of true greatness and the best goal I saw at Maine Road'. Which as he saw virtually every match there would make it the best one!

'We lived around 2½ miles from the ground and we'd walk there and back. Many people also used bicycles and others used trams. The majority of fans, all male with many wearing a flat cap and also smoking, stood on open terraces watching the game. So when it rained most people got soaked. Then when the sun came out there would be steam rising from the crowd as people's clothes dried off' recalls Ian, who the day he was interviewed was anxiously pacing round his flat just 48 hours before the City match against QPR at the end of the 2011-12 season.

That match was played at the magnificent fully covered Etihad Stadium, built at a cost of over £100 million, with a seat each for the 47,435 spectators, including many women fans. Few of those present wore a flat cap, but many were wearing a City replica top or t-shirt. Whereas fans from the 1930s would have carried cash, a front door key and some cigarettes the modern day supporter has a credit card, a mobile phone with wi-fi capability and a season card or ticket. Every moment of the action on the pitch is caught on television camera and beamed around the world.

When he was at school, Ian would join thousands of youngsters in dashing to watch the last 15 minutes of any midweek matches played during a school day. Using the crowd noises they had heard, they'd hazard a guess at the score line. On occasions the race was worthwhile with a late winner or equaliser sending them and the paying public home happy.

In 1936 Ian's dad, Andrew was forced to choose between football and his job. Serving with the Royal Scots he was faced with signing back on for a seven-year-tour, mainly in India.

'My uncle Joe was a railwayman and he and Aunt Mollie had no children and they told my father they would look after me. Problem was that Joe was also a United fan, of which there weren't actually that many at the time. We referred to them as 'the Rags' as they were so poor and not as good as City. Joe had wanted to take me to some away games but I had missed the trains. Joe was also a Catholic and my dad was Presbyterian' explains Ian.

Work was hard to come by at the time but Andrew Niven found a job as a packer, before later becoming a clerk and then chief cashier, and the youngster, whose grandfather played for Dunfermline Athletic, continued his obsession with his favourite team. He was able to quickly recognise that Frank Swift was destined for greatness: 'There was a thrill when he came for the ball as he had a flying action in which he used his weight to catch the ball. Back in those days a 'keeper could expect to be roughly challenged, especially in the air, and there is little doubt that Frank's size was a massive plus.'

Showmanship

Ian can recall the 'keeper regularly chatting away to fans behind the goals and says that without taking away 'his brilliance in using his long reach to dive down and get the ball. Frank wasn't against making a comfortable save into a diving one. There was always a bit of showmanship with Frank Swift and he would have made a good stage actor if he had wanted to be one'.

In the 1930s Swift had yet to refine his distribution skills but it was these that later impressed Ian– whose Army service in the Far East meant that he arrived back from the war much later than those who had served in Europe – so much that he selected 'Frank in my finest City XI as with them he started many an attack. You could see him looking towards his forwards if he had an easy catch to make. He would come down and then throw it to the feet of one of them. For me that just puts him ahead of Bert Trautmann, as for saving shots and dealing with crosses and stopping goals they were equal with one another.'

Swift 'learned to throw a football by watching water polo players flicking a ball about in a swimming bath. I would never be able to match their effortless ease, but once again practise helped. I can clear the half-way line with a throw, which is getting on 60 yards.' (*Football from the Goalmouth*)

He advised 'keepers to practise direction by 'chalking a number of rings on a wall at varying heights, and trying to throw the ball quickly into them' and reminded them that 'a throw can be as valuable as a goal-kick, particularly when forwards are coming in fast'.

On goal-kicks he advised 'keepers to vary their length 'depending upon the position of the other players on the field, the condition of the pitch, and the length and directional ability of the kicker'. He was keen for wingers to 'move back to find open space' and selected Stanley Matthews as the best player to do this saying 'as soon as I catch a high cross-ball, Stanley runs into the inside-left position. I don't need to look for him. I simply send the ball to where I know he will be standing'.

With regard to Frank Swift perhaps making a good stage actor, there are some indications he had the talent. Nan, or Margaret Annie Macdonald was the organiser of BBC's Northern Children's Hour radio programme from 1937 to 1949. She gave many a future star early broadcasting experience including actor and radio presenter Wilfred Pickles, actor and film director Derek Jacobi and film and stage actress Julie Andrews.

Mary Donsworth was a regular listener and just after the war she went on a school visit to see it broadcast. Nan was interviewing Frank Swift and 'when she got a coughing fit he took over and read her questions out and then answered them until she felt well enough to resume her role as the interviewer. He clearly had great presence of mind and it was certainly very enjoyable and funny to watch him in action'.

Soon after, another school trip, this time to the National Portrait Gallery had Mary staring at the Earl of Chesterfield's portrait. As it was Frank Swift's 'spitting image' she got a postcard of the painting, posted it to the 'keeper and received it back autographed.

Mary soon started watching City play at Maine Road, going with her friend Dorothy Scanlan. Their presence sometimes had swearing City fans apologising, but at no time did they ever feel threatened or uncomfortable. At their first game City walloped Sunderland 3-0 in 1947 and the home 'keeper had very little to do and 'so he just chatted with the crowd behind the goal. I couldn't tell you what he said as we always stood in the popular side, or Kippax as it became known. Matches that I saw showed he was solid and dependable. City have been lucky with 'keepers over the years, as we've had some great ones'.

Back at the start of the 1935-36 season City beat Liverpool 2-0 at Anfield in midweek, before travelling north to face Sunderland, Division One runners-up in 1934-35.

Outstanding goalkeeping

It was the Wearsiders' first home game of the season and a large crowd of 45,000 was inside Roker Park. At the end many rose to cheer off Man of the Match, Frank Swift, who had played magnificently.

'Goalkeeping which was little short of marvellous was the outstanding feature of this game at Roker Park. Sunderland's forwards, who have seldom played better, subjected the visitors' goalkeeper Swift to a veritable bombardment, but only once did they succeed legitimately in getting the ball past him into the net as one of the two goals he conceded was an own goal by Bray...Swift's brilliant display included the saving of a penalty-kick slammed hard and low by Davis. No wonder Swift was given a rousing cheer at the interval as well as at the end of the match' reported the *Northern Mail*. It was Gurney who snatched Sunderland's other goal.

Despite the defeat the away side were far from downhearted and smashed six past Liverpool before beating Birmingham City 3-1, at Maine Road.

On 21 September 1935 Manchester City won their third consecutive match, returning from Highbury with both points in a 3-2 win. CLASSIC PLAY BEATS ARSENAL was the headline in the *Daily Mirror* and City was to demonstrate some bewildering play in parts of this game, and deservedly took both points north. The away forwards were fast, wonderfully clever and prepared to shoot quickly. Behind them their 'keeper had a wonderful game with W.H. Bee in the *Daily Mirror* writing 'Swift demonstrated that he is an England 'keeper right enough'.

He was beaten twice, a harshly awarded penalty scored by Bastin reducing the arrears after Herd and Toseland had put City 2-0 ahead. Both were wonderful efforts, Herd juggling the ball in the goalmouth before driving home and then Toseland hitting a top corner shot.

Arsenal equalised when James beat Swift from 10 yards, and might have scored again when Bob Davidson's shot hit the post before the 'keeper twice denied Drake's fine efforts after Tilson had restored the City lead.

Football League selection

After such a fine display and victory there was to be real disappointment over the following weeks for Swift and City. With Harry Hibbs and Moss both injured City's 'keeper had been selected to play for the Football League side against the Irish League. The match was played at Blackpool on 26 September 1935 and the Football League side lined up as follows: Swift, Beeson (Aston Villa), Barkas (Manchester City), Crayston (Arsenal), Barker (Derby County), Robinson (Burnley), Worrall (Portsmouth), Carter (Sunderland), Lythgoe (Huddersfield), Westwood (Bolton), Boyes (WBA).

Only Barker had played in the last League match against the Scottish League the previous October and Swift, Barkas and Crayston were earning their first honour.

The Irish League had never previously beaten the Football League and Boyes opened the scoring on the half hour mark. Distillery's McNally equalised two minutes later with a fine shot and 10 minutes from the end the Derry City left winger Kelly hit a low shot from the wing that flew past Swift for the winning goal. The 'keeper had not played as badly as his outfield colleagues – who were heavily criticised in the papers – but it was to be some time before he was considered for further honours.

In his next outing Swift may as well have been a spectator when Portsmouth came north, but despite non-stop pressure the home side failed to break down a stubborn nine-man Pompey defence in which Bill Rochford and Bob Salmond were outstanding.

Consecutive defeats at home to Stoke City and away to Blackburn Rovers and Preston North End followed before, inspired by a marvellous goalkeeping display from Swift, Manchester City returned to winning ways in a 2-1 home success against Brentford.

Early on he made a brilliant double fisted save from a point-blank George Robson shot, but was powerless to prevent Dai Hopkins putting the Bees ahead. The first half also saw Brook and Brentford right-half Duncan McKenzie dismissed just before the interval. The City man thus became the first from the club to be sent off at Maine Road.

Swift's heroics were rewarded when Billy Owen, with a good header, equalised and then Marshall hooked home a great effort in the second half after Tilson had earlier missed a penalty.

Marshall was to make 355 City first-team appearances, taking his total to 560 League and Cup appearances as he also played more than 200 games for Sunderland before moving to Lancashire in March 1928. He switched from inside-forward, where he regularly found the net and possessed brilliant ball-control, to centre-half in 1934. He joined Stockport County in March 1939.

Swift was also in fine form in the following game when Manchester City beat Everton 1-0. 'The match was characterised by brilliant goalkeeping by Sagar and Swift' reported the *Liverpool Evening Express Football* edition.

The paper then reported that early on 'Cunliffe mightily hit a right foot shot to which Swift leapt and turned over the bar with one hand' and then when Jack Archer crossed 'Swift had to fling himself out to save a winning header from Nat Cunliffe. The 'keeper then twice fisted the ball off Dean's head, once being injured in the process'.

The 'keeper was also injured in the second period. Toseland had put his side ahead when 'Dean let go at point-blank range, the ball striking Swift in the face before rebounding to safety' and then after Sagar had made two outstanding saves from Brook the City 'keeper punched Bill 'Golden' Miller's clever hook shot over the bar.

After having both performed so heroically the two 'keepers both met at the end of the game to congratulate each other before walking off together.

Dixie Dean was a frequent face in Frank's early nightmares: 'His head, crowned with dark, curly hair, was always twisting and turning – and it was the head that gave me most terrors. Dixie could place a header wherever he wished. He knew that a goalkeeper had greater difficulty in dealing with a shot on the ground, especially from close range, than one in the air, so he always tried to get well above the ball to head it down. On his feet Dixie was like a ballet dancer and specialised in placing his shots at the goal. But in the air he was absolutely brilliant.' Despite this praise in 1952, Swift never conceded a goal to Dean in the seven games in which he faced him for City.

On 2 November 1935 Swift was taught a lesson as City were beaten 3-0 away to Derby County when: 'As I went up and out for a high cross, a voice called, 'right Frank', and I let it go. Hughie Gallacher promptly headed it into the net. He walked over and said kindly, 'That should teach you a lesson, Frank. Never be called off the ball.' I have never fallen for that one again.' (*Football from the Goalmouth*, 1948)

Commenting on the jovial Scot, Frank said: 'Most players preferred to shoot with one foot and play the ball to that side of them. Not Hughie. He used to keep it dead straight and close, and bearing this in mind I could never really tell which foot he was going to use. The only certainty was that when he did shoot, he always sent the ball low, placing it with uncanny accuracy.' (*Football from the Goalmouth*, 1948)

On 16 November 1935 many City fans made the short journey to Burnden Park and they cheered loudly when their favourites entered the arena. With both Bolton MPs, Mr C.F. Entwhistle and Sir John Haslam, being joined by the new MP for Darwen, Mr Stuart Russell, there was sustained applause for Bolton captain George Taylor who, it had been agreed, would be paid the gate receipts in return for a decade of service; this was officially known as his benefit match.

The home side, promoted at the end of the previous season, began the game well but were guilty of some poor misses. Jack Milsom then raced clear of the away defence to hit a magnificent shot that was dipping under the bar until Swift, using every inch of his large frame, touched it over with his outstretched arm. Buoyed by this escape it was City who took a half-time lead when Tilson's screw shot beat Bob Jones.

Bolton continued to press in the second period and it was no surprise when Ray Westwood levelled the scores, only for City to race ahead when Brooks scored twice. Bolton were not finished and after Milsom scored with a penalty the away side was forced to defend deeply.

Westwood had the home support dancing with delight when he beat Swift before, in the final minute, the big City 'keeper scrambled across his line to keep out a Milsom header. Monday's *Bolton Evening News* reported 'many at that end of the ground felt it had crossed the line. But Swift takes credit for his pluck in clearing with a heap of players on top of him'. Swift, the paper said 'made the greatest defensive gestures of the day'. It was another fine display by the young 'keeper.

Yet, with City well behind leaders Sunderland, much of his heroics were going to waste and despite a 5-0 thrashing of relegation strugglers Aston Villa, December brought just three points from five matches.

Back at Molineux just before Christmas the away side conceded four goals and lost out by the odd goal in a match they led 2-0 after 35 minutes, Tilson scoring both goals. Like the previous season the Wolves side were inspired by Wrigglesworth and he beat Swift on 44 minutes with a brilliant effort. The left-winger equalised after the interval and then made Cuthbert Phillips' goal before Tom Smalley added a fourth with a magnificent shot. Brook reduced the arrears but the result was a fair one.

Meanwhile just down the road that day one man was writing his name into the record books. Arsenal's Ted Drake lashed home seven goals – his other shot hit the woodwork – in a 7-1 hammering of Aston Villa. It was the third time during the season that the West Midlands side had shipped seven goals.

At Chelsea, City took the lead in the first minute through Herd, but thereafter rarely threatened and Swift in goal had a right peppering' but was helpless to prevent George Gibson and Joe Bambrick – whose six goals for Ireland against Wales in 1930 gives him the international scoring record for the Home countries –from giving the Pensioners both points.

Two days later Manchester City were heavily beaten 5-1 at the Hawthorns, before succumbing 3-0 to Grimsby at Maine Road on New Year's Day.

It meant City faced a difficult task if they were to win their first match of 1936. Sunderland seemed set to replace Arsenal as League Champions, especially after just beating the Gunners 5-4 in arguably the greatest game ever seen at Roker Park.

Keeper's death

The match proved to be a fine one with both 'keepers [Swift and 22-year-old Jimmy Thorpe] playing superbly. Sadly, little more than a month later the Sunderland 'keeper was dead, when following a rough encounter against Chelsea at Roker Park he returned home to rest from his head, eye and face injuries and died a few days later. As a result of what happened the coroner at the inquest urged the FA to instruct all referees to exercise stricter control over the players so as to prevent similar incidents.

Soon after the 'keeper's death the FA set up a committee to examine the circumstances that led to it and both Sunderland and Chelsea were asked to submit evidence. This proved to be a whitewash, with the referee exonerated and Sunderland blamed for allowing Thorpe to play, despite evidence from the club's doctor that Thorpe, who suffered from diabetes, was known to be in good health. The decision meant that 'keepers would continue to receive some very heavy treatment from opposing forwards and Swift was one of those to suffer.

Swift was a great admirer of Raich Carter, who could direct the ball precisely where he intended it to go with either foot. The 4 January 1936 was no different, as on 65 minutes the inside-forward sent the 'keeper one way and the ball the other as he scored the only goal of the match from 10 yards – 'Carter has scored many spectacular goals, but none cleverer than this one', reported the *Northern Mail*.

When Swift selected his finest ever eleven Carter was in it, saying 'he possessed the most uncanny art of anticipation, is the best player in the game without a ball, has one of the hardest shots with either foot and also understands Stanley Matthews so well that after he has slipped the ball through he watches Stanley do his stuff, strolls away from the opposition, and always seems to be in position when the ball comes back'.

Sunderland's victory over Swift's side was to help the north-east club to win the title for the sixth time at the end of the season, equalling Arsenal and Aston Villa's record.

With City having no hope of winning the League there was relief when Portsmouth were beaten 3-1 at Maine Road in the FA Cup third round. In the fourth round a Maine Road crowd of 65,978 saw Luton Town beaten 2-1. Swift had joined the rest of the players and spectators in paying a minute's silence following the death of King George V, the man who had presented him with his Cup-winners' medal at Wembley in 1934.

John McLeod, who had scored against Luton, then continued his fine form in the next match as he scored twice in a 2-1 victory at Portsmouth. Back at the seaside in the FA Cup, McLeod was also one of City's scorers at Blundell Park but there was disappointment as Grimsby won a fine match 3-2.

The match was to mark Matt Busby's last Cup match for Manchester City as a few weeks later a £6,000 offer from Liverpool was accepted. Busby had joined from Denny Hibernians in 1928 as an inside-forward, but had moved to right half-back in an emergency, where he became an instant success.

It was a case of one in and one out, as City spent big to purchase Blackpool's Peter Doherty at a fee of £10,000, just £1,000 less than the then record fee. Earlier in this career Doherty had assisted Glentoran to success in the Irish Cup and his arrival at Maine Road was to turn City into a Championship winning side.

Frank Swift was the first of his new colleagues that Doherty met on his arrival at Maine Road and he 'couldn't mistake the mighty fist that shook mine as he welcomed me – my hand seemed to disappear completely in his huge grip!' (*Spotlight on Football*, 1947)

The Irishman's second game was at Goodison Park where Swift continued his fine form with a good display that helped his side win an undeserved point in a 2-2 draw. He regularly denied Dixie Dean, but was powerless to prevent Torry Gillick's two goals.

Doherty scored his first goal in his new colours when the following weekend Middlesbrough were beaten 6-0 at Maine Road, all the goals coming in the second half. Two weekends later City did even better, beating Bolton Wanderers 7-0. This must have been a bitter-sweet experience for the City goalkeeper as playing in goal for the Trotters was older brother Fred, who had been signed in May 1935 from Oldham Athletic – where he made 55 first-team appearances. So little did the younger Frank have to do that he actually sat down against the post at one point during the second period.

At the other end Fred enjoyed a torturous experience and the Bolton 'keeper was at fault with at least three of the goals. The match was the first time the brothers had faced each other in a 'big game' and before kick-off the pair shook hands as the teams changed ends. At 7-0 it was Wanderers' equal worst-ever League defeat.

The win pushed the victors up to sixth in the table before seven points from the remaining eight games of the season saw them finish in ninth place. Swift played a great game in a 2-2 draw at Villa Park when after having had their two goals lead pegged back the relegation threatened home side poured forward. The away side held out thanks to 'the unhappy goalkeeping of Swift, surely England's best. How he saved one magnificent header from Astley and a host of shots from Houghton and Hodgson bordered on the miraculous'. (*Daily Mirror*)

Chapter 8

Champions

There was little to suggest Manchester City were going to challenge for the title when, on the opening day of the season, they lost 2-0 at Middlesbrough, with Ralph Birkett and Benny Yorston, later a wartime teammate of Swift at Hamilton, scoring. 23,081 watched the action.

After beating Leeds 4-0 in midweek, City then beat WBA 6-2 with all eight goals scored in an amazing first 45-minutes. Herd opened the scoring on seven minutes but within 90 seconds his side were 2-1 down after W.G. Richardson seized on a Marshall sliced clearance to leave Swift helpless and then the Albion man hit a perfectly placed shot from the angle of the penalty area. The lead didn't last long and after Herd equalised on 20 minutes it was Brook who put the home side in front on 30 minutes. Five minutes later Heale doubled the lead before Doherty scored twice to make it 6-2.

After all the excitement it was perhaps not surprising that the second half lacked any quality, with the most interesting thing being the arrival of the police to climb behind the Albion goal and arrest a spectator.

City would also have won the next game, away to Leeds, if their 'keeper had judged a Billy Furness cross correctly. Swift's mistake left Jackie Hargreaves, who had earlier been denied by him on a number of occasions, to head into an empty net. Doherty's headed goal ensured a point apiece.

The following weekend the first derby match in six seasons produced a rousing game before a crowd approaching the then Old Trafford record gate of 70,000.

Defending the Manchester Road End, Swift was soon in action, punching away a high cross. The 'keeper though had no chance when George Mutch found Tom Manley and when his cross picked out Tom Bamford the United centre-forward made no mistake with a powerful shot.

An equaliser looked certain but former Stoke 'keeper Roy John made a brilliant save to deny Doherty as the crowd watched mesmerised. The home 'keeper then amazed the watching public when Brook released a rocket of a shot and as the crowd shouted 'goal' John came from virtually nowhere to save a certain equaliser.

Against the run of play the home side made it 2-0 when Manley's height told as he nodded the ball beyond Swift and things then got a lot worse for the losing team when Barkas was injured, forcing the full-back to go up front with Brook dropping back. Despite the handicap the away side cut the deficit when Bray struck a 15-yard shot through a ruck of players on 42 minutes.

With Herd also injured the away side made a further reshuffle in the second half, the City inside-forward swapping places with outside-right Toseland. Despite the handicaps it was City who scored next when, following a spell of pressure, Heale nodded home Toseland's cross.

When the home side attempted to restore their lead Swift made a good save from another Manley header but with just eight minutes left he was beaten when Billy Bryant ran on to a Bamford short pass to send a low drive flashing into the net for the winning goal. Newly promoted Manchester United had thus collected two precious points, although little good it was to do them at the season's end.

With just five points from five games the losing side sat in mid-table. When they then drew 0-0 at home to Chelsea the 30,047 Maine Road crowd showed their disapproval by slow hand clapping during the second half in which a decent Swift save from Tom Spence was as good as it got. The first half had been little better, but at least Vic Woodley in the Chelsea goal was able to show the sort of form that would shortly win him a place in the England side with good saves from Brook, Toseland and Jack Percival.

The Chelsea side included Sam Weaver, whose League career had started at Newcastle United in the 1929-30 season and included three international caps and two inter-League games. Weaver was renowned for his prodigiously long throw-ins. This was a task considerably more difficult back then as, in order to keep the leather match balls in good condition, dubbin was applied. As a result they usually absorbed water to become waterlogged and heavier. Modern balls have a waterproof coating, so that they remain the same weight throughout the game.

Charlton, in the first ever League game between the sides, also left Maine Road with a point. The promoted Addicks indicated they had enough to stay up, with wingers Don Welsh and Joe Jobling a constant danger. The home 'keeper had no chance of saving a powerful header from George Tadman that equalised Heale's close range opener. In the Charlton goal Sam Bartram played impressively.

City's indifferent start to the season continued on All Saints' Day as Sunderland went home having won 4-2. It would have been a lot more but 'Frank Swift kept the score down'. (Doherty) It left the home side with just 11 points from 13 games.

The week leading up to the game had seen the British public finally being made aware of a possible constitutional crisis when the news that Wallis Simpson had filed for divorce from her husband became public knowledge. During the summer she and King Edward VII had holidayed together in the Eastern Mediterranean on board the yacht *Nahlin*. Yet with the press maintaining a self-imposed silence – imagine that today – few people knew.

With the King making clear that he intended to eventually marry Simpson, Prime Minister Stanley Baldwin explicitly advised him that people would be opposed to such a marriage and indicated that if he went ahead with this [in direct contravention of his ministers' advice], the government would resign en masse.

On Friday 11 December 1936 Edward abdicated after refusing to give up 'the woman I love'. His reign had lasted just 327 days, the shortest of any British monarch since the disputed reign of Jane Grey nearly 400 years earlier. With both Edward and Wallis Simpson known to be admirers of fascism, and Hitler in particular, their departure was a big blow to those parts of the British Establishment that might have favoured a pact with the Nazis.

On Saturday 14 November 1936 Everton arrived at Maine Road following a 4-2 success the previous weekend against West Bromwich Albion in which Dixie Dean had celebrated his 400th League appearance by notching a hat-trick to take his League goal tally to 335, a remarkable record and goals per game ratio that is likely never to be broken in English football.

With the home side in poor form the Toffee's must have fancied their chances. They were quickly behind though when, on seven minutes, Herd's clipped ball sent Toseland free and he finished smartly. Having had little to do, Swift was then beaten by a rocket of a shot from Alex Stevenson but to the Irishman's disappointment the ball came back off the post. The away side were then denied by a brilliant save as Swift dived full length to touch away a Gillick shot. On the stroke of half-time Colin Rodger made it 2-0 and City were worthy 4-1 winners at the end.

Having beaten Bolton Wanderers 3-1 at Burnden Park, they travelled to Arsenal in early December. Signs that the side were now coming towards their best was welcomed by 'a huge contingent of City supporters who bellowed their team to a spectacular and somewhat surprising victory, and wrecked Arsenal's unbeaten home record' said Thomas Tickler in the *Daily Mirror* of 7 December 1936.

All the goals came in the final 20 minutes of a match that City won by adopting a close neat passing game on a rain soaked pitch. Swift had little to do as in front of him centre-half Marshall had a tremendous game and although Ted Drake did manage to hustle through to equalise, after Doherty had scored, that was virtually the only time the prolific striker was able to run free of his marker.

Arsenal were without the injured Cliff Bastin, and his loss on the left was a big blow; after Colin Rodger put City back in the lead it was no great surprise when the same player made it 3-1.

The following weekend Preston were thumped 4-1 at Maine Road but on 19 December Manchester City suffered their first defeat in two months in a game that Sheffield Wednesday would have won more comfortably than 5-1 if Swift had been in poor form. He had no chance when Robinson put the Owls ahead with a low shot after just five minutes. He then did well to prevent Barkas putting through his own goal, but after saving a Starling shot the 'keeper had no chance of preventing Drury netting from the rebound. This put the home side back in the lead after Doherty had equalised.

With half-time approaching Swift made two saves from Mark Hooper, twisting behind to push the ball away and then diving to his left to use his long reach to push the ball for a corner.

His efforts had kept his side – just – in the game but by the 55th they were out of it when Jackie Robinson's effort was followed by a Hooper goal. When Drury was left unmarked he did further damage by heading home to make it 5-1.

Despite that defeat, and a 5-3 loss at Grimsby on Christmas Day, there were over 56,000 inside Maine Road to see City beat Middlesbrough 2-1 on Boxing Day. Nearly 9,000 more were present for the home derby against a fast falling United in which a single effort from Herd was enough to give City both points. Successes against Wrexham and Accrington Stanley also put a resurgent side into the FA Cup fifth round.

Eight goals were then equally shared at Stamford Bridge before Bolton were thrashed 5-0 in the Cup. Four days later City beat Derby County 5-0 in the League in a trouncing that gave real hopes of a first League title. City played masterful football and Swift, after an early save from a Dai Astley effort, had virtually nothing to do except watch the front five demolish the Rams defence. Rodger opened the scoring on five minutes after Jack Howe and Jack Nicholas had dallied. The lead was doubled with a picture goal, Barkas sweeping the ball out to Toseland who centred perfectly for Tilson to score.

When the City centre grabbed his second of the game it was 3-0 after 27 minutes. Brook extended the lead on 64 minutes and Tilson's third nine minutes later ended the scoring.

Victory cut back a point on the top two, Charlton and Arsenal drawing 1-1 with Bastin's penalty miss preventing the Gunners going top. The chasing City then maintained their fine form with a 4-1 success against Wolves with Tilson again scoring three.

Lions roar

Third Division North side Millwall had made it through to the last eight of the FA Cup by beating First Division Chelsea and Derby County en route. A crowd of 42,474 squeezed into the Den to see the tie with Manchester City. The Millwall ground had experienced two incidents of crowd trouble at the Cold Blow Lane end in 1934. In response Millwall had built a covered entrance from the dressing rooms to the pitch in early 1935.

No side from outside the top two divisions had reached the semi-finals of the Cup since a third League had been established after World War One. Only once before had City been beaten by a Third Division side in the FA Cup, when Charlton Athletic had won away in 1922-23.

Inside-right David Mangnall had scored for Birmingham City against Frank Swift on 8 September 1934, and he had netted four times in the 6-1 defeat of Aldershot Town in the FA Cup first round. Against Manchester City he was to score twice before dropping back to help his defence.

The opening goal came on 15 minutes. With City right-half Joe Rogers off the field injured, Mangnall powered home a header from centre-forward Ken Burditt's corner. Twelve minutes later a wonderful centre – one of many during his career – from inside-right Jimmy McCartney was also dispatched in powerful fashion as the City defence failed to mark their men. On the stroke of half-time Swift kept his side in the match with a great save to deny Mangnall a third.

Preferring to stay deep the home side were perhaps asking for trouble in the second half. A raucous crowd helped Millwall. Perched high above the stand one fan tried to push forward the minute hand of the clock. With a circumference of 18ft with hands 8ft long it was the biggest ever installed at a football ground. Electrician Reg Smith, who was lighting up the pitch against City from his outside-left position for the Lions that day, had wired this up.

Playing the game of their lives, Millwall were worthy winners. When the referee Mr Wiltshire from Dorset blew the final whistle Lions fans raced on to the pitch to chair their conquering heroes off the pitch. Pathe News caught the action and sent it round cinemas.

The result meant that if the defeated side were to win a trophy it would have to be in the League and the following match, a 3-0 defeat of Huddersfield Town kept them firmly in contention.

Doherty had put City ahead with a lovely goal but just before half-time only a moment of great improvisation kept City ahead. Richardson's shot seemed net bound only for Swift to dive towards the ball using his feet first and the slightest of touches sent it just round the post. Two minutes after half-time Doherty, who had been criticised at Millwall for keeping the ball for too long, doubled City's advantage with a wonderful goal before Brook completed the scoring in a second half in which Terriers 'keeper Bob Hesford was brilliant.

Despite Swift's own supreme form he was nevertheless not selected for the England trial match held on St Patrick's Day when the Probables beat the Possibles 2-0.

When City journeyed to Goodison Park they faced a side that had only lost once at home all season. With the away side having raced up the table the *Liverpool Echo* headlined its pre-match assessment MANCHESTER CITY'S

MIND AT EVERTON WILL BE ON CHAMPIONSHIP MEDALS and reported 'we expect fireworks, because Manchester City have been a hereditary foe, and their games home and away have been sparkling in every feature. After a dozy start Manchester City have come to their best and brightest.'

With Sagar needing a cartilage operation City found newly signed Harry Morton, Aston Villa's famous 'keeper, between the Everton posts. Swift also found a new attacking opponent facing him in Tommy Lawton. At just 17 years and four days the Bolton born forward had scored a hat-trick for Burnley against Spurs in October 1936. With Dixie Dean coming into the twilight of his career, Everton had paid £6,500 to sign Lawton two months later.

Despite the middle of the pitch resembling a mud bath – reducing City's white jerseys to pitch black by half-time – the game was a very good one and rightfully ended 1-1. City's unbeaten League run was now 12 matches. The away side might even have won it after having a penalty awarded in their favour for handball. Strong Everton appeals persuaded the referee to consult his linesman, who having been much closer to the incident signalled a corner-kick.

Swift in the City goal had an impressive match, using his height to prevent Gillick scoring with a powerful header, touching away Joe Mercer's shot and constantly advancing to punch away dangerous crosses, once being flattened for his bravery. He also enjoyed a touch of good fortune when he misjudged one cross and Dean, expertly heading the ball off the back of his head, beat him only for the ball to finish inches over the bar. Walking to take the goal-kick the City 'keeper wore a smile as wide as the Mersey.

He was beaten on 60 minutes when Stevenson hit a powerful shot. With City rocking the 'keeper then did superbly to prevent a Dean header making it 2-0. With 15 minutes remaining the away side equalised after the referee awarded a free-kick that brought ironic cheers from City fans in the crowd. Jack Percival's punt was missed by everyone and bounced into the goal to give the away side a precious point. It was one of 11 goals that Percival scored for Manchester City in his 161 League appearances.

Six days later and back on Liverpool, City won 5-0 with Brook scoring a hat-trick and Doherty and Herd grabbing the others. The following day, though, Bolton's unexpected point in a 2-2 draw at Maine Road was a blow to Manchester City's title chase. With his brother Fred between the posts for Wanderers, Swift was quickly in action when a long ball over the retreating City defence saw him dash from the box and employing, especially for a big man, some neat skills on the ball he beat George T. Taylor with a little dribble before booting the ball up field.

The away side were playing well and there was a further moment of anxiety when the City 'keeper dropped an awkward shot before quickly retrieving the ball. Don Howe then blasted over with the 'keeper beaten, before the game became a battle for midfield supremacy, neither side ever really achieving it. The home side took the lead with their first real opportunity. A marvellous hook shot by Herd gave Fred Swift no chance, only for Jack Calder to head an equaliser two minutes before the interval.

With City attacking in the second half, the younger Swift was forced to keep himself alert and on the move as sleet belted down. At the other end Fred – in the finest period of his career in which he conceded just six goals in a nine-match period to help drag Wanderers out of the bottom two – performed a diving save to keep out a fierce Brook shot, only for the loose ball to be swept home by Doherty on 68 minutes. Yet with Marshall injured soon after, and forced to play at outside-left, Bolton grabbed an 83rd minute equaliser. Swift blocked Milsom's shot only for Howe to make it 2-2. With Arsenal drawing at Middlesbrough, City stayed four points behind, but with two crucial games in hand.

Two days later, Matt Busby was given a marvellous ovation as he returned as captain of Liverpool, The away side led after five minutes when Fred Howe beat Swift, who in his desperate attempt to prevent the goal cut open his forehead as he dived across the goalmouth. Not for the first time – or last – the 'keeper, after a brief rest and attention from the City trainer, got on with the match.

There was a moment of controversy about the equalising goal; the referee S.L. Clark of London judging that Tom Bradshaw's tackle on a falling Tilson was a penalty. Brook slammed the ball into the roof of the net with South African Dick Kemp well beaten. Now it was all City, their 'keeper watching as Kemp performed heroics to keep the score level at half-time.

The Liverpool 'keeper though could do little to prevent a rampant home side when the game resumed, City bashing home four goals in just six minutes. First, on 53 minutes Dick Neilson met Toseland's cross to head home, before two goals from Herd and one from Toseland took City into an unassailable 5-1 lead, which is how it finished at the end.

City crashed home six goals in the next game. So tight was the top of the table that seventh placed Brentford had a chance to draw level on points with third placed City if they won the match. With 13 wins and only one defeat at home from 19 matches the Bees were in confident mood at kick-off.

Swift was to be beaten twice but with City's attacking line in sparkling form the away side easily maintained their unbeaten run stretching back to Christmas Day. All the forwards – Toseland, Herd, Tilson, Doherty (2) and Brook – netted.

Doherty was the pick of the players on display – producing a 'world class' performance reported G.W. Chisholm in the *Daily Mirror*. Brentford did rally at 3-0, reducing arrears to a single goal but the crowd were then treated to a scintillating forward display as the away side scored three in eight minutes. With leaders Arsenal beating WBA 2-0 City maintained the gap on the Gunners to just three points.

Meantime, with a member of the international selection committee having been present at Brentford, there was speculation as to who he was watching with the headline in the *Manchester Evening News* suggesting 'SWIFT TO GUARD ENGLAND'S GOAL AT HAMPDEN?' It was not to be, however.

City then took advantage of one of their games in hand by beating Brentford 2-1 at home to move within a point of the leaders and at the same time leapfrog second-placed Charlton Athletic.

Swift's side were the superior team but had to wait until 10 minutes from the end for Brook to score the winning goal. This was tough on Brentford's defence, and especially Jack Holliday and Joe James who were outstanding. Heavy rain at the start of the match meant that when the downpour stopped and the sun came out, the pitch became a quagmire.

The game started with two goals in the first eight minutes when Dave McCulloch beat Swift before Doherty equalised. The City 'keeper then had to remain on his toes as on their rare attacks forward Brentford remained dangerous with McCulloch constantly worrying the home defenders.

There were three times as many inside Maine Road for the Arsenal match as had watched the Brentford game, 74,918 pouring through the turnstiles. Having beaten the Gunners in early December the home side knew victory would put them in pole position to lift the League Championship trophy for the first time.

The match pitched the highest scorers – City with 91 – against the tightest defence – Arsenal with 45. It was, though, the home side who were forced to defend for their lives in the first period, as the North London side twisted and turned, dribbled and passed in a way reminiscent of the team that had captured the title for three consecutive seasons earlier in the decade.

Goals would surely have come their way against a lesser defence but with Swift, Dale and Barkas almost forming a blanket round the goal the home side somehow held out. Then on 35 minutes City scored with a shot that would have been worthy of any match. Doherty, receiving a short pass from Tilson glanced up before driving a fierce clipped shot from an acute angle, which no 'keeper (in this case Frank Boulton) in the world would have saved.

Many of City's defenders rushed forward to offer the Irishman their congratulations and the home crowd went wild. Ian Niven was among them. Doherty was his favourite footballer in the City side of 1936-37 and he says of him 'that Doherty rates alongside Colin Bell and as the best players I have ever seen. They were both box-to-box players who could open the tightest of defences. They'd bob and weave past defenders, and sort of glide away from them and the only other similar player was Manchester United's Dennis Viollet, who was a City fan'.

Yet with amateur Bernard Joy totally dominating Tilson there was always the prospect of Arsenal getting at least a draw in the second half. However, although they were never in control of the match, the City side battled on, abandoning their passing game which had taken them to within touching distance of glory to constantly hassle the Arsenal forwards. Behind them Swift was in confident mood and twice punched the ball away when challenged in the box.

On 67 minutes the crucial goal arrived, when after Brook and Tilson had created a half-chance, Toseland scored from close-in. There was to be no way back for the away team and when the referee sounded the final whistle they had found themselves knocked from top spot by their victors. It was a famous victory, one of Manchester City's greatest ever.

Four days later they travelled to Roker Park to face reigning League champions Sunderland. Barkas and Bray, selected to play for England against Scotland at Hampden Park, were absent from the City line-up.

Sunderland had beaten Millwall, City's conquerors in the FA Cup quarter-finals, by three goals to one in the semi and were soon ahead through a smart Tom Wylie header. Things might have got worse but when the scorer then beat the 'keeper with another header the timely intervention of Donnelly, playing for the injured Dale, prevented a second goal.

After a poor first half performance the away side were in much better form in the second. Only some great saves from Johnny Mapson kept his side ahead until on 66 minutes Doherty scored, a feat he repeated 16 minutes later to put City deservedly ahead. Then on 89 minutes Brook put the match out of Sunderland's reach and the 3-1 win put City three points ahead of Arsenal.

In the following game at Preston the home side was, like City, missing key players with Andy Beattie and Frank O'Donnell part of the Scottish side that beat England 3-1. The crowd was a world record of 149,547.

Heavy rain had left the Deepdale pitch soft and heavy, with pools of water glistening on the surface. Former Bury forward Les Vernon led the home attack and when Hugh O'Donnell, brother of Frank, crossed from the left he beat Swift with a fine finish to put his side into an early lead.

Things worsened for the Championship chasing side when O'Donnell and Willie Fagan craftily combined to set up Jim Dougal who, with Swift advancing, slipped the ball into the net. Unlike City, Preston had come out 10 minutes before kick-off to do some vigorous warm-up work and this may have contributed to their flying start.

The League leader's attempts to get back into the game were met with some robust defending, and Mick Burns did well to block a Doherty shot before

Brook shot wide from 10 yards. As half-time approached the away side were in control of the game but still went into the interval two goals down. To make matters worse Donnelly was clearly injured, forcing Brook to drop to full-back as the defender moved out wide on the left.

Remarkably within 10 minutes of the restart City were ahead with three goals coming in three minutes. In the first half Doherty and Herd 'had tried to outwit Jimmy Milne and Bill Shankly by frequently switching positions; but the Preston wing halves had refused to fall into the trap; and we had given it up as ineffective' reported Doherty. Perhaps feeling their job was completed the Preston men were undone when the City duo tried the same exercise early in the second half.

On 53 minutes Dougal's poor back pass was seized upon by Doherty to score, and then the Irishman scored his second when he headed Toseland's cross home. On 56 minutes another right-wing raid carved open the home defence for Herd to hit a low shot just inside Burn's right-hand post. The City fans in the crowd danced deliriously as their side edged towards the title.

Seven minutes later Doherty scored his hat-trick goal, a header after Billy Tremelling had been unable to get the ball away to safety. Ten minutes from the end the plucky Donnelly was the grateful recipient of an unmissable opportunity when Toseland, who had played brilliantly, and Tilson set him up. City's second half display had been as brilliant as their first half display had been disappointing.

What it meant, though, was that after six straight wins Manchester City would win their first League title if they could beat bottom placed Sheffield Wednesday at Maine Road the following Saturday.

The table prior to the game with Wednesday was as follows:

City	40	54
Arsenal	40	51
Charlton Athletic	40	50
Derby	40	47

Owls beaten as title is won for first time

Just before Christmas the Owls had wiped the floor with City at Hillsborough. Then Grimsby had beaten City 5-3 at Blundell Park to drop the losers into the bottom half of the table after 20 matches. A magnificent 20 match unbeaten League run had followed in which the 34 points gained meant the Championship was within reach. Now was the time to make sure, and Wednesday were to be blown away in the first period.

The away side started the match in determined fashion and Swift was quickly forced into action, denying Drury and then rising above Dewar to pluck a dangerous cross from the centre-forward's head.

It wasn't until nearly 15 minutes had gone before the home side opened up the Wednesday defence, but Herd pulled his shot wide.

Four minutes later though Manchester City were ahead, and like many of their goals scored during this historic season it was a wonderful goal. First, surging forward right-half Percival feinted and dribbled up the middle of the field before slipping a smart pass to Doherty. Hemmed in, the Irishman still managed to find Brook with a smart pass. 'In came the home left-winger, and releasing a thunderbolt of a shot from a difficult angle well before anyone expected, Brook saw his fast-travelling and wonderfully directed effort beat Smith'. (*MEN* 24/04/1937) Back in the City goal Swift jumped with joy.

Now totally dominant the second home goal took only five minutes to arrive when Doherty weaved past at least three Wednesday defenders before pushing a pass to Tilson who drove home from 10 yards, 2-0.

With close to 55,000 in the ground the game – and the race for Championship – was as good as over on 31 minutes.

Doherty, Herd and Tilson, with a series of short passes, cut through the visitors' defence as if it wasn't there. Doherty – in each case – putting the ball to his colleagues and running forward for the return, which was perfectly supplied. Tilson's final touch left Doherty clear to complete his dash and shoot past Roy Smith for a goal that brought down the 'house'.

'What a team this City side are at their best! Their combination and positional play was so perfect that one almost felt sorry for Wednesday, who were fighting hard, but must surely have felt that their task was hopeless.' (*MEN*)

Wednesday gamely battled on and Swift was forced to make saves from Robinson, Rimmer and Dewar but at half-time the score remained 3-0.

The second period lacked the action of the first, and few chances were fashioned until on 71 minutes Swift's full-length save from a Charlie Luke shot saw Rimmer follow up to score from the rebound. This was to prove a consolation as in the very last minute Brook was sent clear and from close to the penalty spot he made it 4-1.

When the referee blew the final whistle many of the crowd burst on to the pitch, crowding in their thousands in front of the main stand and the players' entrances to which Swift and his teammates had dashed to escape them. Cheering and singing the crowd was later dispersed by the police after a chorus of *Auld Lang Syne* and *God Save the King*. Manchester City were the 1936-37 Division One champions and Frank Swift now had a Championship winners' medal to sit alongside the FA Cup winners' medal earned in 1933-34.

Praise for side and supporters

After the game City chairman Mr Bob Smith said, 'It has been a fine achievement by the team, especially as they have not been beaten since last

Christmas. On behalf of my fellow directors, and myself I take this opportunity of thanking the players. We are tremendously proud of them and I feel we ought to be proud of our supporters.

There is not a better crowd in the country, and their support has meant a lot to the team in its progress to the Championship.'

Sam Barkas: 'We have been a happy family, and that is one of the secrets of our success.'

Doherty: 'That is very true. When you have a grand spirit allied to a grand team, success is inevitable.'

Chelsea 2 Arsenal 0
Charlton 1 Bolton 0

Manchester City	41	56
Charlton	41	51
Arsenal	41	50

The Championship winning season was to end with a 2-2 draw at Birmingham City. The point gained meant the new Champions had broken the club's previous highest points total of 54 by three points. City arrived at St Andrews after a joint celebration in midweek. After losing 1-0 in the Victoria Hospital Cup at Bloomfield Road, the City players and those of newly promoted Blackpool were the star guests at a banquet and dance given by the Blackpool Corporation at the Empress Ballroom.

The game at Birmingham was typical end of season fare enlivened only by some brilliant Frank Swift saves. He was easily beaten by Seymour Morris on nine minutes but then 'brought the house down with a grand piece of work in deflecting a pile-driver from Morris over the bar'. [*MEN* 1/05/1937] Then he well held a powerful header from Jack Beattie before his best save so far – 'a point blank shot from Dennis Jennings, which the City 'keeper pulled down and then cleared. A great effort and an equally fine save!' [*MEN*]

Birmingham 'keeper Harry Hibbs must have been impressed. Swift was a big fan of the England 'keeper and had been grateful for his help 'when I was a struggling youngster still playing for my place in the first team. He told me never to be afraid to ask his advice, and I took it on many occasions. He was a master of angles, and each time we played Birmingham I learned something new from him.

Particularly did I admire his coolness and calm in the goalmouth. Before the kick-off he used to mark a spot on the six-yard line, which was his central point of operations for crosses from the wing, and for corner-kicks.

So well did he train his defences that I never saw him in trouble. I gave him six inches in height, and have frequently made what seemed amazing saves only because the length of my arms enabled me to reach the ball; yet short as he was, I have seen him make similar saves without any last-minute excitement, purely through his amazing positional sense.' (*Football from the Goalmouth*) Swift picked Hibbs as the 'keeper in his finest ever eleven.

On 47 minutes the away 'keeper was beaten for a second time when Albert Clarke scored from close-in. After this the League Champions surged forward in a desperate attempt to maintain their unbeaten League run. Now it was Swift's turn to admire the Birmingham 'keeper's qualities as Hibbs beat away shots from Tilson, Toseland and Doherty.

It seemed the away side were going to suffer their first League defeat in 22 matches but late goals from Tilson and Doherty, who actually fisted the ball in, were enough to snatch a draw. As they left the field the crowd warmly applauded the new champions. Travelling home the title winners would have heard of Manchester United's defeat at West Bromwich Albion, a result that pushed the Old Trafford side back into Division Two.

Doherty on why City won the League

'Team spirit, I maintain, is the greatest single factor in winning such an exacting and exhausting competition as the League Championship. It is a mysterious and elusive thing; but once it has entered into a team it does not desert you if there is a good feeling, comradeship and unselfishness among the players. I don't know which of these the cardinal virtue is; it doesn't really matter. We certainly had all three of them at Maine Road.

It is only in such happy circumstances that members of a team can produce the best that is in them. Unfailing encouragement and help from the management, perfect understanding and co-operation between the players, and – I must insist on this – an occasional stroke of luck, are the factors, which carry a team to the top. Team spirit plus skill will always produce results.

If there was a good spirit at Maine Road, there was certainly no lack of skill. I have yet to see a better goalkeeper than Frank Swift, and Dale was a model for all full-backs in the precision of his tackling and the cleanness of his kicking. Sam Barkas is a tactician of the highest class; and a full-back who is only really on the defensive when he is on his own goalline; everything else is attack, or designed to promote an attack.

At centre-half, Bobby Marshall was an inspiration to the whole team, the complete footballer with a temperament proof against any strain; and Bray and Percival fulfilled the highest City tradition of half-back play, in that they consistently worked the ball forward and wherever possible, made an opening before pushing it through.

The forward line was not composed of five units, but was a quintet in the truest sense of the word. Were I a centre-half, I am quite sure I should have hated having to mark Freddie Tilson. He wriggled and darted in the most distracting way, and every swoop on a defence had a definite purpose behind it. My bag of goals that season was 30, and had Freddie been a selfish player he would have had a lot of them; but his football skill found a real outlet in making opportunities for others.

Alec Herd is a grand player too. There are not many better shots in the game, nor many so astute and accurate in the use of the swinging pass out to the opposite wing. And, finally, the two wingers, Brook and Toseland, were always a source of danger to opposing defences; their accurate centres brought scores of goals, and Brook's cannon-ball shots were respected by every goalkeeper in the League.

This, then, was the team which gave so many dazzling, bewildering displays; and when injuries or representative games left gaps, as they often did, there were good reserves to call upon – players like Gordon Clark, Donnelly, Heale, Rodger and Neilson, who all fitted in perfectly when an emergency arose. Harmony was the keynote at Maine Road, and it reaped splendid dividends. They were a grand bunch of players, and I was proud and happy to be associated with them.' (Spotlight on Football)

Chapter 9

Charity Shield success and relegation

No one could have predicted that the League Champions would be relegated the following season. No other team had 'achieved' such a feat beforehand and none has done so since.

The season started with a disappointing defeat, a first in 23 League matches, at Molineux where Gordon Clayton's three goals ensured a 3-1 Wolves success. There seemed little to worry about when Herd opened the scoring on 14 minutes but by half-time the home side were two goals ahead.

Four days later, the Champions were in much better form as they beat Everton 2-0 at Maine Road. Swift had little to do and once Herd had opened the scoring there was only going to be one winner after Doherty's thunderbolt doubled the lead.

Two more points were added in a 3-0 home victory over Leicester City in which Swift was again hardly engaged in any serious action. That though was not the case in the fourth match of the campaign. Everton, after leaving Dean out – the centre-forward who had never retaliated to severe on-field provocation having exchanged blows off it with Theo Kelly, Everton's first appointed manager – saw his replacement, 17-year-old Tommy Lawton, strike after 30 minutes at Goodison Park. Eight minutes later Stevenson doubled the home side's advantage and then he added the third when Lawton's pass cannoned off the referee, Mr Hadley, to leave Swift wrong-footed.

On 63 minutes a Peter Dougal drive ripped past Swift and after Brook scored from the penalty spot it was only thanks to their 'keeper that City were not beaten a lot more heavily than 4-1.

Lawton's goal had been a fierce well-placed effort that had given the City 'keeper no chance. Singing along afterwards with his teammates in the communal bath the scorer was as surprised as anyone when Frank Swift entered to congratulate him saying, 'Keep going like that, son – and you'll soon be better than all the rest.' An embarrassed Lawton hardly knew what to say, but when given time to consider his actions he jumped on the train the following day to Maine Road to thank the giant 'keeper for his fine sportsmanship. The actions of the pair were the start of a genuine friendship.

City then suffered a third consecutive away defeat when they were beaten 3-1 by the FA Cup holders, Sunderland, who had beaten Preston North End 3-1 at Wembley in the 1937 FA Cup Final. Playing for the Deepdale side was Bill

Shankly and he later praised his side's conquerors 'In many ways the Sunderland side in 1935-37 played the same total brand of Total Football as the great Holland team of the 1970s. It was a frightening experience to visit Roker Park during the 1930s because Sunderland were such a terrific outfit.'

Although Doherty did manage to draw his side level on 35 minutes, goals either side of the interval by Carter and Burbanks put the game out of reach for a City side that, for once, had been let down by their 'keeper. In coming for a cross Swift failed to push the ball away and Saunders was left with an easy opening goal.

Bravery

After a disappointing start, City ran into better form by capturing five points from six, including two in a 6-1 thrashing of Derby at Maine Road. In early October Swift played his first game against his hometown club, Blackpool. The Seasiders had finished second to Leicester City in Division Two, bringing to an end a four-season spell in the lower League. Former Bolton and England international striker Joe Smith had accepted the challenge of taking over the reins at Bloomfield Road in August 1935. He was to remain for 23 years and lead the club throughout its most successful period. Frank Swift and Smith were to become close friends when the 'keeper became a journalist after he retired from playing.

Playing in their changed strip of all white, Blackpool fell behind to a Brook goal on 40 minutes. A minute later Tom Jones and Swift collided heavily when going for the ball. This brought the ambulance men on to the pitch to treat both men and 'Swift, the referee's coat spread over him and lying still, was taken off on a stretcher as Brook tore off his own shirt and put on the goalkeepers jersey' reported the *Blackpool Sports Gazette*.

To the disappointment of the reserve 'keeper – who reported that he had had no shots to save – Swift wasn't off for too long. It was clear though that he was far from fit and when he stopped Alex Munro's rising centre and threw the ball out quickly it saw 'him stand for a couple of minutes on his line with both hands clasped to his side. He has a lot of pluck, has Frank Swift,' (*Sports Gazette*) and to further prove it he hobbled painfully to put Jimmy Hampson's cross behind for a corner.

The 'keeper had no chance, though, of preventing Dickie Watmough's unstoppable shot equalising the match at 1-1, but it was the home side that took both points when Herd scored the winner. The result put the winners into 11th place.

However, when the champions travelled back to the North East in late October to face Middlesbrough they were without Doherty, playing for Ireland in a 5-1 defeat at home to England at Windsor Park, Belfast. City also lost by four goals. With Brook playing for England, Wardle came into the City XI. The away side were two down on 20 minutes, Tom Cochrane and Norman Higham profiting from indecision in City's defence. Heavy rain ensured that Boro's more direct style kept Swift busy, and he showed his agility to save a well-placed Higham effort.

On 53 minutes the home side struck again when Fenton confidently beat Swift. As the game moved towards its conclusion Swift was constantly involved and one save 'took the eye when Swift came out as Cochrane was veering in, and flinging himself forward punched away the ball from the forward's toe at the expense of a hand injury' reported the *Middlesbrough Gazette*. There was little however the 'keeper could do when with two minutes remaining Fenton was again sent clear to make it 4-0.

Charity Shield triumph

In early November Frank Swift was a member of the first Manchester City side to capture the FA Charity Shield. Opponents Sunderland arrived at Maine Road having just walloped West Brom 6-1 away. Yet it was the League champions who were always in control and, at the second time of asking, Manchester City captured the Charity Shield Trophy.

With their fine passing, Carter, Gurney and Patsy Gallacher might have entertained the midweek afternoon crowd of 12,000, but it was City's inside-forwards, Herd and Doherty who were the more effective and both scored in the second half in a 2-0 success. Swift had relatively little to do, but must have been impressed by the performance of Mapson in the Sunderland goal whose many saves kept his side in the match until Doherty wrapped the game up on 87 minutes.

Despite this success the next eight games in the League were to be disastrous with only one victory and four points gathered. On Christmas Day, Brentford won 2-0 at Maine Road. This was a disappointing result for Swift in that it completed an unbroken four-year run in the first team in which he had chalked up 166 League games and 16 FA Cup matches.

His 167th consecutive League game was at Griffin Park, where the Bees completed the double over their more illustrious opponents before a capacity crowd of 40,000.

In a poor first half McCulloch's shot rattled Swift's knees, and then the centre-forward shot tamely when well placed. However, on 55 minutes Billy Scott headed a good goal before some great footwork in the City midfield opened up the Bees defence for Herd to draw the scores level.

With 10 minutes remaining Bobby Reid scored a hotly disputed winner when, after appearing to handle the ball, he beat Swift. Referee Dr Barton was unwilling to listen to the away side's pleas and City's drop down the table continued, especially after Wolves won 4-2 at Maine Road on New Year's Day.

January 1938, though, was to prove a good month for the League Champions. First City squeezed past previous season's conquerors Millwall in the FA Cup, winning 3-1 at Maine Road after a 2-2 draw at the Den, before easily beating Leicester City 4-1 in the League and Bury 3-1 in the FA Cup fourth round, a game that attracted a crowd of 71,937.

Having beaten Derby 6-1 earlier in the campaign Manchester City repeated the thrashing when the sides met at the Baseball Ground on 29 January 1938. With Heale scoring three times and Doherty once the away side won 7-1, with the latter – in his autobiography – reporting 'we played brilliant football. County's defence was split wide open by a series of crisp, devastating moves, which brought us an avalanche of goals. We looked anything but a relegation side that day'.

Swift had had little to keep him occupied against the Rams, but that wasn't the case in the next match when the League Champions faced Sunderland at Maine Road. The 0-0 result was City's first goalless draw since the match with Chelsea in September 1936.

Swift did enjoy some good fortune when John Spuhler's shot appeared to strike him, but there was nothing lucky about the save that followed from the same Sunderland forward when Swift showed great feet to get across the goal to turn the ball behind for a corner. Further fine saves followed, leading the Northern Mail to report that 'several of Swift's saves were little short of remarkable'.

Despite the point the champions remained just two points ahead of 21st placed Portsmouth. There was therefore some relief that when the sides met the south coast side went home beaten 2-1.

City then qualified for the quarter-finals of the FA Cup by beating Luton Town 3-1 at Kenilworth Road. Back at Maine Road, Arsenal ended City's eight match unbeaten run by winning 2-1.

Having been injured in the Gunners match there was some doubt as to whether Swift would get the chance to play for the first time in the League at Bloomfield Road.

The Tangerines were still getting over the loss of Jimmy Hampson, scorer of 248 goals in 361 games for Blackpool. He and Bobby Finan had scored 44 goals in the previous season. On 10 January 1938 Hampson had gone fishing with some friends. Their boat collided with a trawler and Hampson's body was never recovered.

The match proved a very special occasion for one young Blackpool fan. Four-year-old Margaret (Iris) Swift was watching her father play for the first time. She had already previously been to Bloomfield Road with her uncle Alf who, as a result of having only one leg, watched the game from a wheelchair close to the touchline just outside the players' tunnel. This meant that when the players ran out before the game it made it possible for Alf to grab hold of the City 'keeper and ask him 'do you know who this is?'

'As far as I can remember he said: "I think so", before giving me a hug' says Iris.

She had been born on 22 September 1933 to 17-year-old laundry worker Margaret Dickinson of Eden Street and Frank Swift of Ibbison Street.

'I was told they first met in the Tower and were boyfriend and girlfriend for a couple of years. I later saw Frank working the pleasure boats but I was told not to speak to him if he was with a lady and young girl. I did see them once. Jean, who was my sister, had bright orange hair. I didn't say anything and sadly we never ever spoke before she died,' says Iris.

Margaret, travelling down with a friend on a motorbike, had seen Frank play at Wembley in the 1934 FA Cup Final. She had not been happy about him going to Manchester but her own mother had told the 'keeper, who she greatly liked, 'to follow his talent'.

The pair had considered marrying but according to Iris 'I understand it was the grandmothers who sat down to discuss the future in the days before my birth. Frank's mum made clear that she needed his income to support the rest of the family. She would not give her permission for the marriage to take place, with my dad needing it, as he wasn't then 21 years old.

I also understand there was some discussion about adoption, which my dad didn't want. My grandparents owned a number of shops and it was agreed I would go and live with them. I was born with pneumonia, was lucky to survive and brought up by my grandmother, Rebecca Dickinson, until I was old enough to leave home.

Not long after I was born my mother married Billy Hardman, a good friend of Frank's who worked alongside him with a share on the *Skylark* boat. The couple had three other children, my half-brothers, but I never lived with them as it was seen as 'wrong' that Billy should have to pay for another man's child. Anyway I liked living with my grandmother.'

Still living in Blackpool, Iris is convinced that her mother's lack of humour would have meant that long-term her parents would not have stayed together if they had married.

'My birth certificate doesn't have my father's name on it. I am not sure why. I knew he was my father as I had a photograph of him in my bedroom, although there was a bit of a mystery at times as I was told daddy lives away. Many children's did around this time because of the war, so it wasn't that unusual.

I always lived a life looking in from outside. As I got older and became a young girl then he would hold my hand, but even when you were with him you rarely had his full attention as people were always asking for autographs or to have their photograph taken with him. There was always someone there.

I did see him play a few times for Manchester City and was at his final match against Everton. One time as a youngster I jumped on a bus and went over to Manchester, and when I got there I asked a milkman the way to Maine Road and he took me there and I asked if my dad could get me a ticket and he did. I watched the match and then came home. My grandmother was very, very angry.

I thought he was a good 'keeper; he was big and looked safe when he came for the ball. When the action was up the other goal he would pretend to put sun cream on.

As regards Frank's family then I knew Uncle Alf (*), who was only six years older anyway, and his wife Winnie reasonably well. I didn't know Alice who sadly was killed travelling to watch the open golf in Southport. I knew Fred but our relationship wasn't great.

After Dad finished playing, he was regularly in Blackpool as he would come to watch the matches, and he was very involved with the annual Clubland Command Performance, which he would compere with Stan Mortensen. They'd do a double act of jokes and introductions. It was a major fund-raising charity event held annually in the Winter Gardens and attended by a good few hundred people. Sometimes more.

I myself became a singer at aged 17 and did it for over 20 years until my thyroids were not up to it. I sang under my name, Iris Swift and made a living from doing it, but it's a difficult business in which you can earn decent money for a while and then nothing for a period. I performed across the North West. I was a middle of the road singer.

When my friend died I agreed to look after her son, Andrew Walmsley. He is now in his 40s and has done very well and lives in Las Vegas after success in running the company A1 Sets that designed the sets for *Who Wants to be a Millionaire*. He was the youngest to do a Royal Command Performance, which meant aged 21 he met the Queen.

When he moved to the USA he did sets for American Idol and then he became the youngest to do two sets on Broadway, which were for the Blood Brothers and Buddy. He is aware of Frank Swift.

I would have loved to meet my sister, and I did get a message to her via a contact but, sadly, she did not want to meet me. It's a great shame.

Blackpool's Stan Mortensen would regularly say "I am seeing your dad at the weekend", and I would tell him to say I was thinking of him. I am not sure whether either of us was in a position to do much more than we did. Perhaps if he had lived longer things may have been different.

The day he died in 1958 at Munich I was walking past Hills, a big Blackpool store that later burnt down. It was snowing and I can recall a billboard saying 'Swift survivor'. I had no knowledge what it meant and I carried on walking home, where my gran said 'have your tea, let's leave the TV off'. She knew about the accident.

Soon after, my Aunt Madge came in and said 'as far as I know he is still alive your dad'. I realised immediately what the billboard had meant, although not what it referred to, and my grandma told Madge I didn't know. The TV was put on, my grandfather was also there, and a few minutes later it became clear he had not survived. I was shocked and soon after Stan Mortensen rang and asked if I wanted to go to Germany.

I didn't want to go. If he had been alive I would have gone, but he was dead. I later found out he had lived for a short period of time, his strength having pulled him through a crippling series of injuries. I understand it was recognising my dad that had the doctor at the scene – who had worked in Manchester – saying 'this is a football team'.

I was badly hit when I saw TV coverage of the return of the coffins, as it was obvious, because of its size and length, which one my dad was in. That was possibly the worst day of all. I went to the funeral at St Anne's in Manchester; I stood outside with the crowd, who were there to pay their tribute, which was nice. Dad is buried in Southern Cemetery, Manchester I believe. I did once go to the gate soon after the funeral but I was too distressed to visit the grave.

I thought my dad was wonderful and to achieve what he did coming from where he was, that was a marvellous achievement. I am very proud of what he achieved.'

On a bright Blackpool Spring day in 1938, Iris's dad, after being constantly kept busy for the first 30 minutes, was beaten by Munro before Tilson equalised. Then Frank Swift got back to a low fast narrowly angled Finan drive but from the rebound Tommy Jones followed up to score what proved to be the winner. This was because Brook had his late penalty saved by Alec Roxburgh who was congratulated by dozens of invading fans at the end of the match.

Victory kick-started a five match winning run for Blackpool but City then suffered a third consecutive defeat as Stoke City beat them 3-2 at the Victoria Ground. Further disappointment followed when a Villa Park crowd of 75,500 saw City beaten 3-2 in the last eight of the FA Cup.

Four days later a crowd of only 15,000 were present for the home midweek match against Middlesbrough. The away side had won their last five League matches. After debuting the previous season, local youngster Wilf Mannion had returned to the Boro side and although George Camsell – scorer of a then record 59 League goals when Boro captured the Division Two title in 1926-27 – was coming towards the end of his illustrious career, his replacement Micky Fenton was to prove just as potent in front of goal. Thomas Cochrane was also a fine left-winger and at Maine Road he played what was undoubtedly his finest of 81 matches in a Boro shirt.

Earlier in the day the home side had signed Jack Pritchard from Crystal Palace, a lightly built 22-year-old able to play on either wing. The transfer was the second move, after the earlier signing of Bolton's Jack Milsom, in City's attempts to boost their chances of avoiding the drop.

The new men would be needed. The away side were quickly ahead when, following a mix-up in the home defence, Cochrane pushed Bill Brown's cross past Swift. The 'keeper then did well to keep out John Milne after the outside-right had dribbled through. However from the resulting cross the 'keeper was left with no chance as Cochrane rose unmarked to head home from six yards out.

After the interval things got worse when Fenton hit his 16th goal of the season, and although Milson reduced the arrears on 62 minutes a second goal for Fenton and further two from Cochrane were just reward for a fine Middlesbrough performance in which Mannion showed some of the touches that made him Boro's finest ever footballer.

The home side rested in 20th place. Could the League champions really be relegated? The answer was yes, with only two points being gathered from the next four games. There was relief, therefore, when Pritchard scored his first goal for his new club as Chelsea were beaten 1-0 at Maine Road. Swift had a tremendous match and although he was to be beaten three times in the following home match against Charlton, the City forwards hit five to record welcome back-to-back successes.

However, when City then lost at Grimsby Town and followed this up with defeat at home to Bolton Wanderers the game against West Brom on Easter Saturday became a must win occasion. Fewer than 17,000 saw the action in which the home side showed the form that had won the League title the previous season, and with the Baggies 'keeper, Billy Light, injured in a failed attempt to prevent Doherty making it 2-0 on 20 minutes, victory was never in doubt.

In goal Frank Swift had relatively little to do and the home side left the pitch having won 6-1. Two precious points had been collected and City had boosted their goal average, which took precedence in English football over goal difference until 1976-77, in the tightest relegation battle for many years.

Two days later though Bolton completed the double over their great rivals and for once Swift was culpable when he made a big mistake for the opening goal on 18 minutes, misjudging an innocent-looking centre to allow the ball to slip from his grasp and giving Jim Currier a simple chance to put his side ahead. Bolton should have gone into the interval further ahead only for David Halford to blaze embarrassingly over from six yards.

The travelling side were level on 60 minutes when referee Mr Hewitt of St Helens awarded a dubious penalty for a foul by Jack Atkinson on his old colleague, Milsom. Brook made it 1-1 and when the match resumed several fouls were rightly punished and Atkinson and Milson were constantly at each other's throats.

The winning goal was to be one that no 'keeper would have stopped, Tom Grosvenor cutting inside to hit a shot from an acute angle that flashed beyond Swift with the 'keeper's misery compounded by a heavy blow to the head against the post.

Swift was also to be badly injured in the following match, away to Charlton Athletic at the Valley on St George's Day. SWIFT KNOCKED OUT IN DARING SAVE was the *Manchester Evening News Sports* edition headline. The big City 'keeper had already made a host of great saves when mid-way through the second half he rose to try and collect a high Monty Wilkinson cross and was flattened by Charlton inside-left Les Boulter. The game was halted while he was revived with a wet sponge and some smelling salts. Earlier he had got his body in the way of a close-in Sailor Brown effort, kept out Cyril Blott with a magnificent diving save, and saved a running effort from Brown. In attack the away side also had chances and Sam Bartram made a 'leap worthy of an acrobat' to tip over a Brook shot.

Despite the much needed point the League Champions remained in big trouble and there were huge sighs of relief when, for the second home match in a row, City scored six times as Leeds were beaten 6-2 with Man of the Match Doherty scoring three.

Prior to the final League game of the 1937-38 season the bottom of the table read as follows. All sides had played 41 games.

		pts	gl/average
15th	Everton	38	1.05
16th	Huddersfield	37	0.79
17th	Man City	36	1.05
18th	Stoke	36	0.95
19th	Birmingham	36	0.89
20th	Portsmouth	36	0.85
21st	WBA	36	0.84
22nd	Grimsby	36	0.72

Huddersfield 1 Man City 0
Leicester City 1 Birmingham City 4
Middlesbrough 4 West Brom 1
Portsmouth 4 Leeds 0
Grimsby 1 Chelsea 0
Stoke 2 Liverpool 0
Everton 1 Derby County 1

The final day of the 1937-38 season was perhaps the tensest ever in the history of English football's top flight. At the summit Wolves – who had beaten Leicester City 10-1 in early April – were a point ahead of Arsenal. However with a poorer goal average then victory away to Sunderland was essential if a first League title was to be assured, with the Gunners lining up at home to Bolton Wanderers.

At the bottom seven teams [technically it was eight as if Everton had suffered a crushing home defeat against Derby they could have been relegated if results went against them] entered the final 90 minutes knowing that defeat might spell the end of their time in Division One.

Defeated FA Cup finalists Huddersfield had taken themselves off the bottom of the table with a 3-0 victory at home to Stoke City on May Bank Holiday Monday. The result had pushed City to a place below them in the League in 17th place. If City lost or drew at Leeds Road on 7 May 1938 they would be relegated if four of the five teams below them won their matches. Victory and the reigning League Champions would be safe to play newly promoted Manchester United the following season.

Perhaps unsurprisingly the game was not the greatest, tension being the main winner and Manchester City the biggest loser. In a poor first half the away side were better than their hosts as, prompted by Doherty, they created a number of half-chances without getting the ball past Hesford in the Terriers goal. As half-time approached, though, City should have fallen behind, but from just two yards out former Gunner Pat Beasley somehow conspired to flick the ball over the bar. Then on the stroke of half-time Price broke through and was only denied by a point-blank save from Swift.

At half-time with Birmingham, Portsmouth, Grimsby and Stoke all winning then by drawing City were in the relegation zone with only West Brom, losing 1-0 at Middlesbrough, below them in the table. Victory was therefore needed, and if achieved Huddersfield would go down. Things couldn't be tighter, and it was to be the home side that dominated the second period, and Gordon Clark and Barkas did well to prevent any shots from close-in, the former dispossessing Billy Price from 10 yards out on the hour mark.

When City did get forward it was often Doherty who was the main danger, but Pritchard, Herd, Milsom and Brook all seemed to be unable to play anywhere near their usual standards. Barkas kept his side in the match with a brilliant tackle on Tolley Wienand but with 12 minutes remaining Bobby Barclay, from close-in, forced the ball past Swift for the decisive, match-winning goal.

City, who had remarkably finished as top scorers in the League, had been relegated only a season after winning the League title. Joining them in the lower League were West Bromwich Albion. At the top Wolves' 1-0 defeat at Roker Park and Arsenal's 5-0 victory against Bolton had handed the title to the Gunners, their fifth in eight seasons.

Writing in his autobiography, Frank Swift offers only the briefest of insights into why a team that had 12 months earlier finished top of the pile slumped so badly as to be relegated, saying 'Most of the players were the same in each of the two campaigns, but some of them, like the great Arsenal side just before the war, were growing old together. I really believe that we played ourselves out when winning the title the previous season, and the following term things just didn't go the way we felt they should.'

Doherty also offered little analysis in his autobiography stating: 'We touched the heights during the championship season – and the following year we dropped like a plummet into the Second Division. There was a crop of injuries, of course, and any amount of bad luck; but excuses apart, we failed by a long way to show the sparkling form, which had made us the first team in the country. Many games were lost by scrappy, indifferent displays, and the occasions when we looked like champions were few and far between. Right to the end we strove to pull the game out of the fire; on one occasion the whole City team, in sheer desperation, tried to force the ball through by physical weight alone, and came very near to doing it. But Huddersfield hung grimly on to their lead till the end.'

* It was Alf's daughter Alwynne who first made the author aware of Iris. Only after further enquiries with a number of people did I then interview Iris.

Chapter 10
No quick return

City began their promotion bid with an impressive 5-0 thrashing of Swansea Town at Maine Road. Swift's only serious action was to stretch out his long arms to prevent Bruce from making it 1-1. Success the following Monday, a 3-0 win at Chesterfield, was a big boost but in the third game of the season disaster struck at Bradford Park Avenue.

Before a crowd of 16,738, Swift was beaten by a fierce low drive from John Gallon and then after 15 minutes Doherty was forced to retire from the match. Two minutes later the City 'keeper made a rare mistake when he allowed Martin's weak shot to squirm out of his grasp. Despite flinging himself to rescue the ball the referee, Mr T. Thompson, decided it had crossed the line and Avenue were leading 2-0. Remarkably, especially as Maurice Dunkley was limping, injured, the away side were level at half-time when Brook and then Herd scored.

However, on 57 minutes a fisted save by Swift was met by the onrushing Wesley to make it 3-2 and a late goal gave Bradford a 4-2 success. On another occasion it would have been a case of 'forget about and concentrate on the next match', but Doherty had damaged the internal lateral ligament of the right knee. As he would be out for many weeks then it was a big blow to City's promotion chances.

Dropped
Two home defeats then pushed City down into 14th place. Having conceded 10 goals in three matches, manager Wilf Wild, needed to tighten the defence. New signing Eric Eastwood, playing in place of the departed Barkas at left full-back, was dropped. Joining him out of the side was Frank Swift! It was true that City had conceded a great many goals the previous season and had continued to leak them in the new, but many fans were shocked. Asked by Wild to take a rest, Swift arrived home and found the evening paper reporting he had in fact been dropped. He was to play in the Central League side at Derby, the place where he had made his first appearance in the senior side. Newspaper reporters rushed to Swift's home but failed to find a story as he made it clear that he intended fighting for his first team place through playing well for the reserves. City beat Derby 1-0 in the game.

Making his debut at home to Millwall, Jack Robinson experienced an uneventful first half, which ended with City 1-0 ahead courtesy of a Bray effort. The second was to be a lot more traumatic for the new 'keeper, with

Don Barker, Bill Walsh and Sid Rawlings all scoring within eight minutes of the restart. By the end it was 6-1, leading to one wag on the popular side of the ground to lower City's club flag to half-mast. Robinson was responsible for at least three of the Lions goals.

The following weekend Swift was back in goal. Little good it did a now struggling side as 11 further goals were knocked into the City net in the next three games. Only one point was gathered, leaving fears that far from returning to Division One the side was going to go straight through to Division Three. In the event two draws, including a 0-0 one at Plymouth, steadied things before a first victory in 10, a 3-2 defeat of Sheffield United at Maine Road, brought two welcome points.

In front of Swift a regular back five of Bert Sproston, Eric Westwood, Jack Percival, Louis Cardwell and Les McDowell was being assembled. This stability meant that the months of November and December saw City rush up the table by taking 18 points from a possible 20.

Doherty had also returned to the side and with him City tore apart opposing defences.

On Boxing Day Tranmere Rovers were beaten 9-3 at Prenton Park with Milsom scoring four times. 24 hours later at Maine Road, Milsom scored another hat-trick, as Tranmere were beaten 5-2. Swift was beaten by two penalties.

Having thrashed Norwich City 5-0 in the FA Cup third round there was disappointment when Sheffield United beat City 2-0 at Bramall Lane in the next round. The start of 1939 was disastrous as, in addition to the Cup exit, only five points were gained from eight League games. At the Den the away side had the 'double' recorded over them. Millwall won 3-1, Jack Thorogood and Barker scoring two late 'beauties' to beat Swift and end any outside hopes City might have entertained of gaining promotion.

There was though to be a decent end to the season. Five consecutive games were won, the last at St James' Park when Swift faced, for the first time, Albert Stubbins who started the game by beating three men before firing a shot, which Swift saved acrobatically. Doherty gave the away side the lead before half-time and Heale added a second after 75 minutes.

The good run continued; a further five matches unbeaten making it 10 in total before a last day 2-1 defeat at West Ham United. Swift was in brilliant form with a late save from Len Goulden particularly remarkable. The result left City in fifth place with a goals scored record superior to every other Football League club that season.

Surely next season, Manchester City would regain their place in Division One? Which is just what happened, although not before Hitler intervened to push back the start date.

Chapter 11
Wartime football

There would have been an atmosphere of unreality when Frank Swift reported back for pre-season training in the summer of 1939. Encouraged by an April FA circular, many professional footballers had already joined the Territorial Army. Others had registered with the government's Ministry of Labour, which then directed them where to work.

War was expected and when League football kicked off on 26 August the number of spectators on a full programme of 44 games was, at 600,000, well down on previous seasons. Later that week the evacuation of children from British cities began and within a week over a million had moved into the country.

Yet when Hitler's forces poured into Poland on Saturday 2 September 1939 the FA hesitated and, with the Home Office declaring its support, the games planned for that day went ahead. However, after the declaration of war on 3 September it was clear that the imposition of a ban on the assembly of crowds meant football would have to take a back seat.

In 1914 a belief that the war would be over in months had seen League football continue. However, with many players signing up to fight in the trenches, plus sustained criticism from all quarters then a second season of wartime football was never contemplated. This time, not even a first season was considered, especially as new technology meant a sustained bombing campaign was now a possibility.

With no gate income, clubs in 1939 cancelled player's contracts but held onto their registrations. Out of work footballers could enlist in one of the three services, take essential war work or wait for call-up papers. Players previously signed on as Territorials or with the militia or police reported almost immediately.

Swift thus joined the Bobbies Blue as he waited in anticipation of being called-up. In mid January 1940 he was asked to conduct traffic-control duty in Manchester. The Blackpool lad was all at sea as his giant hand signals totally confused vehicle drivers to create a snarl up that the new police officer 'resolved' by walking away!

By the end of September 1939 a change of attitude at the highest levels of Government revealed regional football was being considered. Following consultation with the FA it was agreed that friendly and competitive matches confined to local and district groups on Saturdays and public holidays could be organised, as long as there was no interference with National Service and the general war effort.

In fact Association Football not only survived but also became a morale-boosting pastime during the war. Writing in the popular weekly the *Topical Times* one police officer said: 'Football is the best teetotal agency we can produce for the worker and others left behind at home. If there is no football each week our cells will be full because the young men of today will have nowhere to go and will fall into mischief. The collection of people at churches is not barred and the collection of football crowds should not be hindered. Let us have them in their customary winter quarters, not on the streets or in the pubs.'

It was even believed that Winston Churchill, who replaced Chamberlain as Prime Minister on 10 May 1940, was supportive on grounds that enemy agents sending crystal set messages back to Germany would be forced to comment that the British people were not worried about the threat of invasion as people were still playing and watching football!

The numbers allowed to attend though were restricted, although in the event it was clear that initially people were not that keen to watch football. As such, on 30 September 1939 City beat Manchester United 3-2 in a friendly and the gate was only 7,000 of the 8,000 allowed to attend. Mancunians were making plans to get their children away to safety and during the war 72,000 children and 23,000 adults were evacuated on special trains and corporation buses.

For the adults left behind there was the need to ensure that those at the war front had the tools to do the job. At the Avro factory, Chadderton the workers were put on 12 hour, seven-day shifts to meet the insatiable demands for the Lancaster bomber that rolled off production lines from October 1941 onwards. 7,377 were built, of which 3,240 were lost in action. They carried the bouncing bombs used on the attacks on the Ruhr dam and also helped sink the battleship *Tirpitz*, which marked the end of Germany's naval war in northern waters.

More controversially 773 Lancasters took part in the raids on Dresden in February 1945; intensive bombing and the firestorm which resulted, killed at least 35,000 people, the vast majority civilians. Those who believe the attacks were justified argue that Dresden, which had previously escaped being bombed, was of industrial importance and that the firepower would act as a warning to the Soviet Union.

Three weeks after their first game, City and United met again at Old Trafford for the opening game of the western area of the wartime League and the away side won 4-0 with Heale, Herd, Doherty and Brook scoring. Back home against Wrexham, the Welsh side were torn apart by City in a 6-1 thrashing.

Things were more difficult at Goodison Park. The game was Joe Mercer's first for the Toffees since he had joined the Army Physical Training Staff and his appearance meant there were 15 internationals on display. A crowd of 7,804 watched an excellent game of football. It had been agreed that a minimum admission price of 1 shilling (5p) would be charged with reductions for servicemen, women and boys. This made it possible to pay players a match fee of £1.50 with no bonuses, a sum too small for anyone to feed and clothe a family on.

Perfectly placed 60 yard free-kick

The opening goal of the match was the result of a well placed free-kick by the away 'keeper. Swift directed the ball from just outside the penalty area to Heale more than 60 yards away, the City forward controlling it superbly before beating Sagar.

Wartime games naturally lacked the keenness and competitive element of League football but there was an opportunity for more skilful football and the crowd was in a good mood as the sides attacked freely. A lovely piece of play by Gillick opened up the City defence and Stan Bentham beat Swift with a great shot. At half-time the score remained 1-1. With Gillick and Lawton scoring the reigning League Champions won 3-1.

In 1952 Swift had this to say about Lawton: 'He could shoot with both feet, was extremely good in the air but perhaps his greatest asset of all was his speed of getting the ball under control and hitting it in the same movement – a most unusual attribute in so big a fellow. And if the truth were known, Tommy was one of the few sharpshooters upon whom I was able to get my own back. When we were practising ahead of an international match, I made him go in goal and I gave him some anxious moments with my left foot drives.'

When Everton and Manchester City re-met on 9 March 1940 Swift was missing for a game that despite featuring many reserves was 'excellent' (*Liverpool Echo*) with both sides scoring twice.

Three days earlier Swift had played for Aldershot against Chelsea in the South C Division of the war League. It was his second, and final, game of the season for the club that had only just completed its seventh season in the Football League in 1938-39. Swift's physical training course at Aldershot was close to completion. In January 1940, the big 'keeper had received his call up papers on the same day as Tommy Lawton. The pair journeyed south together, where walking into the depot at Aldershot an Army captain had England international Lawton sign a number of autographs while ignoring his pal.

The pair were among 154 men from the FA's list of nominations to have been accepted in the first six months of the war by the Services for education courses in physical training. Of these 109 were in the army and 45 in the RAF.

Aldershot's manager was the former Newcastle United and Ireland legend Bill McCracken, the man credited with doing more than anyone to change the offside rule in 1925 from three to two players. After obtaining a pass to the Army barracks in the town McCracken used it to persuade famous football stars to play for the Shots. Yet without a regular 11, Aldershot still did badly, but not when Chelsea came to the Recreation Ground. Swift's side were ahead on just four minutes, with Lawton scoring a penalty after Jimmy Hagan was brought down. Aldershot went on to win 5-1.

Lawton had put on nine pounds during his PT course and considered it harder than anything else he had done. Swift was to make a further 10 appearances for Aldershot over the next five seasons and he and Lawton also played once together in a Charlton side that played at Portsmouth only days before the famous Aldershot victory over Chelsea. Later in the war, Swift also guested for Fulham, playing five times in season 1941-42, one more than he played for Reading in the following season.

Despite his appearances for 'the Shots', Swift still managed to play in 21 of City's 24 League matches in 1939-40 and was between the goalposts when City entertained local rivals Stockport County in December. 5-2 down after 69 minutes the away side produced a marvellous comeback to draw 6-6. Despite scoring five goals, Heale failed to finish on the winning side.

Later in the season Bolton Wanderers centre-forward Jimmy Currier guested for Manchester City and in consecutive weekends in May he bagged four in games at Tranmere Rovers and Port Vale. Clearly determined not to be outdone Alec Herd then did the same in home games against Crewe and Port Vale. In 1940-41, when by scoring 104 goals in regional League games City outscored the other sides, Currier scored 47. Away to Stockport County in a 9-1 victory he scored three, only for Herd to get four. The Bolton player notched 94 goals in 113 wartime matches for his guest club.

Swift played two games for Liverpool at the end of the 1939-40 season. The 'keeper was responsible at the time for directing part of the PT training for the King's Liverpool Regiment. Unsurprisingly football played a major part with regular games organised in Sefton Park in the city. Many of the soldiers Swift worked with were involved with guarding buildings, traffic duties and recovering victims during the May 1941 Blitz of Liverpool. The King's Regiment was to be amalgamated with the Manchesters in 1958.

On 29 May 1940 an Anfield crowd touching 5,000 saw Swift concede three goals as Tranmere were beaten 8-3 and three days later on 1 June 1940 he kept a clean sheet as Liverpool drew 0-0 away with local rivals New Brighton.

That same day Michael Foot (Labour), Frank Owen (Liberal) and Peter Howard (Conservative) sat down together and in four days finished *Guilty Men*. This was a classic book that attacked British public figures for their policy of appeasement, which governed Anglo-French foreign policy during the 1930s and under which concessions were made to the axis powers of Nazi Germany, Fascist Italy and Imperial Japan in order to avoid conflict.

Guilty Men was published in July 1940 and backed new Prime Minister Winston Churchill's decision to reject Viscount Halifax's manoeuvres which were designed to negotiate a peace treaty with Germany that would safeguard Britain's independence and imperial interests. Churchill never believed Hitler would honour such a treaty and thankfully Britain battled on.

Swift was able to play the majority of Manchester City's games in the 1940-41 season. At home to Blackburn Rovers in late October, 'Dickie whipped in a shot that would have beaten many another goalkeeper. Swift somehow got to it' reported the *Lancashire Evening Post*. The game finished 1-1, but when the sides met again in the League War Cup, Blackburn, the previous season's losing finalists to West Ham United at Wembley, were heavily beaten 9-4 over two legs. Having lost the first leg 5-2, political correctness was clearly not much in evidence in 1941 as before the return the *Blackburn Times* called on Rovers to engage in their own 'blitz'.

In 1941-42 Frank Swift played just three games for City and at the Victoria Ground he was beaten five times as Stoke won 5-0. In his absence Robinson and Bill Carey shared the job between the posts as City finished down in 18th place in the Northern (First) League that was won by Blackpool, the first of the Seasiders' three consecutive successes. This was despite Swift's hometown team having been evicted from their ground to accommodate it becoming an RAF training centre, although in the long run 'Pool benefitted from the rent paid by the armed forces as they had their £33,704 overdraft wiped out during the war.

When football resumed in 1942-43 Frank Swift was selected to play for the British Army side against the Army in Ulster. The match was played at the Solitude in Belfast and the away side won 5-3 before a crowd of 14,000.

Going north to star for Hamilton Academical

Towards the end of 1942 Frank Swift was sent across the border to train recruits at Hamilton Barracks. This was the home of the Cameronians infantry regiment that has some of its members listed on the Spion Kop memorial in South Africa that commemorates those killed there in January 1900 during the Second Boer War that pitched the British Empire into conflict with the Afrikaans-speaking Dutch settlers. In 1906, four years after the war ended, Liverpool FC opened a new open-air embankment. When the *Liverpool Echo* sports editor Ernest Edwards referred to it as the 'Spion Kop' the name stuck and has been used ever since.

It wasn't long before Swift was doing battle on the football field for the local side. He made his debut for Hamilton Academical on 28 November 1942 in a Scottish Southern League match away to Hibernian. Hamilton is one of

Scotland's oldest senior clubs having been established in 1874. During the 1930s Hamilton had been at their best and were regularly in the top six of the Scottish First Division.

Hamilton lined up as follows: Swift, J. McGurk, Jenkins, G. McKenzie, J. Lowe, C. Mansley, White, G. Stewart, D. Wilson, A. Herd, A. Smith.

The away side, which contained Swift's City colleague Alex Herd in their starting line-up, were beaten 3-1 with George Stewart scoring for Hamilton. In the *Clydesdale's Sports Gossip* column that appeared in the following weekend's *Hamilton Advertiser* there was a brief mention of the game in Edinburgh of which 'the most attractive feature was a marvellous display of goalkeeping by newcomer Frank Swift'. Four columns on the writer reported that a colleague of his had described Swift as 'the finest goalkeeper I have ever seen'. The writer said that 'coming from him, this is praise indeed'.

The following weekend Swift faced Celtic at Douglas Park and John Lowe, normally a centre-half but playing at outside-right, scored twice in a 2-1 win. Lowe was to become manager at Hamilton in 1956, resigning two years later.

Jock Whiteford had taken Lowe's place at the centre of the defence, in which Robert Wallace, Jimmy McGurk and Gibby McKenzie were to be regulars during Frank Swift's brief Scottish career. All three had played for Hamilton on 14 October 1939 when Airdrieonians had been beaten 5-1 at Broomfield in the Final of the Lanarkshire Cup.

Swift played brilliantly in the match against Celtic with the *Hamilton Advertiser* reporting that 'Swift gave another superb display and was mainly responsible for a blank sheet at the interval'. The following weekend the 'keeper continued his fine form as Falkirk 'were kept at bay by Swift' to help set up a 4-0 success.

On 16 January Frank Swift played his sixth game for Accies in the local Derby match against Albion Rovers. A penalty save helped win the match 3-2 with Lowe scoring once and David Wilson a pair. The latter, hailing from Hebburn Colliery on Tyneside, had been signed by manager Willie McAndrew (in charge at Hamilton between 1925 and 1946) in 1928 and was to go on to become the best goalscorer Hamilton have ever produced. Although he did not score he was a member of the side that beat Heart of Midlothian in the Scottish Cup on 3 March 1937 before a record Douglas Park crowd of 28,690.

Wilson was to score a hat-trick on 20 occasions in Scottish League matches and he formed a fine partnership with Alex Herd.

Two weeks after beating their local rivals, Hamilton were unable to repeat their exploits when they faced Rangers, who ran out comfortable winners 3-0 at Douglas Park. The *Hamilton Advertiser* reported that 'Swift gave another grand display in goal and his marvellous saves undoubtedly kept the score within reasonable proportions'.

On 13 February 1943 Frank Swift played his 10th and final Southern League match for Hamilton, who beat Third Lanark 4-2 at home. Joining Swift as a guest in the team was Middlesbrough's Scottish international Benny Yorston. On his Hamilton debut he scored twice. At just 5ft 5in tall Yorston used his nimble skills, allied to a fine turn of pace, to regularly score goals during his career including hitting 38 in 38 League matches for Aberdeen in 1929-30.

It was to be more than two months before Frank Swift made his final appearance for Hamilton. Having made it through the group stages Hamilton faced Rangers at Hampden Park on 24 April 1943 in the semi-final of the Scottish League Cup. In 1935 Rangers had prevented Hamilton, who finished fourth in the League that season, from winning the Scottish Cup for the first time when they beat them 2-1 in the Final. Twenty-four years earlier Celtic had beaten Hamilton in a replay at the final stage.

There were 60,000 that watched the semi-final action in which Swift's side lost 3-0 but did not go down to defeat easily. Hamilton had chosen to wear their new colours of scarlet jerseys rather than the traditional red-and-white diagonal stripes and were backed by a very large Lanarkshire following. There was early controversy when Lowe breasted the ball home only for the referee to wrongly disallow the effort for handball. The first half then became a dour struggle, enlivened by some fine saves by the Hamilton 'keeper to ensure that at the interval no goals had been scored.

Rangers took the lead when Everton guest Torry Gillick's cross appeared to strike Wallace and the ball swirled over Swift to make it 1-0. Hamilton pushed forward, but failed to make the most of some good opportunities before Venters took advantage of the Hamilton defenders' attacking ambitions by using the space to find Waddell whose shot was handled on the line and from the resulting penalty Young made it 2-0 on 76 minutes. Gillick, who had played for Rangers, against Hamilton in the 1935 Cup Final, before moving to Goodison Park, added the third on the 90 minutes. The *Hamilton Advertiser* reported that 'Frank Swift was the shining light in the Hamilton goal and I am convinced that he stands today as Britain's best. The Hamilton directors deserve all praise for having placed such a box-office attraction before the Scottish football public.'

Back in England
It was during the 1942-43 season that Blackpool were forced to withdraw from the English League North War Cup when they were unable to send a team to Maine Road during a period when there was a ban on the movement of servicemen.

Frank Swift's first football success was as a left-half.

Frank met his wife, Doris, while working with his relations on The Skylark sail boat they ran from Blackpool beach.

Frank Swift's mother, Jinnie was a no-nonsense character.

Fear caused Frank Swift to miss his debut match.

Manchester City | Football Club Ltd.

WINNERS F.A. CHALLENGE CUP, 1904.   FINALISTS F.A. CHALLENGE CUP, 1926.   SECOND DIVISION CHAMPIONS, 1928.

Telephone No. Moss Side 1191.

Telegraphic Address:
"FOOTBALL, MANCHESTER."

Secretary: W. WILD.
& Manager: XXXXXXXXXXXXX.

Registered Office:

MAINE ROAD,

MOSS SIDE,

MANCHESTER.

12th October 1932.

Mr. H. Colley,
Fleetwood F.C.

Dear Sir,

    I am in receipt of your letter of 11th instant regarding Swift and am very sorry to hear of the trouble you were put to in order to find a substitute for him.

    The question of your Club being reimbursed for the cost of the Taxi I will have to mention to my Board, who unfortunately only met last night.   I will bring it up at our meeting next week.

    We have again selected Swift to play in our 'A' Team for Saturday next and you may rest assured that if the lad makes good, your Club will not be forgotten.

    I thank you for your remark re John Bamber and will be pleased to have him watched.

             Yours faithfully,

             W. Wild

Left: Fleetwood were given no warning that their reserve 'keeper was set to play for Manchester City's third team.

Below: Frank Swift for City reserves on 23 December 1933. City's first team lost 8-0 at Wolves on the same day.

SATURDAY, DECEMBER 23rd, 1933.

MANCHESTER CITY Res.

1
SWIFT
Goal

2   3
CANN   DUNNE
Right Back   Left Back

4   5   6
PERCIVAL (J)   LLOYD   McLUCKIE
Right Half-Back Centre Half-Back Left Half-Back

7   8   9   10   11
PERCIVAL (P) COMRIE SYME HADFIELD WRIGHT
Outside Right Inside Right Centre Inside Left Outside Left

ORDER
HYDES
ANVIL BRAND
STRONG
ALE

Referee:
C. FLETCHER, Northwich.
Linesmen:
T. H. BUTTON, Red Flag.
E. B. SMITH, Blue Flag.

KICK-OFF 2-15 p.m.

12   13   14   15   16
SPOONER CHEESMUIR NICHOLAS KILLOURHY OXLEY
Outside Left Inside Left Centre Inside Right Outside Right

17   18   19
HALL JOHNSON SANPY
Left Half-Back Centre Half-Back Right Half-Back

20   21
GREEN HOOPER
Left Back Right Back

22
EARNSHAW
Goal

SHEFFIELD UNITED RESERVES

TUESDAY, DECEMBER 26th, 1933.

MANCHESTER CITY

1
NICHOLLS
Goal

2   3
BARNETT   DALE
Right Back   Left Back

4   5   6
BUSBY   MARSHALL   BRAY
Right Half-Back   Centre Half-Back   Left Half-Back

7   8   9   10   11
TOSELAND   HERD   GREGORY   TILSON   BROOK
Outside Right   Inside Right   Centre   Inside Left   Outside Left

KICK-OFF 2-15 p.m.

ORDER HYDES ANVIL BRAND STRONG ALE

Referee :
R. BOWIE. Newcastle-on-Tyne.
Linesmen :
G. DUTTON. Red Flag.
W. E. TWIST. White Flag.

12   13   14   15   16
DUNCAN   RAMAGE   BOWERS   HUTCHISON   CROOKS
Outside Left   Inside Left   Centre   Inside Right   Outside Right

17   18   19
KEEN   BARKER   NICHOLAS
Left Half Back   Centre Half-Back   Right Half-Back

20   21
COLLIN   WEBB
Left Back   Right Back

22
KIRBY
Goal

DERBY COUNTY

Above: Derby's Jack Bowers makes it 2-0 on Frank Swift's Christmas Day debut in 1933.

Left: Frank Swift's rise to the first team came too quickly to ensure he was listed as playing against Derby County at Maine Road on his 20th birthday.

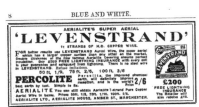
NEW YEAR'S DAY, JANUARY 1st, 1934.

MANCHESTER CITY

1
SWIFT
Goal

2   3
BARNETT   CORBETT (V)
Right Back   Left Back

4   5   6
PERCIVAL (J)   MARSHALL   BRAY
Right Half-Back   Centre Half-Back   Left Half-Back

7   8   9   10   11
TOSELAND   HERD   GREGORY   BUSBY   BROOK
Outside Right   Inside Right   Centre   Inside Left   Outside Left

KICK-OFF 2-15 p.m.

ORDER HYDES ANVIL BRAND STRONG ALE

Referee :
W. R. JENNINGS. York.
Linesmen :
W. BOOTH. Red Flag.
H. HARTLES. Blue Flag.

12   13   14   15   16
WOOD   SANDFORD   RICHARDSON (W.G.)   CARTER   GLIDDEN
Outside Left   Centre   Inside Right   Outside Right

17   18   19
EDWARDS   RICHARDSON (W)   MURPHY
Left Half Back   Centre Half-Back   Right Half-Back

20   21
TRENTHAM   SHAW
Left Back   Right Back

22
PEARSON
Goal

WEST BROMWICH ALBION

No Happy New Year – Manchester City 2 WBA 7.

In 1934, Manchester City were intent on going one better than in the previous season when they lost 3-0 to Everton in the FA Cup Final.

City faced Portsmouth in the 1934 FA Cup Final.

Fred Tilson scored the goals that won Manchester City the 1934 FA Cup Final.

Above: After fainting at the final whistle, Frank Swift need reviving before joining the rest of the City team in collecting the FA Cup from the King.

The 1934 FA Cup winners.

Could City's new 'keeper build on his successful first season?

Frank Swift was a big fan of the Arsenal defender, Wilf Copping (left).

Frank Swift was a big fan of Sunderland's inside-forward Raich Carter (right). The pair were England colleagues.

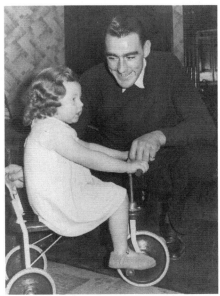

A doting dad, Jean Francis Swift was born on 10 August 1936.

Above: Doherty scored the vital opening goal in City's 3-1 win against Arsenal in the title run-in.

Left: The failure of the FA to act after Sunderland 'keeper Jimmy Thorpe died following a rough match meant Frank Swift continued to suffer some severe challenges.

CROWDS SWARM ON PITCH IN REMARKABLE SCENE

Below: Iris Swift.

Another City Goal Rush: Score Twice in 11 Minutes

Manchester City .... Final: 4   Sheffield Wednesday 1

By STANLEY ELLIS

MANCHESTER CITY are champions of the First Division of the Football League for the first time in their history. To-day they made certain of their honour by beating Sheffield Wednesday 4-1 at Maine Road, and at the same time extended a run without a League defeat to 21 games.

City made sure of the honour with three goals in the first half, but thereafter played easily, but that first-half display was of brilliance worthy of the holders of the honour.

After the final whistle, thousands of spectators came over the barriers and swarmed across the pitch, massing in front of the main stand, cheering and singing, while in general there were scenes of a most enthusiastic kind. But there was no rioting there, and after the playing of "Auld Lang Syne" and "God Save the King," the police were successful in dispersing them.

MANCHESTER CITY—Swift; Clark, Barkas; Percival, Marshall, Bray; Toseland, Herd, Tilson, Doherty, Brook. SHEFFIELD WEDNESDAY—Smith; Ashley, Catlin; Drury, Hanford, Burrows; Luke, Robinson, Dewar, Dearl, Rimmer. Referee: Mr. R. W. Sale, of Middlesbrough.

Wednesday right from the start showed the expected keenness and determination, and it was they who set the pace so that the expectations of a really rousing contest looked like being realised.

ball, which was trapped under the injured player.

In this half City gave the impression of resting upon their comfortable lead, for their play had not quite the same snap about it. Consequently rather more was seen of Wednesday, but although both Robinson and Drury supplied good dribbles there was a lack of finishing power about the visitors.

OFF THE MARK.

Doherty, Toseland, and Brook all had shots off the mark, and the best effort went to Herd's credit, for his powerful drive went barely over the top, and then Smith's fingers were needed to tip it there.

It was only due reward for Wednesday's grit when they scored after 26 minutes of the half. Drury carried the ball up, Dewar slipped it out to Luke, whose shot was well-saved by Swift, but the City goalkeeper at full stretch could only turn it aside, and RIMMER, closing in, scored with a simple shot.

City's show this half in fact proved almost as disappointing as the first had been brilliant. The passing was not so good, nor was the linking up and the fire generally had gone out of their play. The defence tried to get the attack functioning again and Clark once more in every sense proved himself a worthy deputy for Dale.

CITY BELOW BEST

The home team never looked in any real danger, yet this was not now nearly their best. Toseland had a half-centre half-sho...

Owls thrashed as City clinch first League title.

Above & left: Frank Swift was one of many footballer's that became physical trainers for the armed forces during the war.

Three England internationals, Swift, Leslie Compton and Stanley Matthews enjoy a joke together.

Frank Swift could easily pick up a football with either hand.

Doris and Jean Swift.

Swiss fans show their appreciation for a magnificent goalkeeping display.

Above: Frank Swift at Maine Road.

Frank Swift lines up for his full England debut in Belfast in September 1946.

Frank Swift (left) and Joe Baksi, the American boxer, match hand spans. Comparative spans (taken from the little finger to tip of thumb) are Swift 11¾ inches, Baksi 11 inches.

Doris helps her husband sew on his
England badge.

Frank Swift's Great Britain jersey.

Frank Swift's smoking brought him into conflict with England manager Walter Winterbottom.

87, Park St.,
Salisbury,
13·4·48

Dear Mr. Frank Swift,
                          Several of my
schoolfriends and I listened to the
broadcast of the England v Scotland
match on the wireless, and was
thrilled by your goalkeeping, and
I think you played the biggest part
in keeping out the Scots. I was
very sorry to read about your injury
and I hope it will mend to
enable you once again to be picked
to represent England to tour
Spain, Italy, etc.
                  Yours sincerely,
                  Gordon White

Jean Swift collects her dad's fan mail, which included the following letter.

Left: Frank Swift was a big admirer of Ronnie Rooke.

Below: Frank Swift's autobiography was published in 1948.

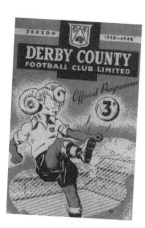

Although Frank Swift conceded two goals in his final match at Derby he kept six clean sheets in 10 matches as his career drew to a close in 1949.

City fan Eddie Humphrys shakes hands with Frank Swift as he leaves the Maine Road pitch for what was planned to be the last time.

Frank Swift runs out at Huddersfield for the final League game of 1948-49.

A magnificent oil painting of Frank Swift.

The final journey.

Frank Swift has been commemorated in a regenerated Hove Road Park, Fylde.

Iris Swift stands next to a magnificent mosaic of her dad.

GOOD GOALIES ARE SCARCE

by JOHN ARLOTT

Fewer goals are scored today, but not because of good new goalies. In that job veterans are still the best

Frank Swift's immense height, reach and hand-span save "impossibles"

Blackpool, for who Stanley Matthews played regularly during the war, gained a measure of revenge the following season when they put City out of the competition en route to losing narrowly to Aston Villa in the final. City had qualified to play in the Cup by having finished 19th in the league, but a 47th place (out of 60 teams) finish in 1944-45 saw them miss out on the 32 who competed in the Cup. Not that this prevented more people coming through the turnstiles. After the first two wartime seasons, football attendances increased as the war front changed from defence to attack.

On Saturday 17 January 1942 just 2,500 had witnessed City beating Burnley 5-0 at Maine Road. Almost exactly three years later even the visit of Halifax Town produced a five-figure gate and with only weeks of the war (in Europe) to run there were attendances of 36,131 and 24,904 at Anfield and Maine Road to see Liverpool beat City twice.

The Halifax match was a special occasion, marking the first time lifelong supporter Walter Allison saw City play. Sam Barkas was absent but his brother Tommy was in the Halifax side and with City winning 2-0 at half-time he scored three second half goals to give Halifax a 3-2 win.

Allison subsequently went to a number of games that season and recalls, 'you arrived not knowing who was playing. The nearby army camp of Wilmslow was a transit camp and so players were often available to play for local sides, City being one of them. Someone would come round with a blackboard on which the names of the players would be chalked up. If it rained then they had to come round again!'

With the end of the war in Europe on 8 May 1945 there was not enough time for a full programme of matches in 1945-46, especially as many players were still on active service and would not be arriving back for some weeks. Swift's colleague Flight-Sergeant Jackie Bray was to be demobbed after being awarded a British Empire Medal. Serving with the RAF he had transferred to a unit that rehabilitated wounded fighter pilots. Inside-forward George Smith had lost his lower forearm, amputated at the wrist after he suffered a shotgun wound in South Africa. It affected his balance, but he was to play again and made his official first-team debut in 1946. He was to score 75 goals in 166 League appearances for Manchester City and later notched 98 League goals in 250 appearances for Chesterfield. Full-back Eric Westwood, who had guested for Chelsea at Wembley in the wartime 1944 Southern Cup Final had fought on the Normandy beaches and was mentioned in despatches.

They were the lucky ones, Eric Stephenson of Leeds United was killed serving with the Ghurkha Rifles in Burma in 1944 and the Peacocks also lost centre-half Leslie Thompson and centre-forward Maurice Lawn. Liverpool's England full-back Tom Cooper was killed serving as a sergeant in the Military Police when his motorcycle collided with a bus on 25 June 1940.

Albert Keeling had played just the once for Manchester City, a 5-2 success against New Brighton on 14 September 1940 in which he played at right wing with Swift in goal. The Flight Sergeant was reported missing presumed killed during an operational flight in December 1942, months earlier he had brought down a Junkers 88 in the Bay of Biscay.

Chapter 12
Playing for England

England had played five wartime internationals during World War One, ending with a 2-0 victory against Wales at the Victoria Ground, Stoke just 24 days before battlefield hostilities ceased on 11 November 1919.

Exactly 20 years later the two countries again locked horns in an unofficial international. This was played at Ninian Park, Cardiff before a 28,000 crowd. In goal for England, Chelsea's Vic Woodley was beaten by Grimsby centre-forward Ernest 'Pat' Glover in a 1-1 draw with Len Goulden of West Ham United scoring for the away XI.

One week later, on Saturday 18 November 1939, and with the newspapers speculating the Nazis were planning to invade Britain soon, Frank Swift was given his chance between the England posts when the sides re-met at the Racecourse Ground, Wrexham. Blackpool's Dai Astley, later to manage Inter Milan, put two past him but England narrowly triumphed 3-2 with an own goal from Tommy Jones, and efforts from Aston Villa's John Martin and Liverpool's John Balmer.

WALES: Cyril Sidlow, Bill Hughes, Arthur Smith, Bill Burgess, Tommy Jones, Doug Witcomb, Idris Hopkins, Bill Redfern, Dai Astley, Bryn Jones, Reg Cumner.

ENGLAND: Frank Swift [Manchester City], Bert Sproston [Manchester City], Walter Crook [Blackburn Rovers], Ken Willingham [Huddersfield Town], Stan Cullis [c] [Wolverhampton Wanderers], Joe Mercer [Everton], Stanley Matthews [Stoke City], John Martin [Aston Villa], Tommy Lawton [Everton], John Balmer [Liverpool], Eric Brook [Manchester City].

Referee: McCarthy (Wales)

Swift had been joined in the side by teammate Bert Sproston in defence and Eric Brook up front. Unlike Swift, both had played for England at official level with 11 and 18 appearances respectively. In May 1938 Sproston was a member of the England team that played against Germany in Berlin. It was a game the Nazi regime were desperate to win, and before which a reluctant England team, at the behest of the British ambassador, Sir Neville Henderson, gave the Nazi outstretched arm salute.

On the pitch things proved more palatable with England playing their opponents off it to win 6-3. Sheffield Wednesday's Jackie Robinson got two before a crowd of 110,000. After the game Sproston, reported Stanley

Matthews, had told him: 'I know nowt 'bout politics and t'like. All I knows is football. But t'way I see it, yon 'itler fella is an evil little twat.' Sproston, of course, was right.

A year earlier Manchester City's players had refused to perform the same actions when following their Championship success the club had organised a five-game tour of fascist Germany. The fourth game was watched by over 70,000 at the Berlin Olympic Stadium when City faced what was, except in name, the German national side who had been sent away to special camps to prepare for the match. Looking to benefit from the ensuing propaganda Hitler had requested that the City players give the Nazi salute.

The away side had enjoyed wonderful hospitality throughout the tour. Nevertheless as Peter Doherty later recalled: 'When we were expected to give the Nazi salute at the line-up before the match started we decided merely to stand to attention. When the German national anthem was played, only 11 arms went up instead of the expected 22!'

City in fact lost the game, which was recorded by television cameras, 3-2 after an uncharacteristic mistake by Frank Swift and a series of misses from the normally reliable Doherty.

The England national team were also later required to give a fascist salute when they faced World Cup holders Italy at the newly opened San Siro Stadium in Milan on 13 May 1939. Despite the furore over the salute to Hitler the FA still told the players in no uncertain terms that they should salute Italian tyrant Benito Mussolini. Hardly surprisingly when news reached home there was fury – Eddie Hapgood, Vic Woodley, Stanley Matthews, Frank Broome, Ken Willingham and Len Goulden were unfortunate enough to be forced to make both salutes in Germany and Italy.

There were just 17,000 at the Racecourse Ground for a match billed as 'the Red Cross' international, and the entrance fees they paid helped send a cheque for £1,060 to the charity and the Order of St John, a body which was also empowered to raise voluntary aid detachments under the War Office Voluntary Aid Scheme. The organisations had worked well together during World War One and when hostilities resumed they combined to form the Joint War Organisation.

The game was a thrilling one for the Welsh crowd, who saw their side take a two-goal lead in the second half only for England captain Stan Cullis to rally his troops and produce a stirring comeback. The first half was a very even affair, with Willingham, Matthews and Martin down the English right finding it difficult to break down the Welsh defence in which left-back Arthur Smith played heroically.

Good first-half performance

In attack the Welsh forwards had enough purpose to constantly worry Swift in the England goal, and when Derby County's Bill Redfern broke clean through the City 'keeper showed his quality by the way which he parried the ball. Bryn Jones then gave Swift cause for concern with a shot that flashed narrowly wide before Astley struck the angle of the bar. The 'keeper then had to be smart to clear in a goalmouth melee before for the second time Wales, on this occasion by Reg Cumner, hit the woodwork.

Wales took the lead on 47 minutes when Swift in collecting a high ball from Cumner was heavily challenged by Redfern. Today it would be a free-kick, a melee of protesting defenders and a yellow card. In 1939, when the Manchester City 'keeper was forced to drop the ball, it was 'play on' and when it went out to Astley he drove it back to find the net. Two minutes later the scorer swerved away from Cullis to beat Swift for a second time.

England though were not beaten, and as if by a switch of a light the away forwards suddenly clicked. Initially Everton's inspirational centre-half T.G. Jones seemed to be unbeatable but when his club colleague Tommy Lawton drilled a low shot he was unable to get out of the way and the ricocheting ball beat Cyril Sidlow to make it 2-1. Then out on the England left, Brook began to weave his magic and from one of his centres, Martin equalised. Then a perfect pass from the winger opened up the Welsh defence for Balmer to strike what proved to be the winner. All five goals had come in a 10-minute spell, and at the end the crowd – many in khaki or Air Force blue – cheered the teams to the dressing room.

Writing in the North Wales regional newspaper *The Leader* X.Y.Z felt England had deserved to win and that 'Swift, Sproston, Crook, Cullis, Willingham and Mercer made up three fine lines with efficiency written all over them.'

Swift was missing for the next wartime match at Newcastle, where England beat Scotland 2-1, and also for the defeat to Wales at Wembley, a 1-1 draw at Hampden, a 3-2 defeat to Scotland at Newcastle and a 4-1 beating of Wales at the City Ground, Nottingham – a match in which Charlton Athletic's Don Welsh, later to manage Liverpool, scored all of England's goals – but the 'keeper returned to the side against Scotland at Hampden Park on 3 May 1941.

It was a weekend when American President Theodore Roosevelt said 'the American people are ready to fight again for the existence of democracy'. In the event it was not until more than six months later, after the Japanese attack on Pearl Harbor, before they did so in earnest. Meanwhile Britain was being battered from above and the city of Liverpool, in the third night of raids, was to be badly hit by the Luftwaffe on the night of 3 May.

Perhaps in the event it was no surprise that the eight-page *Daily Mirror* could find no space to report on a match that attracted 78,000 spectators, including many servicemen, in which Welsh scored another two as England won 3-1.

Scotland had taken the lead on just 10 minutes, when Alex Venters beat Swift, and thereafter England were hard pressed to prevent the home side adding to their lead with the 'keeper making a number of smart saves. Then on 42 minutes Welsh, wriggling clear of his marker Jimmy Dykes for the first time, showed a poacher's touch to beat 'keeper Jerry Dawson.

Things got even better for the away side in the second half when an injury to Venters left him almost incapacitated and when Wilf Mannion whipped in a cross Goulden headed powerfully home. On 87 minutes, Welsh from fully 25 yards drove home a beauty and the smallish number of spectators still there when the referee sounded the whistle gave a big cheer for the winners who had started poorly and finished brilliantly.

After his success with England there was no surprise that Frank Swift was selected in September 1941 to represent the Army side in a Friendly match against Ireland played at Windsor Park, Belfast. The idea of the fixture had been first discussed in the Irish FA Emergency committee meeting of 5 September 1940, the aim being to raise money for the Army FA for purchasing football equipment. The gate money (minus expenses) was split between the IFA and the Army FA.

The sides were as follows:

IRELAND: Tom Breen (Belfast Celtic), Bill Hayes (Huddersfield), Bertie Fulton (Belfast Celtic), Harry Walker (Belfast Celtic) Jack Vernon (Belfast Celtic), Tom Brolly (Linfield), Norman Kernaghan (Belfast Celtic), Jimmy McAlinden (Belfast Celtic), Dave Martin (Glentoran), Alex Stevenson (Everton), Michael Kelly (Derry City).

BRITISH ARMY: Frank Swift (Manchester City), Jimmy Carabine (Third Lanark), Andy Beattie (Preston North End), Cliff Britton (Everton), Stan Cullis (Wolverhampton Wanderers), Joe Mercer (Everton), Ralph Birkett (Newcastle United), Tommy Walker (Hearts), Don Welsh (Charlton Athletic), Jimmy Hagan (Sheffield United), Denis Compton (Arsenal).

Referee: Flight Lieut. Jimmy Jewell (RAF)

An attendance of 30,000 at Windsor Park witnessed a 4-1 away win in which Hagan scored a hat-trick and Mercer a single goal with Martin replying for Ireland.

Playing at right-back for the Army was Jimmy Carabine, the man Swift rated as the finest right-back he ever saw. They were to play in many army representative sides and before the first the Third Lanark man had told the 'keeper to 'let me know how you want me to play'. Writing in his autobiography, Swift described Carabine as 'ice-cool'.

Swift was back in Belfast playing for the Army against Ireland the following September and this time finished on the losing side. The home side won 3-2 but according to Peter Doherty it could have been plenty more if not for Frank Swift:

'The Army side contained six English and four Scottish internationals, including Swift, Carabine, Busby, Herd and Lawton; and although the Irish team was perhaps not the best that could have been selected, it proved more than a match for this star-studded British XI. Every man in the Irish side pulled his weight magnificently, and but for the brilliance of Swift in the Army goal our score might well have been doubled. Frank made himself a great favourite with the crowd, some of his tremendous clearances, which travelled almost from one goal to goal, winning loud applause.'

When the sides re-met in September 1942 another magnificent display from the Manchester City 'keeper kept the score down to Ireland 4 British Army 2.

After his appearance against Scotland, Swift missed the next nine wartime international matches. These were a 3-2 win in Wales, a 2-0 Wembley victory over the Scots, a 2-1 win against Wales at St Andrews, a 3-0 win against Scotland and a 5-4 reverse at Hampden Park – in which Tommy Lawton scored a hat-trick for the losers – a 1-0 defeat in Wales, a dour 0-0 Wembley draw with Scotland and a further two matches at home to Wales that saw both countries win a game each.

He returned for his third match for England at Hampden Park on Saturday 17 April 1943. This time there were no other Manchester City players in the line-up. Playing at full-back were Middlesbrough's George Hardwick and Arsenal's Les Compton. Captaining the side, for a game in which the sides were introduced to Czechoslovakian President Mr Jan Masaryk, before kick-off, was again Wolves centre-half Stan Cullis.

Bill Shankly was selected at right-half for Scotland and playing at centre-forward was Dougie Wallace, scorer of two of his side's goals when the Scots had won 3-2 at Newcastle earlier in the war.

Off the pitch, Spain had offered to mediate between the United Nations – now consisting of, among others, Britain, France, the USA and the Soviet Union – and the Axis Powers of, among others, Germany, Japan and Italy. The offer had been quickly rejected by the Allies, with US Secretary of State Cordell Hull saying they only sought 'unconditional surrender' on a weekend when British Forces pounded mainly German troops on the Tunisian tip. Victory there and an advance on Italy would be opened up.

Also opened up was the Scotland defence, as England played one of their finest games to win 4-0. Down the England right Sunderland's Raich Carter and Stoke's Stanley Matthews ran riot, combining brilliantly, with the Wearsider scoring twice. As both came in the first 10 minutes England cruised to victory with Denis Westcott and Denis Crompton completing the scoring.

With Cullis rarely putting a foot wrong, and totally blotting out Scottish centre-forward Willie Buchan it wasn't the most difficult of games for Swift, although Willy Waddell did hit the outside of the post from a corner, and then in the second half he made a clawing save to prevent Bill Shankly's 30 yard shot from hitting the top corner of the net, before touching away a curling Waddell shot.

Writing in the *Daily Record* its match reporter felt that 'The Saxons are more used to playing together and every movement revealed a ready-made co-operation that the Scots were always striving for in vain.'

Future Wolves star picks up some tips

Among the massive 105,000 crowd was a 12-year-old up-and-coming 'keeper, Malcolm Finlayson from Alexandria, Dumbarton. He had already seen Swift play in the Scottish wartime League for Hamilton Academical in a 2-2 draw against Dumbarton and had become a big fan.

'I was that impressed that whenever he was playing locally, and I could afford to go and watch the game, I made it my business to do so. In those days most Scottish grounds had a semi-circular terrace directly behind the goal so that you could get close to the action and the players. Wanting to improve as 'keeper I watched everything he did and more or less tried to base my game on his,' says Malcolm.

It clearly didn't do him any harm, as after a short spell in Junior football with Renfrew, he was asked to go on trial with Second Division Millwall in February 1948.

He did so well 'the Lions' immediately signed him up as a professional and 16 days later he made his debut in a 1-1 draw against West Bromwich Albion. It was the start of a fabulous 16-year career in which during his time with Wolves, between 1956 and 1964, he won 2 League Championship and one FA Cup winners' medal. In one famous game for Millwall against Walsall he was rushed to hospital from the Den with his team losing 3-1, only to return patched up during the second half and play on to help the side win 6-5.

'What I liked about Frank Swift was how he commanded the area. Of course 'keepers are the only players who can see all of the action and I followed his attitude, which was that if I am coming for the ball then defenders should get out of the way – or else! He wasn't a shouter, but at corners and free-kicks he would let players know where he wanted them. He also punched the ball well, and when he chose to catch the ball he usually did so,' says the man who on his retirement from playing football became a successful businessman.

On this particular day Frank Swift didn't have a great deal to do. What Finlayson particularly remembers is a high ball into the box with both Swift and Wallace, noted for charging down everything, seeking to get to it first. When the 'keeper did so 'he then stepped to one-side and ruffled the Scots centre-forward's hair as he flashed past'.

Wallace was later involved in a moment of controversy in this game when at a free-kick he grabbed Cullis where it hurts. Cullis collapsed and required treatment and Wallace never played for Scotland again.

Finlayson, who even now regrets not having the courage to approach Swift to ask for his autograph when he later saw him get off the train in Dumbarton, has still kept the cutting from a local south London newspaper that, soon after making his Millwall debut, called him 'the second Frank Swift'. 'I wasn't, as he was the best 'keeper I ever saw play, but I was still delighted.'

Three weeks after the match at Hampden, Swift played in a 1-1 draw against Wales at Ninian Park. With Allied troops having taken Tunis and Bizerta in a lightning raid there was also heartening news from Russia, where the Red Army continued to push the Germans back towards their own homeland.

The City 'keeper then missed out on a first return to Wembley since the 1934 FA Cup Final when England beat Wales 8-3 at the famous stadium in September, a game in which Stan Mortensen, England's 12th man, made his international debut – for Wales – by replacing Ivor Powell who had broken his collar bone.

Mortensen's experience has parallels in that when England beat Scotland 2-1 at St James' Park in December 1939 the home side contained Scotsman Tom Pearson, a regular for Newcastle United. He was included after Sam Barkas and Eric Brook were involved in a car accident on the way to the game and Pearson joined his club colleague Joe Richardson in the England side.

England 8 Scotland 0

On 16 October 1943 Swift was back in goal for England at his old stamping ground, Maine Road. With the Germans in full retreat from the Red Army around Kiev, Scotland were also pushed back on the football field and were slaughtered – not literally, of course – 8-0. England even missed a penalty to make it 9-0. Tommy Lawton had finished top scorer in Division One in

1937-38 and 1938-39, where he was equal with Mickey Fenton of Middlesbrough, and he was on fire as he scored four times with inside-left Jimmy Hagan, of Sheffield United scoring twice.

ENGLAND: Swift, Scott [Arsenal], Hardwick [Middlesbrough],Britton [Everton], Cullis [Wolves] captain, Mercer [Everton], Matthews [Stoke], Carter [Sunderland], Lawton [Everton], Hagan [Sheffield United], D Compton [Arsenal].

Frank Swift, like Tommy Lawton, rated the England XI that day as the finest team he ever played in.

He said: 'Taking into consideration that it was a wartime game, with both sets of players affected by wartime conditions, and lack of training facilities, long hours of travel to get to the match – it was a magnificent, if one-sided match. And I've yet to see such perfection of movement, unselfishness, or team spirit as England showed that afternoon. Or the courage to equal that of the Scots, beaten though they were, but never humbled.

'It was sheer delight to be the goalkeeper on this great side. For long periods I was able to watch the machine swing into action, to note the brilliant half-back play of the three musketeers, Britton, Cullis, Mercer, the terrific shooting of Lawton, the methodical destruction of the Scottish defensive plan by Carter and Hagan, and the sheer wizardry of Stanley Matthews.

Well though everybody played, I think it will go into history as Stanley's match. At times he seemed to bamboozle the whole of the Scottish rearguard on his own. When he got the eighth goal, entirely on his own, the whole crowd rose as one man and cheered for minutes on end and even some of the Scots clapped their hands.'

Keeper sets up England's seventh with a great throw

As might be expected the England 'keeper hardly touched the ball, but when in the second half, Scotland's left-half, Campbell struck a fearsome long-range drive into the left-hand corner of the home goal Swift leapt like a salmon and tipped the ball over the bar, before getting up, performing a theatrical bow and receiving rapturous applause from the crowd. Poor Morton was left scratching his head in amazement. Lawton's fourth and England's seventh was also the result of a marvellous long throw from the 'keeper, the England centre scoring without anyone else touching the ball.

Such had been England's brilliance that Frank Butler in the *Daily Express* wrote – 'I doubt if an English crowd will enjoy a football exhibition as much again.'

He was backed by Ivan Sharpe – respected writer and former England amateur international who won an Olympic gold medal with the Great Britain side at the 1912 Olympics in Sweden – who said: 'the 1943 team that defeated Scotland 8-0 was perhaps England's best since 1907. For this there was a reason. Service football brought them more into action more frequently than is possible in normal times. They developed understanding.'

Swift missed out on being selected when England played, and beat, Scotland 6-2 at Wembley in February 1944 but returned on 22 April 1944 for the match at Hampden Park.

This was the first time the City man had played in the same England side as Stoke City's right-half Frank Soo, the first non-white player to play for the country. Born in Buxton in 1914 Soo was of mixed Chinese and English parentage. He was to go on and make nine wartime appearances but never played in a full international. One of a batch of players produced by Stoke during this period – the others including Stanley Matthews, Joe Johnson, Freddie Steele, Billy Mould and later Neil Franklin – Soo was a neat player who Mortensen rated highly saying, 'He seemed incapable of a clumsy movement'.

The biggest raid ever by the RAF was being mounted the weekend of the game, with attacks on targets in France, Belgium and Germany. The D-Day Normandy landings were less than two months away and while many waited to literally do battle, 133,000 Scots were happy to see their favourites fight 'The Auld Enemy' on the pitch. Lawton was again in good form, and his two goals with one from Carter saw England narrowly home 3-2.

To beat Scotland, England had to come from behind to win, Swift being deceived by a 19th-minute Jimmy Caskie shot from distance. His mistake was quickly forgotten when England scored three times from the 21st minute onwards. With Cullis again outstanding it wasn't until 66 minutes before Dodds cut England's lead to a single goal, but after which, despite continuous pressure, Scotland failed seriously to trouble the England goal. England ran off 3-2 winners.

In the next match, Swift was missing when England beat Wales 2-0 in Cardiff but was then again selected for the FA Combined Services tour match against Ireland played at Windsor Park, Belfast on 9 September 1944.

Britain's Second Army had broken through stiff German defences and was now only 25 miles from the German border. It surely couldn't be too long before 'real' competitive football was back on the agenda? Not that this particular game failed to sparkle. The FA side won 8-4 with Carter opportunistically scoring four times, while Swift had to pick the ball out of the net four times courtesy of his Manchester City colleague, Peter Doherty, an Irish Cup winner with Glentoran in 1932-33.

The match attracted a then record Windsor Park crowd of 49,875 who paid record gate receipts of £4,597. Many of the crowd had come to see the RAF's Stanley Matthews and poor Joe Barr, the Cliftonville amateur left-back making his debut, was led a merry dance for most of the match.

After defeats in 1942 and 1943 the Services had chosen their strongest side with seven England internationals and two Scotland internationals – Busby and Archie Macaulay and one from Wales – Walley Barnes. Only Mortensen had yet to play for his country.

Swift had to pick the ball out of the net when Doherty equalised from the penalty spot on 18 minutes.

'Taking a penalty-kick when Frank Swift is between the posts is a difficult task, because he positions himself intelligently, and his bulky frame seems to leave very little space in which to shoot!' said Doherty afterwards.

A minute later the 'keeper was beaten again when Belfast Celtic's Pat Bonnar crossed accurately for captain Doherty to push his side ahead. Almost immediately, Carter equalised and when Ireland again pressed Swift rose high above defenders and forwards alike to take control of the ball.

At half-time, with the score 2-2, a tight match seemed certain, especially when Doherty then equalised Jimmy Mullen's early effort. However, after Mortensen put his side back into the lead the brave resistance of the home side was broken when Jack Vernon, the Irish centre-half, was forced to leave the field injured. Against 10 men, the Combined Services side scored two more quick goals through Carter and went on to win convincingly.

Rous takes charge
With the FA England selection committee having had to be abandon the task of selecting the International team it was passed for the first time ever to one man, FA Secretary, Stanley Rous, the referee at the 1934 FA Cup Final between Manchester City and Portsmouth.

For the following week's match, at Anfield, he selected Swift for his seventh wartime international. The match finished England 2 Wales 2. Wales took a two-goal lead before Lawton created an opening for Carter and then headed home Mullen's cross. Mortensen made his debut for his country in the game.

Narrowly avoids being killed in a plane crash
The Allies had blasted into Germany and two further weeks later it was considered safe enough for Swift to join his FA service colleagues to play in Paris against France at the end of September. He nearly didn't make it, with City's programme for the 7 October match at home to Crewe Alexandra reporting 'the British Services' team nearly collided with another Allied 'plane. Only 20 feet separated the planes from a collision, and I am told that

the "near miss" caused one famous international in the party to be violently sick.' Swift would have been sitting in the rear of the Dakota. He had taken to riding there because he had noted that during the war many tail gunners had survived after being thrown clear when their bombers crash-landed.

The match was played at the Parc des Princes, Paris. The ground had been used as a concentration camp for political prisoners but Paris, following a seven-day battle, had been liberated on 25 August 1944. In his autobiography Swift recalled a 'wonderful stay. The French people were still almost delirious with excitement at their liberation from the Nazis, and we, in common with other British troops, were feted by these warm-hearted people'.

The Russians had fought their way past the German defence and into Warsaw. The French couldn't do the same against the England back-line and with [another] hat-trick from Carter the FA Services XI won 5-0. The match was well attended, and included, Frank Swift noted 'large numbers of fashionably-dressed girls'. Well it was Paris!

A day later, on 1 October 1944, and with the Trades Union Congress, as part of a plan to revitalise Britain, calling for the nationalisation of key industries once hostilities ended, Swift moved on to play against Belgium in Brussels.

Although still at war he found Brussels to be a more vibrant place than blacked-out England. Bumping into an old schoolfriend he had a great time off the field, going to the dog-racing, and enjoying pure white bread and huge baskets of grapes. The FA Services XI, containing two Welshmen and a single Scot in Matt Busby, won 3-0. Huge numbers of British troops witnessed the victory, including a thousand who had marched 30 miles and on finding they were locked out simply took up picks and shovels to bring down the wooden fence to gain entry.

Back at Wembley

Less than two weeks after the match in Brussels and 10 years after the last time, Swift walked back out at Wembley. A crowd of 90,000 saw him do so and, like in 1934, he left the field at half-time a goal down, this time to Scotland for whom Middlesbrough's John Milne opened the scoring on just four minutes.

Three second-half goals by Lawton – including a wonderful equalising shot – and efforts from Carter, Goulden and Brentford's Leslie Smith saw England home comfortably, 6-2. England forwards' spreading of the ball constantly worried the Scots defence and Swift had relatively little to do.

When the sides next met, in early February the next year, England won 3-2 at Villa Park. Stan Mortensen, playing for the second time for his country, scored twice, his first successes for England. He might have got many more but the Scots 'keeper, Bobby Brown of Queen's Park, played brilliantly with one save from a Lawton header drawing gasps of approval and the huge cheers of the 65,780 crowd packed inside Villa Park. The 'keeper also did well to block Mortensen's fierce drive on 75 minutes but was powerless to prevent the Blackpool man knocking home the rebound for the winner.

In a sure sign that the end of the war was near Villa's stand seats, commandeered for use in Birmingham's communal air-raid shelters had been returned and refitted for the game.

WARTIME INTERNATIONAL
03/02/1945, Birmingham, Villa Park, 65.780
ENGLAND 3-2 SCOTLAND [HT 1-1]
Scorers:
England: 'Sailor' Brown, Stan Mortensen 2
Scotland: Jimmy Delaney, Jock Dodds

ENGLAND:
Frank Swift, Laurie Scott, George Hardwick, Frank Soo, Neil Franklin, Joe Mercer [c], Stanley Matthews, 'Sailor' Brown, Tommy Lawton, Stan Mortensen, Leslie Smith.
SCOTLAND: Bobby Brown, Jimmy Harley, Jimmy Stephen, Matt Busby, Bob Thyne, Archie Macaulay, Jimmy Delaney, Willie Fagan, Jock Dodds, Andy Black, William Liddell.
Referee: T. Smith (England)

Off the field, the US Army were now only 30 miles from Cologne, making it safe for another FA tour to the Continent in March 1945. Back in Brussels a FA XI beat Belgium 3-2 with Lawton scoring all three. Swift was left out in favour of Walsall's Bert Williams but was back for his 10th wartime international when England travelled to Hampden Park on 14 April 1945. Despite his two goals against Wales, Mortensen was left out of the side.

With American President Franklin D. Roosevelt having died two days earlier there was silence prior to the match with only the strains of the *Last Post* to be heard.

When the 133,000 crowd did find its voice it was to roundly boo Swift, after the Hibernian forward Tommy Bogan careered over him in the first minute and was carried off with an injured knee. With Swift using his huge hands to take the Scot towards the stretcher on the halfway line there were cheers when he returned back to his goal. These though were dwarfed on 12 minutes when Willie Waddell shot the ball past him into the net. Disappointed by seeing the effort chalked off for an earlier free-kick awarded in their favour the Scots fell behind to a Carter goal, whose partnership with Matthews was the outstanding feature of the 90 minutes.

However, after equalising through substitute Leslie Johnstone of Clyde the home side must have fancied their chances when the half-time whistle sounded at 1-1.

On the restart Scotland were the better team but were to be foiled by the England 'keeper. The unlucky forward was Tony Harris whose 'two flashing shots in the second half, when the score still stood 1-1, would both have been scorers against a goalkeeper not possessed of the superlative ability of big Frank Swift'. [*Daily Record*]

Inspired by their 'keeper England took a two-goal lead when Charlton's 'Sailor' Brown and Lawton scored in the 61st and 64th minutes.

Outwits former City colleague Matt Busby

The margin might have been cut in the 75th minute when Scotland were awarded a penalty. Having failed to persuade two of his fellow Scots to take the spot-kick, his former Manchester City colleague Matt Busby failed miserably with Swift 'figuring it would be easy, as long ago Matt had taught me all there was to know about saving penalties. And so it proved, for I stopped his shot'.

Swift had been delighted to briefly meet before the match Field Marshal Montgomery who 'a few weeks later was involved in a much bigger battle – the D-Day landings which were to win us the war'.

Late goals from Matthews, Brown and Lawton saw England extend the lead to 6-1, and although the scoreline flattered the away side there was no doubt they deserved to win and Swift was also grateful to the injured Bogan who made clear after the match that his injury was an accident. 'Anyone who knows Frank Swift is well aware he would not intentionally hurt a fly' reported the *Daily Record*, as it condemned those who had booed him.

Although it was wartime, England was playing some wonderful football. Because they were playing much more regularly together than during a League season the England players were able to build partnerships with each other and enjoy an opportunity to discuss tactics – and the opposition's strengths and weaknesses – before each match. As Stan Cullis later wrote, 'We saw an awful lot of each other…without quite realising it we built an international side like a club team and that was an important part of the success.'

Following the Hampden victory, Williams replaced Swift in goal for the 3-2 victory at Ninian Park on 5 May. Twenty-four hours earlier the two 'keepers had listened, along with Joe Mercer, Stanley Matthews, Frank Broome and Stanley Rous, to the BBC announcement that German forces had surrendered in north-west Europe. The Manchester City 'keeper then also missed out playing in the 2-2 Wembley draw with France on May 26 that marked the end of official European hostilities after Germany unconditionally surrendered on 7 May 1945.

Chapter 13
Touring with England in post-war Europe

At the end of May 1945 Swift played for the army team in Italy under the direction of manager Matt Busby with Arthur Rowe, later the architect of the 'push and run' style of the successful Spurs title side in 1951, as trainer. Following their flight the party travelled overland by a bumpy army truck to entertain British troops enjoying a well-earned rest. All those present were required to wear uniform, but there was plenty of time to see some unforgettable sights with a visit to Pompeii, buried by volcanic ash when Vesuvius erupted in AD79 among the highlights. The war was over.

Games in Naples, Rome, Ancona and in Florence, where everyone was impressed by the magnificent stadium, were organised. The 'keeper had left behind his boots, making him the butt of all the other players' jokes but with his side easily winning the first match against No 3 Army Division – consisting of players from units stationed between Bari and Gibraltar – Swift was offered by tourists' captain Joe Mercer as a replacement for the losing sides injured 'keeper, Notts County's Jack Reid.

For the big 'keeper this was too much of an opportunity to enjoy himself. Between signing dozens of autographs and joking with the crowd, he produced a string of outstanding saves before prancing around his goalmouth when a last-minute penalty was awarded. Such was Tommy Lawton's helpless laughter that he passed on the spot-kick to Duggie Hunt to make it 6-0.

The next morning all the players piled into an Army lorry to make the 150-mile journey to Rome. En route they witnessed the destruction wrought by years of fierce fighting in which over 450,000 civilians and military personnel were killed, including Bolton captain Harry Goslin who lost his life on 18 December 1943 when a bomb exploded on his observation point during the battle of the River Sangro. Serving with the 53rd Field Regiment RA (Bolton Artillery), Goslin had already fought alongside many of his Wanderers colleagues in both France and North Africa. Goslin, in one of his four wartime appearances for England, had played in front of Swift at Hampden Park in the 3-1 success in May 1941.

Arriving in the ancient Italian capital city there was a surprise in store for the players when they discovered they were to meet the Pope. A somber mood was quickly replaced by excited voices as they entered the opulent Papal palace. Everyone was on their best behaviour except, recalled Tommy Lawton later, Frank Swift who whispered that he was not going to 'kiss any man's ring!'

When the magnificently-robed Pope appeared, carried in by his Swiss guards, he blessed all the players and despite Frank Swift's joking every player was immensely proud to have been blessed by Pope Pius XII. Some of the players later had their 'revenge' on their popular 'keeper for his non-stop larking around when they had him chucked overboard in Ancona Harbour after he had turned the fire hose on them.

When the side reached Florence they were delighted to find a magnificent Stadium on which to play the game. The Fifth Army XI opponents were able to call upon members of the Brazilian Army, which was then attached to the Allied Forces locally.

For the first time during their tour, the touring soccer greats were met with hostility from some in the large crowd, who reckoned they had stayed safely at home playing football while they and others were fighting and dying. Lawton, Mercer, Busby, Swift and the rest of the party were accused of being draft-dodgers. Stung, the Combined Services tore into their opposition and won 10-0.

After such unpleasantness, Swift would have been delighted to hear the respected BBC radio commentator Raymond Glendenning declare that players who had stayed at home and play for morale had 'done more for this country's prestige than is generally realised' and that the Combined Services tourists had been 'our first ambassadors to liberated Europe'.

Beaten but chaired off

Less than a month after his return home Swift journeyed to Switzerland and was between the posts for two unofficial England games against Switzerland and Switzerland B. The team almost didn't make it, with only the last-minute arrival of the first Swiss passenger plane into England since 1939 enabling them to travel.

The side, travelling in civilian clothes, enjoyed tremendous hospitality off the field, but on it England played poorly in the first match and Swift suffered his first defeat, losing 3-1. The chance to enjoy some sumptuous food, hot weather, an enthusiastic welcome, a bumpy pitch and a game played above 10,000 feet all contributed to a disappointing result. Some 35,000 spectators packed into the little ground and the result flattered England, who were saved from a thrashing by their 'keeper. Certainly he was the star of the show and to show their appreciation he was carried off the pitch, shoulder high. In the second game England played much better to win 3-0.

In September 1945 Swift played in the Victory International in Belfast where Mortensen's single goal was enough to see England beat Northern

Ireland 1-0. He was omitted from the game against Wales – which England lost 1-0 – but was delighted to play against Belgium at Wembley in a game England won 2-0 and in which Wolves half-back Billy Wright made his debut for his country. Brown and Jesse Pye scored the goals. For the first time England players were given tracksuits to wear, and following the example of the great Russian side Moscow Dynamo, who had toured Britain in the summer of 1945, the team were given match balls to engage in a pre-match kick-about.

Swift was delighted to receive at the after match banquet, held at the Dorchester Hotel, a crystal ash-tray as a present from the Belgium side and had been impressed at the shooting power of Francois Sermon during the game itself.

ENGLAND: Frank Swift, Laurie Scott, George Hardwick, Billy Wright, Neil Franklin, Joe Mercer [c], Stanley Matthews, Jesse Pye [Notts County], Tommy Lawton [Chelsea], 'Sailor' Brown, Jimmy Mullen [Wolverhampton Wanderers].

BEL: Francois Daenen, Robert Paverick, Joseph Pannaye, Antoine Puttaert, Marcel Vercammen, René Devos, Victor Lemberechts, Henri Coppens, Albert de Cleyn, Joseph Mermans, Francois Sermon.

Referee: G. Reader (England)

Scotland 1 England 0

Returning to Hampden Park in April 1946 Swift was on the losing side for the first time in a wartime international. England, with Bradford Park Avenue's Len Shackleton playing for his country for the first time, looked like escaping with a draw. With England's half-backs, Mercer and Wright, never allowed to the settle the away side had been under severe pressure in the second half – during which Swift bravely played on after being revived when knocked unconscious during a goalmouth scramble for the ball with Billy Liddell. There were only 22 seconds remaining when Partick Thistle's John Husband's free-kick – 'beautifully placed' wrote Swift, was headed forward by Waddell and with Liddell and Jimmy Delaney lunging forward the latter shot the ball home from close range.

This was a moment in which Swift said he 'had never heard or seen such excitement, with the Hampden Roar threatening to burst its bounds'. Scotland had won 1-0 and even the 'usually stolid Glasgow policemen beamed their delight' as news also came through from Murrayfield that in the Rugby Union International, Scotland had beaten England by a record margin, 27-4.

Still suffering the effects of his earlier injury Swift was the last England player to leave the field, his Scottish counterpart Bob Brown racing the length of the pitch at the final whistle to shake his hand and walk off with his arms around the big England 'keeper. Brown, who is still alive today and living in Helensburgh, later became the first full-time Scotland manager and led his country to a 3-2 Wembley success against England in his first game in charge in 1967.

Fundraiser following football disaster

Eleven days after the match in Glasgow, Scotland and England met again at Maine Road. Thirty-three people had been killed at an FA Cup match between Bolton Wanderers and Stoke City at Burnden Park on 9 March 1946. The game was played to raise funds for their families. It ended 2-2 with Welsh scoring twice and Bill Thornton doing the same for Scotland and 70,000 paying fans watched it.

Swift was chosen, for the first time, as England captain saying 'I got a terrific kick out of leading the England team on to the field on my own ground. And I was greatly bucked by the ovation the crowd gave me when I ran to my favourite goal for the kick-in. I'm afraid it upset me a little, for I had a nervy sort of game' blaming himself for missing Liddell's corner and Thornton's subsequent headed equaliser in the second half.

England had promised, after the previous year's tour, to play Switzerland at home and did so on 11 May 1946. A crowd of 75,000 packed out Stamford Bridge. Charlton Athletic's Sailor Brown had played in the previous weekend's 4-1 defeat against Derby County in the FA Cup Final. Consolation – of a sort – came with a goal in a 4-1 victory over the Swiss.

The England squad had been sent to Twyford for training, and under the managership of Arsenal trainer, Tom Whittaker, had worked out how to combat the lightning speed of the Swiss team. It was intended to keep it tight in the first and open up in the second. The plan worked but on 57 minutes the Swiss took the lead through a beautiful goal from Friedlander. Debutant Bert Johnson played a part in the passing movement that created space for Carter to equalise with a powerful drive from 20 yards and after which England tore the Swiss defence apart.

The game marked Swift's last wartime international as in the final game Bert Williams, now playing for Wolves, represented England in a 2-1 defeat in Paris. Swift played in 14 wartime internationals of which 11 were won, and one was lost. Disappointingly these matches were ruled by the Football Association as not being worthy enough to be classified as full internationals and so despite having lost six years of his career to the war no caps were awarded to him, or any of the players involved.

In addition Swift played four times for the combined services against Ireland, of which two games were won, twice for the FA XI – both games being won, twice in unofficial internationals in which England won one and lost one and the drawn Friendly with Scotland to raise funds for the Bolton disaster. By anyone's standards this is an impressive record.

Wartime internationals

1939	Wales (A), England won 3-2
1941	Scotland (A), England won 3-1
1943	Scotland (A), England won 4-0
	Wales (A), England drew 1-1
	Scotland (H), England won 8-0
1944	Scotland (A), England won 3-2
	Wales (H), England drew 2-2
	Scotland (H), England won 6-2
1945	Scotland (H), England won 3-2
	Scotland (A), England won 6-1
	Northern Ireland (A), England won 1-0
	Belgium (H), England won 2-0
1946	Scotland (A), England lost 1-0
	Switzerland (H), England won 4-1.

14 wartime internationals – 11 victories, 2 draws and 1 defeat.

Chapter 14
The return of competitive football

Manchester City started the 1945-46 season with a 2-1 home win against Middlesbrough. that was watched by a crowd of 25,000.

On 24 November 1945 City drew 0-0 at Ewood Park, a game in which Swift was at his very best: 'ROVERS FOILED BY SWIFT – Swift's wonderful and spectacular save from Coates just before the interval of the Rovers' match against Manchester City at Ewood Park on Saturday will be remembered long after other incidents in the game have been forgotten. It was a great drive, which would have beaten most 'keepers. But Swift was always sure. He had an inspired day, dealt brilliantly with shots from all angles and generally frustrated the hopes of the home forwards.' (*Blackburn Times*)

In addition to his duties between the Manchester City posts Frank Swift continued to turn out regularly for the Combined Services side and on 13 December 1945 his presence, along with seven other England internationals, helped draw a crowd of 8,000 to Layer Road, Colchester, for a match against the Colchester Garrison. The 'keeper forsook his normal place in the side to play at left wing.

On Saturday 5 January 1946 'real' football returned with City involved in the FA Cup for the first time since losing to Sheffield United in January 1939. Since the FA had agreed that every round would see teams play each other home and away, there was a crowd of 19,589 inside Maine Road to see the 1934 winners take on Division Three North side Barrow,

The City line up was: Swift, Clark G., Barkas, Robinson P., Cardwell, Walsh, Pritchard, Herd, Constantine, Smith G., Bootle.

Missing from the team was Peter Doherty. The Irishman and City's directors had clashed during the war. Soon after it started Doherty had unsuccessfully applied for work with Leyland Motors and Vickers Armstrong. Then, when he was offered a job in Greenock he was instructed by City to remain in Lancashire and told by the City chairman that he would not be allowed to play football for any Scottish side. Even though he was found a chauffeur's job by one of the club's directors he quit after a few days. Like a number of Blackpool residents he eventually found work at the ordnance factory at Risley, near Warrington.

However rather than wait to be called up he volunteered for the RAF. Stationed initially at Skegness he often found it impossible to return to Lancashire and he played several games for Lincoln City and Grimsby Town.

One weekend when he could make it home he wired to City to report his availability but after arriving in Blackpool he found a letter saying Albert Malam, a registered Doncaster Rovers player, would keep his regular place in the side. For Doherty no expenses were paid.

After he was then refused permission by City to play for certain clubs, on grounds that their size and funding restricted their ability to properly insure him, Doherty's dissatisfaction with his employers grew: 'I was annoyed with City's uncompromising attitude. Once again, in spite of the fact that all contracts had been cancelled, I was receiving orders as if I were a full-time player getting a normal weekly wage.'

Derby County [with whom he did guest on many wartime occasions] – helping the Rams to win the 1945 Midland Cup by scoring five times in the second leg of the Final against Aston Villa – offered £6,000 for his services in December 1945. When it was accepted it meant he lined up in the FA Cup on 5 January 1946 for Derby against Luton Town. In 133 League and FA Cup appearances for Manchester City the Irishman had knocked home 81 goals, a fine goals tally for an inside-forward.

Playing alongside him for the Rams was Raich Carter, signed from Sunderland in the same month for £6,000. The pair provided the class to take Derby to a first ever success in the FA Cup, Charlton Athletic being beaten 4-1 in the Wembley Final in which Doherty scored one of the winning side's goals. How City could have done with a player of Doherty's stature in their side.

Against Barrow, with Herd and Jimmy Constantine both scoring three times, Manchester City won the first leg 6-2. In the return, played at 2pm on a Thursday, the sides drew 2-2. City progressed 8-4 on aggregate to face Bradford Park Avenue, who they had only weeks earlier beaten 6-0. No one knew it, but City were set for their record home defeat!

Playing away in the first leg, and before a crowd of 25,014, City, with two late goals, won handsomely 3-1. Swift had a decent match, using his long legs to prevent Bert Knott opening the scoring and then diverting the centre-forward's splendid shot over for a corner. With the game tied at 1-1 and only seconds of the first period remaining 'Swift saved City with a save which only he could have made – a magnificent backward leap to turn a header from Shackleton over the bar, when a goal looked a certainty'. (*MEN*)

The second leg was sure to be a formality. Avenue, though, had in their side a number of good players and during the war had beaten sides rated their superiors. On his day Len Shackleton – the Clown Prince of Soccer – could be almost unplayable and the match at Maine Road on 30 January 1946 was to be one of those days.

Writing in his autobiography the future West Ham and England manager Ron Greenwood, signed from Chelsea at the end of the war, recalled 'Our cause seemed hopeless and to rub things in our coach ran into a blizzard right on top of the Pennines on our way to Maine Road for the second leg. The wind howled, the snow swirled and our coach struggled. Len Shackleton said "let's turn back…we don't stand a chance anyway". That seemed a fair assessment, but we pushed on and eventually got to the ground with less than 20 minutes to spare. Our trouble proved worthwhile, even though the pitch was covered by pools of water and a gale blew across the pitch.'

It was City, though, who were blown away, beaten 8-2, with Jackie Gibbons, the former Spurs amateur centre-forward, scoring four times. It was to be a famous day for the West Yorkshire side.

Ron Greenwood: 'The sight of the great Frank Swift picking the ball out of the net eight times is something I shall never forget. Everything went right for us. It was one of those days.'

Returning home Len Shackleton's dad consoled him when he reported the score as 8-2. He didn't believe his son when he said Avenue had won and it needed the sight of the score in the newspaper the following morning to convince him. City fan Geoff Ireland had seen the first match, and he too couldn't believe the score even after seeing the result in the paper!

Earlier in Swift's career City had on their staff a youngster, Jackie, who had aspired to be a 'keeper. Drawing on his experience the City 'keeper told him that 'after every match in which a goal has been scored against me, I make a practice of sitting down and drawing diagrams to see where I was at fault'.

Leaving Maine Road after Avenue's success Swift bumped into the same youngster, who was, by now, a very smart sergeant major and after a small chat the pair parted with Jackie informing the beaten 'keeper that he 'had plenty of homework to do this evening!' (*Football from the Goalmouth*)

To a lesser man such humour might not have been as well received, but Swift had already seen the funny side of being beaten so heavily. With the papers suggesting he was shortly to be transferred to Anfield, Walter Allison recalls some in the crowd shouting out 'When are you off to Liverpool then?' 'Read it in the papers' was the reply, accompanied by a broad smile.

Then after Gibbons – who had a record of doing well against City – had fired in the seventh Swift had been reduced to laughter. Lying prostrate in the mud the 'keeper heard teammate, the newly married Bert Sproston, telling the scorer to 'go away, Sonny Boy, there's plenty of room to play at the other end'.

Allison also recalls, 'at the end of the game Swift went out of his way to congratulate the Avenue players, to shake their hands. He wasn't sour or bitter, and this was always a part of his game, he was a genuine sportsman was Frank Swift and that made him a decent man also in my view'.

Still a youngster, Allison should have been at school. When his mother discovered he had bunked off a word with his father saw him reported to Hardwick Central School Headmaster Mr Peake, who was 'an awesome immaculately well dressed man who caned me and my brother Tom. It was worth it as Shackleton that day was a genius. Totally unplayable'.

Sproston had signed for Manchester City from Spurs in November 1938 for a fee of £10,000. Capped 11 times by England his record of 134 first team appearances for Manchester City would have been greater but for the war.

Despatched from the FA Cup. City continued to compete in the wartime League and in early April they played Manchester United home and away at Maine Road. Now managed by Swift's former teammate Matt Busby it was to be a long time before United were able to return to Old Trafford. During the war nearby Trafford Park had become a major new centre for war production that saw employment rise there by 25,000 to 75,000.

After first bombing the Port of London on 7 September 1940 – when 436 people were killed – the German Luftwaffe had extended their targets north. Old Trafford was first hit during a heavy bombing raid on Trafford Park over Christmas 1940 that left over 700 Mancunians dead.

Although football resumed at Old Trafford in early March another raid on 11 March 1941 destroyed much of the stadium. From then on games were switched to Maine Road and when the local rivals clashed twice in April 1945 a total of 112,000 watched the action. Crowds everywhere were streaming through the turnstiles and the post-war boom was to reach its peak in 1948-49 with a record aggregate of 41,271,414. With a UK population of 50 million it was the equivalent of four in every five people having seen a live match.

Over the summer of 1946 Frank and Doris Swift enjoyed visiting Norway as part of a coaching course organised by FA secretary, Stanley Rous. Arriving in Oslo after a pleasant flight they were taken by car to Larvik where Doris's request for a cup of tea was met with blank stares and a wait of 70 minutes. The small whaling town was very picturesque and Frank enjoyed a great reception when he arrived at the local sports ground, with its athletics track around the pitch, prior to a League match that evening.

With the game tied at no score he was able to offer some words of advice at half-time and when Larvik scored three without reply it marked 'a very good start to a very happy association with some of the grandest people I've ever met'.

Over the next few weeks he organised four three-hour sessions a week, taking the two senior sides, a junior team and a boys' eleven. He was delighted with the enthusiasm of the players and was extremely proud when one of his players, Gunnar Thoresen, was capped at inside-right for Norway during his time there. At senior level the team rose from near the bottom to second in the Championship being beaten only once in 15 matches.

Meanwhile there was plenty of time for the married couple to take in 'some of the finest scenery I've ever seen' and every day the pair would go swimming at the nearby Lake Farris or at a seaside resort called Goon. As his coaching trip came to an end Swift joined other British players, who had also spent the summer coaching, in a match against a Norwegian international eleven played at Oslo. Arsenal's Curtis scored the only goal of the game. The night before he returned to England, Doris and he were guests of the Larvik club and left with souvenirs of a 'very happy stay in hospitable Norway'.

Chapter 15
Promotion at the second attempt

After a seven-year break Manchester City returned to League action on Saturday 31 August 1946. With the fixture list remaining as it was for the 1939-40 season a journey back to Filbert Street saw City capture both points in a 3-0 win against Leicester City in which Les McDowall, Bill Walsh [scoring his only City goal in over 100 League and FA Cup appearances] and Harry Jackson scored the goals.

Of the side that had faced Chesterfield on 2 September 1939 there were five players representing Manchester City in the game with the Foxes – Swift, Sproston, McDowall, Dunkley and Herd.

Swift, Sproston, Barkas, Percival J., McDowall, Walsh, Dunkley, Herd, Jackson H., Black, Smith G.

The first day success marked the start of a bright opening. Unbeaten in the first seven matches it was clear that Swift's side were going to be among the promotion hopefuls. Against Bradford Park Avenue a measure of revenge for the previous season's FA Cup hammering was gained in a 7-2 success at Maine Road. Andy Black got a hat-trick.

The eighth game of the season brought a first defeat, West Ham winning at Upton Park with a late Archie Macaulay goal. An unidentified spectator at the match later recalled being behind 'Swiftie's goal in the second half. He was joshing with the crowd about the Hammers' inability to score; mind you City hadn't scored either. The Hammers had a throw in on the left. The ball was touched on to Archie Macaulay. He rose and planted the ball into the net. We went mad and Swiftie had a lot of stick to take. He took it all in good spirit, grinned and called out 'fluke' as he got the ball out of the net. Swift believed in entertaining the crowd but he was also the best goalie I ever saw, and I include the great Russian 'keeper Lev Yashin, Gordon Banks and Peter Shilton.'

On 2 November Black also got another three, as West Brom were beaten 5-0 at Maine Road. The result pushed City to fifth. City beat Coventry City 1-0, in the next home match where Swift was able to shake hands with Alf Wood, who during the war had acted on many occasions as his deputy when he was unavailable to play for the Army. Wood was to miss just two Sky Blues games in five seasons after the war. This was a remarkable achievement considering that towards the end of it he had been diagnosed with spinal meningitis and told he would never play football again. Wood retired from playing in 1958, aged 43.

Later in November 1946 City's reserve 'keeper Jack Robinson decided that it was time to move on. He had waited nine years for Frank Swift to become ordinary and had now grown tired of waiting, taking the chance to transfer to Bury.

Recalling that after every match the pair would go over the goals that had been conceded Robinson told the *Daily Mirror*, 'Frank passed on as much of his skill as he could. I consoled myself that he couldn't go on forever. I've realised that I'll have to move on or I'll never reach the top. Frank just goes on and on and never plays a bad game. It will be a wrench, because Frank and I are the best of pals.'

Paying tribute to his patient understudy, Frank Swift said: 'If ever a player deserved to be in a first team it is Jack. He's a grand lad, and there's a big future for him.'

In December Manchester City surged to the top of the table, taking 11 from a possible 12 points on offer, including two at war-damaged Home Park on Boxing Day, Plymouth losing 3-2. The previous day City had beaten Argyle 4-3, scoring a late winner after Argyle recovered from three down to draw level.

Meantime, after 14 years in the managerial seat [the longest of any City manager in the club's history], Wilf Wild had decided to return to the administrative role that he had first assumed in 1920 under Ernest Mangnall, City manager from 1912 to 1924. Stepping up to the hot seat was former captain Sam Cowan, whose inspirational skills on the pitch were now to be utilised off it.

The new man had limited managerial experience with just one season in charge as player-manager with Cheshire League side Mossley. Nevertheless he was given a salary of £2,000 a year, five times that of the senior players and allowed to spend at least part of each week in Brighton where he retained business interests. He took charge for the first time against Newport County at the start of the December and was to lead Manchester City back to Division One before quitting after a disagreement with club officials over his insistence about continuing to spend time on the south coast.

On New Year's Day 1947 City outclassed Fulham 4-0 at Maine Road, the largely unoccupied Swift watching Andy Black and Herd both score twice. Black's goals were among the 52 he scored for Manchester City in 146 appearances between 1946 and 1950.

Twenty-six-year-old Joe Fagan, who later managed Liverpool so successfully, made his debut, more than eight years after joining City, against the Cottagers. Although he lined up at right-half he soon made the centre-half position, where he had played for the Navy side during the war, his own and his powerful performances at the heart of the City defence played an important part in the side's success in 1947.

Fagan and Swift were good friends, lived close to one another and the latter affectionately bestowed the nickname 'Patsy' on Joe, a reference to the popular

Irish folk song *Hello Patsy Fagan*. After training finished the pair were a regular team against Joe Hart and Jackie Bray at head tennis in the Maine Road car park. Games would continue until Fagan, who joined City in 1938 after they offered him a £1 a week more than home club Liverpool, and Swift won.

Three days after beating Fulham, 20,000 squeezed inside Saltergate to see the visitors beat Chesterfield 1-0, where Harry Jackson scored the only goal but Swift was the Man of the Match with an impressive display against a rough forward line. It was City's fifth consecutive win and the record rose to seven after victories over Gateshead in the FA Cup and Millwall in the League.

The match against Bolton Wanderers at Burnden Park in the FA Cup fourth round attracted 41,286 and they saw the home side race into an early 2-0 lead through goals from Billy Wrigglesworth and Nat Lofthouse before two goals from Black and a Capel effort tied the scores at 3-3. Malcolm Barrass also scored for Bolton. Back at Maine Road a massive queue on the Tuesday morning saw all stand tickets snapped up. Swift recovered from a chill to play and the big 'keeper made a great save in the second half to keep out a powerful Lofthouse drive and thus help ensure Westwood's early goal was sufficient to take his side through to play Second Division Birmingham City in round five.

There was disappointment, though, when Swift was left to pick the ball out of the net five times as Birmingham City won 5-0. After twice seeing the away side hit the woodwork a slip on an icy pitch by McDowall helped give the Blues a vital second, courtesy of Cyril Twigg. In order to avoid a colour clash the home side, for who outside-right Ambrose Mulraney was outstanding, had played in red with City in white.

Despite this defeat it was Manchester City who took both points in a 1-0 win at Maine Road when the sides met in a crucial promotion match in the middle of March. It was Smith who got the all important goal, one of 75 he scored for City in 166 League and FA Cup appearances.

The highlight of the game, though, was Swift's save from Mulraney, which City fan Geoff Ireland recalls was 'hit point blank at him from the edge of the goal area and he turned it round the post. It was memorable and only the save Bert Trautmann made to deny Denis Wilshaw of Wolves in the 1950s was as good'.

The previous weekend City's game at the Hawthorns had been called off as the chill winds that brought much of Britain to a standstill throughout February and March 1947 meant the frost bound pitch was unplayable. The large number of postponements were to mean the League season was to run into June, the latest ever in its history.

This was to present problems for those footballers who also played professional cricket in the summer and in mid-March the *Daily Mirror* speculated on which sport would be given precedence among the likes of Denis and Les Compton at Arsenal and Sunderland's Willie Watson.

In the meantime and despite playing for a Second Division side, Swift was picked for the Football League side against the Irish League in mid February. The game was played on an icy pitch at Goodison Park and Middlesbrough's George Hardwick captained the Football League.

A 40,000 crowd saw the home side win 4-2. Burnley's amateur outside-left Peter Kippax gave himself a great chance of earning a call up to the England side by scoring two goals with Lawton also scoring twice. Highlights of the action were shown on Pathe News.

Despite his goals Lawton was dropped for the 12 March Inter-League match at Hampden Park and Frank Swift, with Ted Ditchburn going in goal, joined him on the sidelines.

There was, though, good news for the 'keeper on Grand National Day, Saturday 29 March when it was announced he had been selected for the England side to face Scotland at Wembley. This brought him a step nearer his ambition of being selected for the Great Britain team to face the Rest of Europe on 10 May 1947 at Hampden Park.

If the 'keeper was celebrating then so too were any punters who had stuck money on 100-1 outsider I Caughoo, whose jockey E. Dempsey had a 50,000 crowd cheering him to the winners' enclosure.

Over Easter 1947 City were almost guaranteed promotion when five points from three games were collected in back to back fixtures with Luton Town and away to Southampton.

At Kenilworth Road the away side wrestled a point in a tight 0-0 draw. In the second half Swift brought down Allenby Driver for a penalty, but when Harry Cooke knocked it well wide the diving 'keeper injured himself and required a sponge from trainer Barnett before play could restart. Later on he kept out former Derby man Dally Duncan's shot at the far post.

In the following match City won 2-0 at Oakwell. Watching was a mad keen young Tykes fan, Arthur Bower, whose dad and granddad were present on that famous April 1912 day at Bramall Lane, Sheffield when Barnsley beat West Bromwich Albion 1-0 in the replayed FA Cup Final.

Still a regular at Oakwell in 2012, Arthur has watched football at all levels. He was present the day Hungary walloped England 6-3 at Wembley in 1953, and saw virtually all of Manchester United's FA Cup games in 1958 when the post-Munich side almost won the famous trophy. Arthur says, 'It was a privilege to be at those games. As a Barnsley lad we felt we were honouring the great Tommy Taylor, who like Frank Swift, was tragically killed in the plane crash.'

Arthur is a big fan of some of the greatest 'keepers including Gordon Banks, Peter Shilton and Pat Jennings. He rates Frank Swift, though, as better than any of them, saying: 'I'd select Frank Swift as the goalkeeper in my finest eleven. The others were very good, but Swift's height and physique, allied to his ability to dive for the ball as well as any 'keeper, meant he could reach further and therefore get to shots placed that little bit nearer the corner of the net. He was just that little bit better than the rest. Swift was a good distributor of the ball and could throw it accurately over a long distance. He was also a real character and he would chat to the crowd behind his goal and when he made a good save the Barnsley fans would be happy to applaud and shout out "well played Frank". In addition to seeing him against Barnsley I also saw him play for England against the Netherlands at Leeds Road.'

The Barnsley game was to be Swift's last City game for almost a month, as a combination of matches for England and Great Britain kept him out of the side throughout May. In his absence Alec Thurlow played competently as City won twice and lost twice to maintain their place at the summit.

In Swift's absence, promotion was secured on 10 May, when with Birmingham drawing at Nottingham Forest, City beat Burnley 1-0 with a goal from Herd. A crowd of 67,672 watched the action. Gates everywhere had rocketed after the war. Against a background of austerity, the game provided a relief for millions of people. So too did the cinema: this was a time when that art form had a regular attendance of 30 million in Britain.

After two seasons – divided by six years of war – Manchester City had returned to Division One. Swift returned to the side to play in the last two matches as the title was clinched, the last game taking place on 14 June 1947, a 5-1 home win against Newport County at Maine Road in which Smith scored all five to take his League total in the season to 22. With City directors looking to the future, new signing Roy Clarke from Third Division Cardiff City played against Newport and this meant that when he played the first game of the next season he had played in the third, second and first divisions in consecutive matches. City had also bid £14,000 for Frank Swift's England colleague Stan Mortensen but Blackpool were unwilling to part with their star centre-forward.

City were back in the big time nine years after being relegated. Frank Swift also had a Division Two winners' medal to go with his League Division One, FA Cup and Charity Shield winners' medals.

Pay rise

To cap a great season the 'keeper had been awarded, like the rest of his delighted colleagues, a pay rise. The maximum wage had originated in 1901, and at £4 a week it was substantially less than many of the top players were already earning. In 1906 Manchester City's breaching of it through under the counter payments to their top players had led to FA sanctions and the subsequent loss of many fine players to Manchester United. As a result it was to be more than two decades before City recovered their place as the best side in Manchester.

By this time the maximum wage had been increased to £5 in 1910 and then £9 in 1920, only for it to be reduced to £8 – and £6 in the summer months – in 1922. More than a quarter of a century later the figure remained the same. At £8 a week this meant Frank Swift was paid the average working wage in 1947. Little wonder that like other top players he felt they 'did not get enough out of football' and wanted a more decent return, especially as gates were booming.

The Players' Union aimed to increase the sums paid by £4 a week and also hoped to raise the minimum wage to £7. They also wanted transferred players to be paid a percentage of the fee and for players to be given a free transfer if not offered a living wage. Union membership had grown considerably in the years after the war, but Football League Clubs were unmoved.

Twice a strike was threatened – and slight improvements were made through the Football League management committee – before the Players' Union under its secretary, Jimmy Fay, broke the deadlock by urging the Labour Government under Clement Attlee to establish a National Tribunal, a practice introduced during the war to resolve industrial or trade disputes.

Parties to the trade dispute were the clubs themselves and 'Workmen: Members of the Association Football Players' Union employed as professional footballers by the above-mentioned employers.'

Headed by Lord Terrington, the five panel members, after three days of hearings, awarded the players an increase to £12 and £10 for the maximum wage and £7, with £5 in the summer, as the minimum. The players' proposals on transfer fees were rejected.

Swift was pleased to see his and other players wages being increased and believed that 'Fay had really done a fine job of work for the professional footballer. The Players' Union fight was not particularly for the star-player, but rather that the minimum wage should be a living wage, and also that the lesser-known and young players should receive some protection.' (*Football from the Goalmouth*)

Chapter 16
Full England honours and captaining his country

International football returned for England in September 1946 with matches in Belfast and Dublin. Swift was delighted to be selected for his first peace-time international and joined the party at their base in Newcastle, County Down. Preston's Tom Finney replaced the injured Stanley Matthews in the 13-man squad.

In his 1948 autobiography Swift recalled 'some beautiful scenery, as well as some general larking about and mischief making, the sort that helps bonds a team together and builds friendships'. Raich Carter, a brilliant passer of the football, used his skills off the pitch to become squad pool champion.

Windsor Park, Linfield's ground, was bursting at the seams for the game between the whole of Ireland and England on Saturday 28 September. So much so, that the referee Mr Willie Webb, a Scots train driver during the week, had to delay the kick-off by 10 minutes while the crowd was pushed back over the touchline.

The tone of the game was set with a no holds barred challenge between the Irish centre forward Eddie McMorran, a Belfast blacksmith who later moved from Belfast Celtic to play at Manchester City, and Swift. This had the crowd roaring its approval, but it was silenced when England went up the field and Carter – whose combination at inside-forward with fellow north easterner Wilf Mannion was one of the highlights of the game – put the away side in the lead.

England dominated the game thereafter and at the final whistle came off 7-2 winners, with all five forwards having scored. In his first official international Mannion got three. The result was an excellent one for Walter Winterbottom, who had been appointed during the summer as England's first ever-permanent manager. Since he was a former Manchester United player, he knew Swift well.

After a performance described by Irish captain, Peter Doherty as 'brilliant' it was no surprise that Winterbottom kept the same side for the match two days later at Dalymount Park, Dublin with the Republic of Ireland – organised by the FAI in Dublin. Full-back Bill Gorman, who played his League football for Brentford, and Manchester United's Johnny Carey, who had both played in Belfast, were selected to play for Eire. It was England's first match in Dublin for 34 years and their first-ever game against Eire.

A noisy 32,000 crowd helped inspire the home side, and England were fortunate to win courtesy of a fumble by Shamrock Rovers' Tommy Breen in the Irish goal that was punished by Finney knocking home on 80 minutes, the Preston man's first England goal.

A greasy surface had proved difficult, and the men in green never gave up with the O'Flanaghan brothers – Arsenal's Kevin and Bohemians Mick – constantly threatening the England back line. Mick had been serving in his father's bar before the match, only to receive a call to get his boots and help out his country. It was Everton's Alex Stevenson though who came nearest to giving the home side the lead. His shot beat Swift but came back off the crossbar, the ball leaving a distinctive splash mark as a constant reminder of the Irish number 10's misfortune.

Faultless performance

What wasn't lucky though was Swift's almost faultless performance. Before the game he had met the Republic's Premier (Taoiseach) Eamon de Valera, whose pre-match reception for the visiting players was the first time such a function had been held. The two appeared to get on well and beaming photographs of the pair – with Swift a couple of inches taller – later appeared in many papers.

De Valera had hoped for a tighter encounter than in Belfast and Swift had agreed, intending to earn the £20 he got for each appearance for England. After a series of 'plucky fine saves' reported the *Mirror* the big 'keeper was helped out when he dropped a late Tommy Eglington cross and was glad to see Laurie Scott kick clear.

England had won, but in Johnny Carey, who constantly switched positions throughout the game, Ireland had the man of the match. Swift had been England's best player and he thoroughly enjoyed the magnificent after match banquet at the Gresham Hotel in Ireland's capital city.

Winterbottom selected the same side for the Home Championship match against Wales in November 1946 at Maine Road. It was a busy time for the City ground, because as well as hosting City's games the destruction of Old Trafford by the Luftwaffe had also left United playing there until reconstruction work could be completed. A player from both Manchester clubs was on display, Swift and United left-half Henry Cockburn.

The England manager's decision not to recall Matthews had raised eyebrows in the press, but with Mannion scoring twice, the first after some beautiful midfield passing tore open the Welsh defence, England won 3-0. This was an injustice on the Welsh side that on more than one occasion broke free of the England defence only to find Swift swooping to grab the ball at the onrushing forward's feet.

At one point, reported the *Daily Mail*, 'Swift caught one ball from Ivor Powell in trapeze fashion, with his 13st 7lb parallel with the floor, but a foot off it...rolled over, sat up, stood up, feinted to kick clear, had a look at the maker's name on the ball, then effortlessly threw it 40 yards, straight as a die to Langton.'

Two weeks after beating Wales, England played the Netherlands at Leeds Road, Huddersfield. Heavy rain kept the crowd down to 32,500. Frank Swift was beaten twice, but England scored eight with Tommy Lawton getting four. Swift described it as 'one of the finest displays I have ever witnessed from a centre-forward'.

The highlight though for him was the after match banquet at Harrogate. At this the Netherlands Football Association President, Karel Lotsy, said his country could never adequately repay England for the help given during the war in saving the lives of Dutch children, some of whom had also perished by helping Dutch underground workers and British spies. With everyone aware that Lotsy had been an active underground worker himself then you can imagine there wasn't a dry eye in the room.

Swift's fifth international was a much more difficult affair. It was his first competitive match back at Wembley since 1934, with England playing Scotland. Training at Brighton the England players were visited by American boxing heavyweight Joe Baksi, a regular contender for the World title in the late 40s. The boxer and 'keeper compared hand spans and Swift won by ¾ at 11 ¾'s compared to 11.

With Matthews recalled in preference to the younger Finney there was also a full debut for Wolves Jimmy Mullen. With the Scots redheads Archie Macaulay and Alec Forbes playing magnificently at half-back it was no great surprise that Scotland led at the interval courtesy of an Andy McLaren 16th minute effort. Hibernian's Billy Steel had created the goal, when after turning the defence he delivered an incisive pass. Jimmy Delaney constantly threatened to double the lead, but Swift was having a fine game and England emerged after the break more confidently and equalised on 56 minutes through Raich Carter, playing almost to the day 13 years after he had made his England debut against the Scots in 1934.

With Scotland desperate to regain the lead the ball was played into England's box and Delaney found himself just unable to force it home after the home 'keeper's long arms plucked it from just in front of him. To make matters worse for the Scot he hurtled headlong into the post. With Swift urging the trainer to make haste there was a delay while he received treatment. In the event England took a point in an undeserved draw. Facing a different 'keeper Scotland would surely have won.

No wonder the *Daily Mirror*'s reporter at the match, John Thompson, praised the England number 1 for 'being the 'keeper we have long regarded him to be'.

On Saturday 3 May 1947 Frank Swift played his sixth full international. 54,389 were at Highbury – Wembley being used for the Rugby League Cup Final – to see England beat a poor French side 3-0. With Stoke locked in a four-way-battle, with Liverpool, Wolves and Manchester United, for the League title the Potters centre-half Neil Franklin might have preferred to be at Elland Road, but in his absence Stoke still narrowly won their League game to stay in with a chance. This was despite Stoke manager Bob McGrory's bizarre decision not to play Stanley Matthews after he had recovered from a knee injury in February. Matthews put in a transfer request, and although this was refused the increasing tension between manager and player could not have helped in a season in which Stoke would have won the title if they had beaten Sheffield United on the final – delayed – day of the season, 14 June.

Replaced by Finney, Matthews missed the France game, as well as Stoke's last three matches of the season as on 10 May, immediately after playing for Great Britain against the Rest of Europe at Glasgow, he signed, aged 32, for £11,500 for Blackpool. If Stoke thought they had done well to get so much for the winger they were to later bitterly regret letting Matthews leave.

Great Britain 6 Rest of Europe 1

Matthews helped Great Britain whip the Rest of Europe X1 6-1 in front of 135,000 spectators at Hampden Park. The GB team was: Frank Swift (Manchester City/England), Billy Hughes (Birmingham City/Wales), George Hardwick (Middlesbrough/England), Archie Macaulay (Arsenal/Scotland), Jack Vernon (West Bromwich Albion/Ireland), Ronnie Burgess (Tottenham Hotspur/Wales), Stanley Matthews (Stoke City/England), Wilf Mannion (Middlesbrough/England), Tommy Lawton (Chelsea/England), Billy Steel (Greenock Morton/Scotland) and Billy Liddell (Liverpool/Scotland).

Rest of Europe: Du Rui (France), Peterson (Denmark), Steffen (Switzerland), Carey (Republic of Ireland), Parola (Italy), Ludl (Czechoslovakia), Lambrechts (Belgium), Gren, Nordahl (both Sweden), Wilkes (Holland), Praest (Denmark).

The match had been arranged by Stanley Rous to celebrate the return of the home nations into FIFA in 1946. Britain's relationship with Football's world governing body had always been a difficult one and none of the home countries' associations were among the founding fathers of it in May 1904. When soon after they did join it wasn't for long, as in 1920 they all dropped out. This was partly in protest at the involvement of nations that Britain had been at war with, but mainly because having invented the game there was a general feeling that there was now too much foreign influence.

It meant that when the World Cup started in 1930, Scotland, Wales, England and Northern Ireland were absent. Now all four Home Nations would have the chance to participate in the 1950 finals in Brazil.

The side selected to represent Great Britain was probably not as strong as it should have been. There was no doubt that Swift was the best 'keeper but the inclusion of Steel, who had played just the once for Scotland, was intended to balance up the side internationally as Raich Carter and Peter Doherty were clearly superior players.

At the same time, the opposition was viewed by Matthews not to be as tough as it might have been, and in his autobiography the winger cited the absence of German players and the late withdrawal of some Italian players. Both countries had recently been at war with Britain, but surely this was football? Whatever the make up of the teams the match was keenly anticipated and those who saw it were lucky to do so.

Wilf Mannion set the ball rolling with the opening goal on 22 minutes, only for the tall, elegant Swedish international inside-forward, Gunnar Nordhal to equalise 90 seconds later. Mannion then stepped up to net a 33rd minute penalty (2-1), ably assisted in Steel's goal soon afterwards (35 minutes) and eight minutes before half-time Lawton grabbed a fourth.

After Nordhal's goal, Frank Swift had hardly been troubled in the first period, although he did pull off two decent saves to deny Nordhal a further goal and the Austrian Rappan.

In the second-half GB continued to dominate but chose to display their skill rather than humiliate their opponents. They managed to score twice more, courtesy of Italian defender Carlo Parola, who sent one past his own 'keeper on 74 minutes, and a sixth from Lawton in the 82nd minute. At the other end Frank Swift saved low down to deny Praest of Denmark from breaching Great Britain's defence for a second time.

Swift rated Praest highly saying: "He was an instinctive goal-getter who could shoot with both feet and did so when least expected. He was also a very clever ball player who occasionally would whip in a toe-poke towards goal or send in a grub-hunter, a low ground shot which scuttled along the floor."

First defeat
New Blackpool player, Stanley Matthews was included in the England squad that travelled to Switzerland and Portugal at the end of May 1947. Neil Franklin too was included, and on arrival in Zurich the England players enjoyed a marvellous welcome.

With the game being played at well above sea-level the squad were put through some heavy training sessions that were overseen by Winterbottom, trainer Wilf Copping and masseur Walter Max. Off the practice pitches many of the players enjoyed a round of golf, with Matthews especially keen on the game.

Visiting Zurich, Swift found it a very modern city, but was less impressed with the Grasshoppers pitch and ground, feeling it was cramped. The large attendance meant a rope needed to be tied round the playing field, stopping the 'keeper from making a run-up to take a goal-kick. In addition, having lost the match-ball, the French referee Monsieur Sdez started the game with a practice ball.

In the event England could have done with using it a lot more before kick-off as they played poorly and lost 1-0. Coming on the same day as Scotland lost 2-1 in Belgium the *Daily Mirror* reported that after having beaten the Rest of Europe any of 'Britain's pride had been lost, humbled on the Continent against national teams…there was no excuse for England. The Swiss, all amateurs, were a good combination, and thoroughly deserved the one-goal victory'.

It was however, by Jacques Fatton on 27 minutes, one that Swift was convinced should not have been allowed being 'certain that the ball was travelling so fast across the goal, and at such an awkward angle that it was not possible for the scorer not to have diverted it past me except with his hand'.

With 63 minutes remaining though England had plenty of time to, at least, draw level, but aside from Matthews – who later wrote he felt many of his teammates were guilty of underestimating the opposition – the England forwards were poor.

When England did look like scoring Erwin Ballabio – who Swift rated as 'about the best 'keeper on the Continent' was equal to their efforts. This time another after match banquet did not go down quite so palatably and when an experimental England side then failed to score in a 0-0 draw against Switzerland B in Geneva it meant that the England players knew they would be heavily criticised if they lost their next game in Lisbon. The Portuguese were a far superior side to the Swiss, and it would be a much tougher encounter especially as there would be warm conditions to contend with.

Portugal 0 England 10
With Bobby Langton injured Tom Finney played at outside-left with Stan Mortensen replacing Carter for his full international debut. For Carter the Switzerland match was to be the end of his international career, in which he had played 13 official games and scored seven times.

Unlike in Switzerland the ground in Lisbon was massive, the National Stadium being built in a natural hollow. It had cost £350,000, a colossal sum at the time, and down one length of the pitch was mounted a huge colonnade for the Portuguese Prime Minister Antonio de Oliveira Salazar to sit and watch the game. Like the rest of the 65,000 crowd it must have been an uncomfortable Sunday afternoon for the man who presided over and controlled Portugal from 1932 to 1974.

One or two of the England players remarked Swift afterwards had suggested the arena bore the appearance of the Rome Coliseum. On this particular day Portugal were slaughtered, 10-0. Neil Franklin had only just made it on to the pitch, being put through a rigorous pre-match training session to test out an injury. The Stoke player was desperate to make it home to play in his side's second last match of the season, against Aston Villa, but not that desperate that he wanted to miss out playing for his country. Times have changed since 1947 – today's footballers would surely sit out a similar match? In fact they would probably have never even travelled.

Franklin played well, but so did every England player including Swift who had plenty to do in the first half and was praised for his 'highly polished performance'. His counterpart in the home goal, Joao Azevedo, had enjoyed a rapturous reception prior to the kick-off but he was beaten three times in the first 11 minutes.

The home side had wanted to use a size four ball, used then only in England by schoolboys, and after the first goal in just 17 seconds they replaced the larger one that had been used at kick-off. Little good it did, scorer Lawton heading forward for Mortensen to score his first England goal after just two minutes and make it 2-0.

When Finney made it 4-0 on 21 minutes the game as a contest was over. Swift rated it one of the greatest he ever saw, the Preston plumber picking up the ball in his own half, dribbling forward before twice recovering after having his legs whipped from under him, before flicking the ball over Azevedo and tapping home. Six minutes later the 'keeper developed a mystery injury and disappeared – to the jeers of the home crowd – down the tunnel to be replaced by Manuel Capela. Substitutes were only allowed for injuries and two minutes later full-back Alvaro Cardoso also found himself unable to continue and Vasco de Oliveira replaced him, England's questioning of the officials proving of little use. On 38 minutes Lawton wrapped up his hat-trick and England led 5-0 at half-time.

Despite such an impressive lead, trainer Wilf Copping urged England to go for more. Matthews three times beat the full-back and from his crosses Mortensen with two, thus completing his hat-trick, and Lawton made it 8-0.

Mortensen made it 9-0 and then with five minutes left Matthews again destroyed a withering home defence to make it 10. It had been a superb performance and although many of the crowd had gone at the end, the more sporting stayed to give England a great cheer. Their attitude proved to be in complete contrast to the Portuguese team who failed to turn up for the after match banquet. Later all the home players were suspended by the Portuguese FA.

Swift was disappointed his opponents didn't enjoy a meal with him saying 'it was a pity, because we never had a real opportunity of praising their gentlemanly conduct and sportsmanship on the field'.

1947-49: Becoming England captain

Away to Belgium in September 1947 saw Derby County's Tim Ward awarded his first – and only – cap and like in Lisbon in the previous game, Tommy Lawton scored early, this time in just 12 seconds. Mortensen struck his fifth international goal and although Belgium at one point reduced the arrears to 3-2 a second Finney goal and another from Lawton, soon after saw England comfortably home, 5-2. The match was played at the Heysel Stadium, which was later the scene of the tragedy in which 39 fans lost their lives in May 1985 prior to the Liverpool-Juventus European Cup final match.

Finney, who went on to make 76 full appearances for his country, was a big fan of Frank Swift. In Paul Agnew's authorised biography on the Preston legend the forward is quoted as saying, 'England has been blessed with some outstanding goalkeepers throughout my life span. You only need to think of Bert Williams, Ted Ditchburn, Frank Swift, Gordon Banks, Peter Shilton and David Seaman. With good justification you could pick any of these but I must go for Frank Swift as the best.

Frank was a giant of a man, capable of picking the ball off the ground with one hand and then, quite effortlessly, tossing it half the length of the field and beyond. At well over six feet tall, he had a huge frame but was surprisingly agile, particularly quick at getting down to low shots, which is so often a weakness in big 'keepers. He was a master at reducing angles and anything in the six-yard box was his. When the ball came into that danger area it was bad news for anyone, opponent or colleague, who had the misfortune to be standing in his path.

He had some rare old tussles with the likes of Trevor Ford and other robust centre-forwards who could rough things up a bit and enjoyed the physical side. And Frank played in an era when bodily contact was part and parcel of the game and referees were slow to offer protection to the men in green jerseys. He also had a magnificent attitude and was a laugh-a-minute joker in the dressing room. Swiftie would be my number one every time.'

A few weeks after the Belgium game, England again won away by three goals. Liverpool's Phil Taylor made his debut at Ninian Park, and with fellow half-backs Franklin and Billy Wright in inspired form the Welsh forwards, including Arsenal's star-man Bryn Jones, toiled.

England raced into a three-goal lead after just 25 minutes, Mortensen scoring one to take his overall total to six in three games. If Swift had much to do then it's not clear from reports in the *Daily Express* and *Mirror*, as he doesn't even get a mention.

Brilliant Doherty

On 5 November 1947 England played (Northern) Ireland at Goodison Park in a Home International match. As the game moved towards its conclusion the away side led through a Dave Walsh goal. Ireland had been the better side and twice Swift had denied his former City colleague Peter Doherty, now playing for Huddersfield Town. Carey had kept Matthews out of the match and the large Irish following in a 67,980 crowd were set to celebrate a famous victory.

They had cheered when Mannion had seen his 70th minute penalty well saved by Fulham's Ted Hinton and had been thrilled to see Belfast butcher Jack Vernon keep Lawton under wraps.

Billy Wright though could unpick many a defence and Mannion swept his fine pass home with just six minutes remaining. Complaints that the 'Boro man had handled were waved aside by the referee. To add further insult Lawton finally wrestled clear of Vernon to score what seemed a certain winner.

Then with the final touches of the game an Eglington cross cut out Swift and launching himself at the ball Doherty powered a header home, before hurtling injured on to the turf. As the final whistle sounded the Irish players raced forward – ignoring the scorer's pain – to jump with joy on top of him. When the joyous frenzy had ended Doherty was tended to by the Irish trainer and was helped off the pitch by Swift, the City 'keeper's disappointment at having lost out on victory tempered by his concern for his friend.

Afterwards, Carey was full of praise for Doherty saying, 'No other footballer in the world could have done that.' Although England hadn't played well the selectors immediately announced the same side for the match against Sweden in two weeks' time. It was Swift's 12th full-international.

Mortensen had not scored in his fourth against Ireland, but cracked home a hat-trick in a 4-2 success in a match played at Highbury. The Blackpool man's tireless energy lifted the England team, and he was the Man of the Match. His goalkeeping colleague also played well with the *Daily Mirror* reporting:

SWIFT OBLIGES

> Frank Swift, that champion of Soccer showmen, gave the 44,000 crowd the kind of display spectators everywhere have come to expect from him. He never lets them – or England – down.
>
> Once he was injured in the midst of a Swedish attack. A shot had beaten him all the way, but Hardwick headed out from the goalmouth. The bulk and agility of the man must have filled the Swedes with despair.

Lucky 13

Game number 13 proved to be one of Swift's finest appearances for his country. His counterpart, Southampton 'keeper Ian Black was making his Scottish debut and the sides both contained a member of Field-Marshal Monty's Eighth Army in Finney and Willie Thornton. Scotland's captain, 6ft 2in George Young had been given the task of holding Lawton, who had stunned the football world by signing for Third Division North side Notts County, and he was successful in preventing him adding to his 21 international goals.

Scotland dominated the first 20 minutes. According to Matthews they would have taken an unassailable lead if not for the performance of Swift and in front of him Franklin, saying 'Such were the heroics of Swifty and Neil during those early exchanges that I felt proud just to be in the same team as the two of them'.

Turning defence into attack

Matthews' Blackpool colleague Stan Mortensen was also impressed by Swift's accurate clearances that turned defence into attack. Writing in his autobiography *Football is my Game* he recalled that 'it was from one of Frank's kicks that England went ahead. He put the ball nicely to the forward line, [Stan] Pearson passed out to Finney, and Tom went for goal like a streak of lightning. Holding the ball cleverly away on his left side so that two tackles failed to dispossess him, he finished up with a cracking shot'. After dominating the first half Scotland were behind on 44 minutes.

On 64 minutes Lawton picked out Mortensen as he dashed beyond the Scottish rear-guard. Many spectators felt the Blackpool man was offside but waved on by the referee he beat Black to put his side 2-0 ahead. Never looking too comfortable England held out without conceding a goal.

That was quite remarkable, as Frank Swift had suffered two broken ribs in a collision with Billy Liddell. The Liverpool man – who largely carried the Anfield side in the mid 50s – had wanted to shoulder charge the big 'keeper as he comfortably collected the ball. He describes what happened next in his own autobiography saying 'Big Swifty, realising the danger, twisted to one side to avoid me. But I was going at such a rate that I couldn't help barging into him'.

Even though the Scouse legend bounced off the Manchester one and ended up on the ground the 'keeper had been badly injured. With no subs and George Hardwick, the man selected to go in goal if he had left the pitch, injured with a torn ligament and limping out on the left wing then Swift decided to stay put. Taken to a Glasgow hospital afterwards, Swift insisted on going home and when he was met by his wife at Victoria Station, Manchester then not even the huge cheers of those who recognised him were enough to stop him collapsing on the platform before a friend's car took him home to recuperate.

Swift hadn't fancied staying in Glasgow saying 'Manchester air is what I need' and according to Liddell when the pair next met said to him 'I know you didn't do it on purpose, Billy. If I thought you had, I'd have soon settled your hash!'

England captain and hero:

Italy 0 England 4

The Scotland match proved Hardwick's last for England, the Middlesbrough player having played 13 times and in all of which he captained his country. Five weeks later England had a new captain in Frank Swift and the game against Italy proved to be his finest for his country.

The reigning World Champions chose to play the match in the cauldron of Turin's Stadio Comunale in May 1948. In front of 58,000 baying home supporters, and with the temperature touching 90 degrees, Swift had a brilliant match and his genius and courage between the posts turned the Italian FA's 50th anniversary celebrations into a wake. In fact, Italy's fans were calling for the head of manager Vittorio Pozzo long before the final whistle!

It was tough on Pozzo for there was no way he could foresee Frank's wonder show... or indeed, the blinding destruction delivered by the Blackpool centre-forward Stan Mortensen.

Before the game, business was brisk for the ticket touts lingering outside the stadium. There was pulsating tension in the air and one could sense all round that the stakes were high!

The Italians were reputedly on bonuses of £1,000 each to win, whereas the England players, whatever the outcome, would pick up £20.

Recalled Tom Finney 'Italy opened up breathing fire and it looked as if we could be in for a beating. But we stuck in there and after four minutes they were in disarray, victims of a sucker punch. Stan Matthews fed his Blackpool teammate Stan Mortensen who cut inside left-back Eliani before hammering the ball home from the tightest of angles.

Then it was backs to the wall for England's defence as the Italians swarmed forward in numbers with the Torino trio of Mazzola, Gabetto and Loik all looking dangerous. But Frank quickly became the star of the show, pulling off three stunning saves to deny Italy an equaliser – one being quite breathtaking from a close range header by Carapellese.'

Then, totally against the run of play, England scored again. Frank Swift's precise throw-out found Billy Wright who moved the ball forward to Stanley Matthews who in turn flicked it on to Mortensen near the halfway line. He darted away, raced past two defenders and pulled the ball back perfectly for Tommy Lawton to fire, hard and low past Bacigalupo.

As Italy pegged England back in their own half, Swift pulled off three more outstanding saves – one of them at point blank range to deny Gabetto who sank to the ground and beat his fists on the turf in frustration. Italy also had two goals disallowed as England hardly mustered an attack during the first quarter-of-an-hour of the second half.

But then, with home players arguing between themselves, England mounted an attack down the left. Wilf Mannion bore down towards the penalty-area and when the opportunity presented itself, he crossed perfectly for Tom Finney to volley home from 12 yards.

It was all over bar the shouting, and with the barricades down, England poured forward once more and rubbed salt into the Italian wounds, with a fourth goal 20 minutes from time, scored in style by Finney, who slammed the ball high into the net after fine approach work by Henry Cockburn and a surging run by Mortensen.

'I rate it the greatest display I've ever seen from an England team. Under a blazing sun, faced by a fine team, England fought to a 4-0 win, and as we walked off the field, the Italians giving us the big hand, I know how proud we all felt to be Englishmen.' Billy Wright, writing in 1958.

After such a magnificent performance against Italy it was no surprise that Swift – kept his place – and captain's role – for the next England game, playing in Copenhagen on 26 September.

The 'keeper had also sought to improve his already refined distribution skills that had been so openly on show at Hampden Park the previous season. Coming home from Italy, England played two games in Switzerland and Mortensen recalled that in addition to 'allowing the opposing centre-forward in the second match to charge right up to him, before playfully lifting the ball over his head before clearing…Frank repeatedly half-volleyed the ball so that it came down right at Matthews' feet.'

Off the field the big Blackpool born 'keeper had also proved to be an essential part in helping build the team spirit that is so essential in any side, Mortensen recalling that on arriving tired and thirsty in Turin after a day's travelling the Manchester City man took it in his stride when the players were met by a welcoming committee. Pushed forward he was all smiles as he received a huge bouquet of flowers.

'Swift', said Mortensen, 'Is always a great help in the dressing room as he is so full of life and gaiety and yet not the sort of licensed humourist of whom one can tire so readily. He knows when to jest, and when to be serious. He knows just the match when he can introduce a pinch of clowning into the game, and just the match in which he must be "On the job" for the full 90 minutes.'

Despite this there were reported tensions with Winterbottom and his staff. Best-pal Lawton was more outspoken about the attitude displayed towards the England players by the selectors, coaching and administrative staff. He particularly resented being called by his second-name and having to constantly justify every small expense occurred going to and from matches. He and Frank Swift had an enduring fondness for a fag to steady their nerves, a practice Winterbottom strongly disapproved of.

The two players did what all professionals do; they 'hid' it from their bosses by locking themselves in the toilets. Of course with steam coming over the cubicle tops there was never any doubt what was going on. Things reached a peak when Winterbottom reacted furiously as the pair took out cigarettes from their pockets as they left the field at the interval. Unable to take the England manager too seriously the two players laughed their heads off at him and Swift told him that 'it helps our breathing'. As a concession to the manager's authority they disappeared behind locked cubicle doors for a smoke.

Swift was 35 when he played his last game for England so this unusual flouting of authority clearly didn't affect his International career, but Lawton played his final match in Denmark in September 1948. He was 28 and at the time had scored 24 goals in 23 full-time international matches with a further 22 in 23 unofficial internationals.

The match against the Danes was a very poor one with Len Shackleton, making his official England debut, and the much more experienced Jimmy Hagan, playing in his only full international at aged 30, both missing early chances. Despite almost total possession England failed to score and the game ended 0-0. It might have been worse. The England 'keeper had only been called once into action, when he pushed a 40-yard Axel Pilmark shot round the post, before with just two minutes to go the Danish right winger Johan Ploeger fired in a shot that went through his legs and into the net. Much to England's relief the linesman's flag was up for offside.

Shackleton and Hagan were omitted from the following match against Northern Ireland away. Newcastle's Jackie Milburn replaced Lawton. It was the Irish number 10 Charlie Tully who should have scored first but after running the ball round Swift and with an open goal in front of him he cleared the bar with a wild shot on eight minutes.

Ireland did equalise on 50 minutes, Dave Walsh replying to Matthews' first half effort. But after which England poured forward, Mortensen got his third international hat-trick, Milburn opened his account and Manchester United's Stan Pearson got his first goal. England won 6-2.

One month later England faced a much more difficult encounter against Wales – especially when Laurie Scott, playing in his 17th full international, limped off the field with a sprained ligament on 25 minutes. It proved his last action as an England man for the player who had made 16 wartime appearances.

Swift, replaced as captain by Wright, did well to prevent Trevor Ford from giving Wales an early lead and late on Man of the Match Roy Clarke, his Manchester City colleague, might have done better when well placed. In between Finney stole the all-important winner, his 11th goal in 14 England appearances.

Swift now had 17 caps, but when England played Switzerland on 2 December 1948 he was missing in goal. The last time that had happened in a full international had been when Chelsea 'keeper Victor Woodley had played the last of his 19 matches for England against Romania on 24 May 1939. Coming in for his first – of six – appearances was Tottenham Hotspur 'keeper Ted Ditchburn.

The new 'keeper had little to do and an experimental England line-up won 6-0 with West Brom's John Haines scoring twice in his only international game. Another debutant, Jack Rowley of Manchester United also scored in this game and he was highly rated by Frank Swift: 'He was quick to shoot. It was the unexpectedness rather than the strength, which made his shooting so dangerous. Although his right foot was good, I was always worried when the ball was running on to his left. He was always looking and determined to have a crack at goal whatever the angle or distance.

I was sat in the stand at Highbury in 1948 when I saw Jack; playing for England against Switzerland, score a stunning goal with a terrific shot from fully 35 yards. The ball never rose above three feet off the ground. It was some shot – one of the strongest I had ever seen.'

On Saturday 9 April 1949 England, with Swift back in goal, faced Scotland at Wembley in the Home Championships. Milburn struck his third goal in England colours, but coming in the 75th minute it proved a consolation effort as a fine Scotland side won 3-1 to take the title with six points.

Much of the away side's success was down to a fine goalkeeping display by Jimmy Cowan, who especially in the first 15 minutes played magnificently.

With Derby County's Billy Steel at inside-left giving Wright a hard time, England were pushed back and Jimmy Mason scored on 29 minutes before Steel doubled the lead on 52. With England's defence in disarray Lawrie Reilly added to the Jocks advantage on 61, and it was the Scottish banners that were flying highest at the end of the match. Frank Swift – who had been injured in a first half collision with Houliston that had left him unable to use his feet to clear the ball – was now 35. As an intelligent man he must have realised his finest days as a 'keeper were behind him. He must therefore have been unsurprised to find the Mirror's John Thompson saying 'the time has at last come for Ted Ditchburn to take over the job Frank Swift has held with such distinction'.

When England played Sweden in Stockholm on Friday 13 May 1949 Ditchburn played his second game for England. The away side, and the new 'keeper, though played poorly and lost 3-1. So on 18 May 1949 Frank Swift, who had announced his retirement at the end of the season, stepped up to play his final game for England. The away side were far too strong for Norway, but the amateurs did well to keep the score down to 4-1.

Four days later, away to France in Paris England experimented by bringing in Wolves 'keeper Bert Williams and once 'the Cat' was up and jumping he soon made the number one spot his own, even though he did concede a first minute goal on his debut. Williams went on to play 24 times for his country. He was a fine replacement for Swift, who retired having made 19 appearances for England in which he was 14 times on the winning side and only twice – against Switzerland and Scotland – a loser. Frank Swift was a winner.

Full internationals record
1946
Ireland (A), England won 7-2
Republic of Ireland (A), England won 1-0
Wales (H), England won 3-0
Netherlands (H), England won 8-2

1947
Scotland (H), England drew 1-1
France (H), England won 3-0
Switzerland (A), England lost 1-0
Portugal (A), England won 10-0
Belgium (A), England won 5-2
Wales (A), England won 3-0
Ireland (H), England drew 2-2
Sweden (H), England won 4-2

1948
Scotland (A), England won 2-0
Italy (A), England won 4-0
Denmark (A), England drew 0-0
Ireland (A), England won 6-2
Wales (A), England won 1-0

1949
Scotland (H), England lost 3-1
Norway (A), England won 4-1

19 appearances – 14 victories, 3 draws and 2 defeats.

1947
Great Britain 6 Rest of Europe 1

Chapter 17
Back in the big time

Having played his final League match in mid-June, there was little more than two months before Frank Swift was back in competitive action for City in August 1947. Cowan's departure after winning the Second Division title saw secretary Wilf Wild step back into the manager's seat while a longer-term replacement was sought. Also joining the managerial fray was Sam Barkas, who became manager at Workington Town.

In a bid to further strengthen the side Manchester City had signed Irish international Eddie McMorran from Belfast Celtic and he made his debut in City colours in the first public trial match, which saw the Blues beat the Reds 3-1. The striker scored and linked up well with Roy Clarke, who had cost City £9,000. Outside-right Jackie Wharton had also arrived from PNE and the trio had cost a combined £25,000. Meantime, City had a new captain in McDowall.

For Manchester City's first match in Division One since May 1938 a 65,809 crowd was inside Maine Road to see if Wolves, third the previous season, could be beaten. Despite being densely packed, fans were more than willing to help late arriving youngsters keen to see the action. Rick Sumner, who first saw City play in November 1940, recalls 'at big games being picked up and passed over the heads of the crowd to the front. The first time was very scary until I realised I couldn't fall as the crowd was so dense there was no space to fall into. To the fans we were their kids'.

Wolves' stylish centre-half, Stan Cullis, had retired at the end of the previous season to become assistant manager to Ted Vizard. A natural leader, Cullis skippered Wolves for several years. Although he was a powerful tackler and strong in the air it was his passing ability that marked him out as special.

Sportsman
Cullis's final game was against Liverpool on Saturday 31 May 1947. If Wolves won they captured the league title for the first time in the club's long history. But if Liverpool could take home both points they would go top of the table and hope that Stoke City would fail to win at Sheffield United on 14 June. That would allow the Merseyside club to capture the First Division trophy for the fifth time.

Liverpool scored early through Jack Balmer. The key moment of the match came, however, midway through the first half when a chipped ball over the Wolves defence left Albert Stubbins in the clear. Cullis was left stranded; stopping his opponent would mean bringing him down from behind. Today it would be a certain sending-off, but not so back in the 1940s. Cullis refused to consider fouling Stubbins who duly notched the second to set Liverpool up for a 2-1 win. When Stoke later lost Liverpool were crowned Champions. Cullis played hard but fair, his attitude summed up perfectly by his later statement that 'I didn't want to go down in history as the man who decided the title by a foul'.

Frank Swift's best ever eleven included Cullis, and he would have made him captain. There was also 'no other player that I, as a goalkeeper, would "allow" to play so much football in the penalty area in front of me'.

With all three new forwards on display, the home side won a seven-goal thriller in which Clarke and McMorran scored to add to Smith and Black's efforts.

City: Swift, Sproston, Westwood, Fagan J., McDowall, Emptage, Wharton, Black, McMorran, Smith G., Clarke.

Everton, though, showed that City's new men might need time to settle, the Merseysiders winning back-to-back matches 1-0. Villa Park proved a happier hunting ground, Clarke scoring in a 1-1 draw against a Villa side containing ex-Swansea forward Trevor Ford, who City had courted for many months the previous season.

Walter Allison recalls that the likes of 'Ford, and others such as Scotland's Jack Dodds and Jack Stamps of Derby, meant that Frank Swift, like all 'keepers of that era, would often choose to punch the ball as he would be aware they intended to hit him hard in order to intimidate him. 'Keepers were offered much less protection than today and they rarely protested. In those days I stood behind the goal, as close to the pitch as possible and I could see how Frank Swift dominated the area. He would tell defending players where to stand, he wouldn't shout and often it was just a little move of his head, or a little touch on the shoulder which sent a defender into a particular spot. He'd stand at the far post for corners and come for the ball if it was floated towards him, either to punch it away or if unchallenged to catch it.

Swift could throw the ball and also roll it out, but that depended upon the state of the ground, as if it was wet then the ball would get stuck in the mud. Often the conditions meant a long kick was the best any 'keeper could do. Frank was great at getting down to shots that seemed certain to beat him. He did concede a lot of goals compared to 'keepers today, but back then teams aimed to outscore their opponents and many more games finished say 3-3 or 4-3 or had scorelines such as 6-3.'

McMorran and Clarke were again on the score sheet as Sunderland were beaten 3-0 at Maine Road. Then, with Swift playing for England against Belgium, he missed the first derby match since January 1937. A 78,000 crowd packed inside Maine Road to witness a highly competitive match that ended 0-0. Swift also missed the return fixture with United as he was away again on England duty.

Huge celebration as Swift makes mistake

When City faced Blackburn at home in late September, Jack Smith drove his side ahead before being denied a second by a typical brave Swift dive at his feet. By the end it mattered little though as Rovers – boosted by a fortunate penalty that Jackie Oakes stroked home – won easily, 3-1.

The victors later beat City in a 1-0 win at Ewood Park. Swift was responsible for the goal: 'If ever a footballer looked as if he wished the pitch would open up and swallow him up it was England's super 'keeper when Leslie Graham, with a shot that was almost too weak to cross the line, scored the winner midway through the second half. The 31,033 crowd gasped unbelievingly for several seconds before the realisation dawned upon them that 'the great, the incomparable, Swift had blundered' reported the *Blackburn Times*.

To drive home this remarkable event the paper even went to the trouble of illustrating affairs with a drawing of events. In the long run it did Rovers little good as they slumped to relegation.

Watching the game as a youngster was Bryan Douglas, a man many would argue was Rovers finest footballer. 'Yes, Swift did make a poor mistake but he also made a number of very good saves in that game. You could see his class. I never got the chance to meet Frank, but when he was working for the *News of the World* as a columnist in the 1950s he made some very flattering comments after I had got into the first team. Tom Finney did the same and when such great footballers start praising you then it really does boost your confidence. Later when I got selected for England it was well known that Frank referred to the manager Walter Winterbottom as Mr Cold Arse.'

The following weekend Frank Swift was back home as City drew 1-1 at Blackpool. Having, late in the previous season, signed Stanley Matthews from Stoke City, the Tangerines (the Blackpool board having officially adopted the colours in 1939) were assembling a fine side that was set to make three FA Cup Final appearances in six seasons. Large queues started forming outside Bloomfield Road three hours before kick-off and early on Swift saved a delightfully struck Matthews half volley. Wharton grabbed his first goal for Manchester City, with Mortensen knocking Blackpool's goal past his good friend in the City goal.

Against Portsmouth at home the arrival of new signing Billy Linacre boosted the attendance. Leading 1-0 through an effort by Smith, the home side were rescued when Swift slid out to boot the ball to safety as Jack Froggatt and Bert Barlow dashed through.

Two weeks later City maintained their impressive home form when, with Smith scoring three times, Charlton Athletic was beaten 4-0. The previous weekend Middlesbrough's Micky Fenton had continued to plague Swift when he scored twice as Boro beat City 2-1 at Ayresome Park.

Off the pitch there was good news as City announced that Everton coach and former Scottish international, Jock Thomson, had agreed to become manager at the end of November. Like Cowan, Thomson arrived with little managerial experience.

Meantime that same week Manchester United announced plans, at their shareholders meeting, to re-open Old Trafford with a capacity of 120,000. In addition 'United's system of training local boys for the future, rather than paying fabulous transfer fees for ready-made players was supported by the shareholders'. (Tom Jackson)

Given time this was to produce the world famous Busby Babes, with whom Frank Swift was to spend his final moments in February 1958 at Munich. One of the Babes was a big City fan from a City supporting family. However, when he was badly treated by the club it didn't stop Frank Swift intervening to get him started at Old Trafford.

Swift had watched talented schoolboy Dennis Viollet play on many occasions. Born in 1933 Viollet was good enough to play in any forward position and at half-back. He was a lethal goalscorer and in 1949 many several First Division clubs sought his signature. All of his family were 'Blues' and yet no one had been in contact about signing for the club.

Swift set up a meeting with City's youth scout, but, after waiting for an hour, the youngster and his father were informed the scout had left for another appointment. No apology or explanation was offered and, not surprisingly, both left in a hostile mood.

City's loss was to become United's gain. Joe Armstrong, United's chief scout, had taken a keen interest in Dennis's schoolboy career and he kept Matt Busby informed of his progress. The Scot then visited the Viollet household to speak to the youngster's parents about joining the club, returning a few days later with Armstrong and assistant manager Jimmy Murphy. They laid out United's blueprint for future success and left a deep impression with Murphy telling the parents: 'Don't let young Dennis miss out on the opportunity of joining this wonderful club.'

Uncertain as to what to do next, Dennis Viollet's parents sought Frank Swift's advice and guidance. Big Swifty was annoyed at the treatment they had received from his own club and spoke quite candidly to them about Manchester United's offer for young Dennis to join them. He told them; 'I played with Matt Busby and he is a wonderful fellow. You won't find a better boss or a better club.'

It was the clincher and Viollet duly signed for Manchester United, telling anyone who asked about why he had not joined City that it was because no one had ever asked him.

England international Viollet was to collect two Championship winning medals with Manchester United and played in the 1958 FA Cup Final. With 32 League goals he was Division One top scorer in 1960 and later helped Stoke City to win the 1962-63 Second Division Championship, where he got on the end of many of Stanley Matthews's crosses to score some vital goals.

For the home game with Liverpool in November a thumb injury saw Swift fail to pass a pre-match fitness test. After 15 years Swift had finally failed to make the City first-team for injury reasons.

He returned for the December match away to runaway League leaders Arsenal. No side had won at Highbury so far in the season, yet with 83 minutes on the clock that record seemed set to be broken with the away side leading through a Black goal. A late penalty was harsh on City but in Ronnie Rooke the Gunners had one of the surest shots in the land and his successful effort left the scores tied at the end of a fine game. Walking to meet each other, the City 'keeper walked off the pitch with his arm round Rooke as the pair engaged in deep conversation.

Rooke's goal's was one of the 33 he scored in the 1947-48 season, good enough to put him top of the Division One scorers' charts. The striker was an unmistakeable figure on the pitch with his bandy legs, shirtsleeves flapping and black, wavy hair on top of a craggy face dominated by a 'Roman nose'. His goals helped ensure Arsenal won the League title by a distance.

'With the ball in front of him, there was no more deadly a shot than Arsenal's Ronnie Rooke. He imparted a swerve – I never found out if it was deliberate or natural – and if the ball was curling away, it was almost impossible to reach' was Frank Swift's verdict on a man who netted almost 400 goals in 472 first-team matches for Arsenal, Crystal Palace and Fulham.

Captain of Manchester City

With McDowall missing through injury, Sproston had been made captain but against Huddersfield away, the day after his 34th birthday, the 'keeper was asked to captain the City side for the first time. The match finished 1-1.

Early in the New Year, Manchester City beat Barnsley 2-1 and then Chelsea 2-0 in the FA Cup. With no replays the second match had gone into extra-time when Linacre and Smith put out the Pensioners, a nickname derived from the nearby Royal Hospital Chelsea, a retirement home for former British Army members.

Swift was the star of the show when, after being badly injured in the second half, he carried on to inspire his side to victory in extra time when he hobbled so painfully across the pitch that spectators doubted he would ever reach the goalmouth.

'It was a nasty injury. His courage in carrying on had a good effect on the rest of the team,' said secretary Wilfred Wild.

Sadly, City stumbled in the next round, beaten 1-0 at home to Preston North End. Four successive home League victories, though, meant that when Charlton were beaten 1-0 at the Valley Swift's side had climbed to sixth in the table.

The 'keeper had played well against the Addicks and his fine form meant (the *Manchester Evening News* reported) that he was favourite to be voted as the first Footballer of the Year Award with Matthews, Stan Mortensen and Hardwick also in contention. In the event, with Blackpool winning through to the FA Cup Final, it was wingman Matthews who became the first winner of the prestigious award.

Stanley Matthews later commented in his autobiography: 'I was voted Footballer of the Year in 1948. Frank came third behind my colleague Stan Mortensen, but in fact, he should have won the prize that year after some quite brilliant performances for England especially. He was one of the best goalkeepers I ever played with and against. He often preferred to throw the ball out to a colleague rather than kick it downfield, had hands like spades, was a great shot-stopper and such a kind chap both on and off the field, and what a comedian!'

The idea for an annual award had been proposed at the inaugur meeting of the Football Writers' Association in October 1947 by Roy Pesk of the *Daily Mail*. Peskett worked throughout 1947 and 1948 to edit Fr Swift's autobiography which was launched at the end of the season. *Foo from the Goalmouth* was published by Sporting Handbooks Ltd and cc 6d (47.5 pence today). It was 180 pages long and Frank Swift n number of bookshop appearances, especially across the North V England, to autograph purchased copies. While it contains a nur inaccuracies the book is an enjoyable read and was one of very fe then published on great footballers.

The game against Charlton proved to be Swift's penultimate the season for City. Playing with a damaged leg against S

Hampden Park he suffered two broken ribs and missed a further three matches.

After his injury the big 'keeper said to local reporters he was 'keeping my fingers crossed that I might be fit for the FA tour in May'. To demonstrate that was the case he was back between the posts for the final game of the season in which City lost 2-1 at Bramall Lane to finish in 10th place.

It had been a good first season back in the top flight for City, but with Manchester United beating Blackpool in the FA Cup Final attention naturally centred on Matt Busby's side.

The 1948 summer football break, meantime, saw the attention of sports fans directed towards the Ashes series and the Olympics, then being held in London. Having not lost a Test since the war, Australia were strong favourites in the cricket and legendary captain Don Bradman publicly expressed his ambition of going unbeaten through his final tour before retirement.

As such Australia won 10 of their 12 lead-up matches, eight by an innings. The England team, however, had several notable players themselves, including Len Hutton, Denis Compton and Alec Bedser. Nevertheless, the final result was a 4–0 series win for Australia, with the Third Test drawn. By remaining undefeated for their entire tour the winning side earned themselves the sobriquet of The Invincibles.

Three players in particular stood out for the winners. Bradman averaged 72.57 runs an innings but lost out on an overall career test match average of 100 by making a duck in his final innings. Ray Lindwall, one of the greatest fast bowlers of all time, and Bill Johnston both took 27 test wickets, with the latter taking over 100 wickets on the tour.

At the Olympics, the US sprinter Harrison Dillard equalled Jesse Owens' 1936 Berlin record for the 100 metres of 10.3 seconds to take the gold medal. He added a second as a member of the 4x100 metre relay team, repeating his relay success four years later in Helsinki before adding a fourth Gold medal by winning the 110 metre hurdles.

The 1948 Summer Olympics were the second occasion that London had hosted the Olympic Games, the first having been in 1908.

The event came to be known as the Austerity Games due to the economic climate and post-war rationing. No new venues were built for the games and athletes were housed in existing accommodation. In comparison the third London Olympic Games in 2012 cost the nation over £9 billion, much of it spent on a new 200 hectare Olympic Park, constructed on a former industrial site at Stratford in East London.

In 1948, 4,104 athletes, including 390 women, represented a record 59 nations. Because of their roles as aggressors in World War Two Germany and Japan were not invited to participate. The USSR was invited but chose not to send any athletes. The United States team won the most total medals, 84, and the most gold medals, 38. Britain won 23 medals, three of them gold, two in rowing and one in sailing.

Chapter 18
The final hurrah

Swift's final full League season was in 1948-49. He featured in the following side against Burnley on the opening day: Swift, Sproston, Westwood, Fagan J., McDowall, Walsh, Linacre, Black, McMorran, Smith G. and Clarke.

A single goal defeat and three points from the first six saw manager Jock Thomson reshuffle his forward line with Linacre pushed to centre-forward in place of McMorran and Jackie Oakes, signed from Blackburn Rovers, coming in on the right wing. A 3-1 victory away to Preston, with Linacre scoring, raised hopes of a Championship challenge but City were inconsistent throughout the season.

Set to celebrate his 35th birthday at Christmas there were also signs that Swift's place between the posts was not so certain. He had made an elementary mistake in the opening home fixture against Preston North End, being beaten as he was still throwing his cap into the back of the net by Bobby Langton after just seven seconds; this is the earliest goal ever conceded by Manchester City.

Against Charlton at the Valley the City 'keeper also played badly. He was at fault with at least two of Charlton's goals and even though Verdi Godwin, signed from Blackburn Rovers, scored twice for the away side they lost 3-2.

According to the *Daily Mirror* his performance threatened his place in the England team as: 'Walter Winterbottom, international team manager, watched the match at the Valley. The present form of Swift cannot have impressed him. The rest of the City defence seemed to be affected by the absence of their usual supreme confidence in him.'

In the event he was to keep his place for the England match with Denmark, captaining the side in a disappointing 0-0 draw.

Playing in his first League derby match in a decade the City number one kept a clean sheet in a third consecutive 0-0 draw between the sides. He was fortunate to do so when he made an early positional mistake only for Johnny Morris's shot to clip the upright. Late in the match, though, after pulling a leg muscle the 'keeper – for the umpteenth time – showed his bravery by refusing to leave the field and making two splendid saves.

Unable to recover in time he missed the following game at Birmingham City where, with Thurlow between the sticks, the away side lost 4-1. Jackie Stewart scored all of Birmingham's goals. City's reserve 'keeper enjoyed a better day at St James' Park where he defied newly promoted Newcastle United in a 0-0 draw, before also keeping out Sheffield United in a 2-0 success at Bramall Lane. Back in goal Swift blocked out Middlesbrough in a 1-0 home success. However a combined 11 goals conceded to Sunderland, Wolves and Bolton, where Malcolm Barrass scored four times, had Swift regularly reaching for the back of the net as only a single point was gathered.

With England's selectors, meantime, looking to the future Ted Ditchburn was given the goalkeeper's jersey for the Football League side against the Irish League. Frank Swift did though play one more time for the Football League, when before a 90,000 crowd at Ibrox Stadium he helped his side record a 3-0 win against the Scottish League on 23 March 1949.

There was better news at club level as in December City, with eight points from 12, climbed up the table. A 3-2 success at Stoke on the first day of 1949 then pushed the Maine Road side to within six points of leaders Portsmouth.

However, just one point – another 0-0 draw against Manchester United – from the next three games appeared to put to an end any hopes of Swift winning a second League winners' medal and there was also no chance of a second FA Cup success when Everton beat City 1-0 at Goodison Park.

Swift played three good games in February, refusing to be beaten as City defeated Newcastle, Middlesbrough and Sheffield United all by 1-0 and rose to within seven points of leaders Portsmouth with two games in hand.

Defeats at Villa Park and the Baseball Ground, split by a 1-1 draw at home to Blackpool, in which Swift was unimpressive in goal, ended any hopes of a late title surge even after six points were gathered against Bolton, Liverpool and Chelsea in which City won each match 1-0.

Swift played against Bolton and Chelsea, giving him a fine record in his 10 previous appearances of just seven goals conceded and six clean sheets. The 'keeper may have been 35 years old but he was playing some of the finest football in his illustrious career.

However, even the greatest of 'keepers have to eventually call it a day. City's directors clearly didn't think it would be until, at least, the end of the following season but after Easter draws at home to Sunderland and away to Chelsea the board were handed a letter by Swift announcing his decision to quit.

On 20 April 1949 City chairman Mr Bob Smith told journalists 'Swift's letter came just before yesterday's board meeting. It staggered everyone. We had not the slightest indication that he was contemplating retiring from the game. It is very disappointing for the club.'

The 'keeper though was now employed by the catering firm Smallman's, was training part-time and had started to look to the future by buying his home on Wyverne Road in Chorlton-cum-Hardy from the club a few weeks earlier.

In his letter he wrote 'I am very sorry to leave the club but the break had [to?] come sometime. ...you will be aware that for sometime I have been engaged in commercial pursuits, and have been finding an increasing proportion of my time is taken up with my occupation.'

Despite his long years of service, the City directors were not at all pleased and Swift reported that despite their request he would not be changing his mind about retiring; a farewell party set for 28 April 1949 would be going ahead, even though the directors had indicated they would not be attending.

As a result when the City bus departed for Molineux after a pre-match meal at a nearby hotel it was not a pleasant place to be. That was because Frank Swift departed from his usual jocular mood, designed to help everyone relax, with neither the 'keeper nor the accompanying directors speaking to one another.

The game was Frank Swift's final match at Molineux. City's 8-0 hammering there before Christmas 1933 had given him his chance in the first team, but the ground had not proved to be a lucky one with five defeats in which he conceded 15 goals. In the circumstances a 1-1 draw wasn't too bad.

Prior to kick-off Swift was given a wonderful ovation and on reaching his goal area he was met by the Wolves mascot who shook him by the hand. There were huge cheers.

Opposition captain Billy Wright was a player Swift admired and he selected him to partner his now manager, Stan Cullis, when he chose his best ever eleven saying: 'He does everything with a flourish, gets through an amazing amount of work, and yet is probably the fittest player on the field at the final whistle. Perhaps the greatest tribute I can pay him is that when I have sat down later to analyse a game in which we have played, he is the boy who had cropped up most in my thoughts.' By the time Wright finished playing for Wolves in May 1959 he had made 541 appearances as well as a then record breaking 105 international caps for England. Today there is a statue of him outside Molineux.

On Monday 25 April City's directors had clearly seen sense. Huge numbers of letters to local papers had reminded them of Swift's talents and his contribution to previous successes. It was reported that Swift and the board had settled differences over an occasion to mark his retirement – 'an occasion of special character will probably by dated for the close season.' (*Manchester Evening News*)

On 27 April what was intended to be Swift's final League match at Maine Road saw crowds turn up early to cheer the 'keeper prior to kick-off. The result might have been better, a 3-0 win for Arsenal showing a big gulf in the sides.

Walter Allison recalls that when Jimmy Logie scored the Gunners third 'he collided with Frank Swift, who smiled and shook his hand in congratulation'.

A more lasting memory – not least because it was caught on camera – was that of Eddie Humphrys at the end of the game. With all the City players lifting Frank Swift shoulder high he was taken on a lap of honour. He was still being carried down the tunnel when 'I shook hands with him. I actually don't remember how I had ended up on the edge of the pitch but it was a great feeling and I could hear the fans and officials close by cheering. Swift was a big hero for City fans and well loved by football fans of all clubs'. Humphrys later got Swift to autograph a photo of the moment when the pair shook hands.

Two days after the Arsenal game hundreds of City supporters turned up for a farewell party for Frank Swift. It was held at the Waterloo Hotel on Waterloo Road, Hightown. Fans queued to shake his hand and have their photographs taken with the big 'keeper, who was happy to enjoy a pint or two.

On Saturday 7 May 1949 Swift ran out at Leeds Road to face relegation threatened Huddersfield Town. He had been hoping to face his former City colleague, Peter Doherty, but an injury left the Irishman on the sidelines in what would have been his final Division One game before becoming Doncaster Rovers player-manager. Also joining him in the managerial seat was McDowall, who took charge at Wrexham after making over 100 first-team appearances at Manchester City. The midfielder, who was born in British India, was to be soon back at Maine Road and under his managerial reins City were to capture the FA Cup in 1956, beating Birmingham City 3-1 in the Final. McDowall left in 1963 after City were relegated to Division Two.

Not surprisingly Swift chose Doherty who, as manager of Northern Ireland, took his country to the quarter-finals of the 1958 World Cup in Sweden, as a member of his finest ever eleven: 'Peter was at his most dangerous when, seemingly, he had lost control of the ball. Many's the time I have seen him score a great goal, or make a perfect pass when you could bet almost anything that he was going to fall over. Peter is such a delight to watch, for it is obvious to all that he loves to play football.' According to Harry Gregg [the man who played in goal for Northern Ireland at the 1958 World Cup] 'Frank Swift would often talk about Peter Doherty when you were in his company.'

Swift also rated Doherty as among the three deadliest penalty takers in football during his time in the game, the others being Blackpool's Willie Buchan and Arsenal's Denis Compton.

Swift was handed a sprig of heather by a young enthusiast before the match that the Terriers won 1-0 to escape the drop by a point. The City 'keeper played brilliantly with the Huddersfield Examiner headlining Monday's back page with: SWIFT ALMOST PROVED INVINCIBLE and reporting that 'he alone seemed to hold Town's fortunes in his hand'. At the end he was carried from the pitch on the shoulders of celebrating City and Huddersfield fans. The result meant that City finished seventh in the League while for Swift there was the prospect of ending his career at the top, the FA having chosen him as a member of their end of season tour to Scandinavia, Holland and France.

Airplane tragedy

Football on the continent had suffered a real blow on 4 May 1949 when the entire Torino squad, winners of three consecutive Serie A titles between 1946 and 1948, were killed when their plane, returning from a friendly match against Benfica in Portugal, crashed into a hill near their home city.

Thirty-one people – including 18 players and manager Andrea Agnisetta – were killed including 10 Italian internationals of which seven – Mazzola, Loik, Menti, Grezar, Gabetto, Bacigalupo and Ballarin – had been in the Italian side beaten 4-0 by England in Turin the previous summer. Torino were to complete their season fielding a youth side, their four opponents also fielding their youth sides as Torino won a fourth title. The Italian club have yet to win a fifth.

Over the summer of 1949 Frank Swift was looking forward to becoming a City fan. On 3 August it was reported that he had applied for stand season tickets for himself, his wife and two friends. His request was placed on the list behind those with priority, last season's ticket holders.

In response to several clubs having approached him, particularly as an assessor of young talent, Swift said: 'If I do anything of that nature on Saturday afternoons, I'd rather do that for City.'

Frank Swift had also by this time become a Freemason. Michael Horwich, a director at Manchester City for many years, later recalled his attendance at his mother Lodge, Trafford No 1496 in West Lancashire Province before and after he was himself initiated in January 1950. The pair had met in 1947 when 'Frank told my father that he was attending his Third Degree ceremony'.

Chapter 19
Brief return before new career dawns

As reserve to Swift, the 1949-50 season was now Thurlow's chance to make the number-one spot his own and therefore there was a surprise when he was missing for the City trial match with Ronnie Powell in goal for the Blues and his brother Tom for the Reds.

Both youngsters were not ready to play first-team football and just three days before the big kick-off at home to Aston Villa it was announced that following the 'unfortunate withdrawal of Thurlow that Frank Swift had come out of retirement' to help out City by playing in the fixture. He would be again facing Trevor Ford.

With Westwood, who made 248 first-team appearances in all for the club, appointed as the new City captain the 39,954 crowd inside Maine Road gave 'A special cheer for Swift' prior to kick-off, the game finishing 3-3.

Amid rumours that City were set to spend a five figure sum on a new 'keeper there were also reports that the players were considering a scheme to provide financial aid to Thurlow, who had been diagnosed with tuberculosis and had gone to Norfolk to convalesce. Sadly, the 'keeper was to die in 1956. He was just 34.

At home to Portsmouth, Swift showed some of his finest talents, dealing confidently with crosses and corners, punching when under pressure and getting down smartly when twice the ball was slid beyond the City back four to onrushing attackers. With Smith scoring the only goal the home side won 1-0.

Swift retained his place for the derby match with Manchester United, the first to be played at Old Trafford since 1936. He collected dangerous crosses as United started brightly but was later powerless to prevent two efforts from Stan Pearson cancelling out Jimmy Munro's single goal for City in a match refereed by Halifax's Arthur Ellis, who later became famous for his compère role in BBC1's *It's a Knockout*. This good-natured competition pitched towns and cities against each other, attracted a nationwide audience of millions and ran from 1966 to 1982.

Four days later, Swift played what proved to be his final competitive game for Manchester City as they drew 0-0 with Everton before a midweek crowd of 27,265.

Manchester City: Swift, Williams, Westwood, Walsh, Fagan J., Murray, Linacre, Munro, Smith G., Black, Oakes J.
Everton: Sagar, Saunders, Dugdale, Farrell, Jones T.G., Lello, Corr, Wainwright, Catterick, Fielding, Eglington.

The 'keeper was, in fact, due to feature against Fulham the following Saturday but on the day it was reported he had not recovered from an injury sustained against the Toffees. With Powell in goal Manchester City won 2-0 and it was to start a 10-game run in the first team for the 'keeper. But with only one further win and five defeats City were on the lookout for a 'keeper of stature to replace the now (finally) retired Frank Swift. The choice was to prove unpopular, and the new man even conceded seven in his third game as Derby overwhelmed City 7-0 at the Baseball Ground. But given time the new man was to be just the man to follow 'Big Frank' in the City goal.

Former German Prisoner of War Bert Trautmann was to become a big City star, but up front in 1949-50 the side struggled and between mid-September and early April no goals were scored in 14 consecutive away League games. A 13-game winless run that started after Christmas meant that despite a late winning run, Manchester City returned to Division Two after just three seasons in the top-flight.

Swift had welcomed Trautmann to City and he made clear his opposition to a possible fans boycott of games in which he played. Still officially signed as a City player, Matt Busby's request to the City board to be allowed to sign him as a reserve to long-serving Jack Crompton were not entertained by the player himself or those who held his contract.

Busby said of Frank Swift: 'Swifty was a mere boy when he played with me in City's winning Cup Final against Portsmouth in 1934. The occasion proved too much for him and at the end of it he fainted. Trying to pull himself together in the dressing room afterwards he stammered: "Have we won?" He developed into the cheeriest dressing-room man in the game of football, whether playing for Manchester City or England. In any company he was a brilliant raconteur. In the dressing room his infectious good humour brought a smile to even the most nervous beginner.

On the pitch he was the first showman goalkeeper. But first he was a magnificent goalkeeper and second a showman. He believed in entertaining the crowd. He played with a smile and with banter to match. Some opponent would send in a mighty shot. The big hands of Big Swifty would envelop it as if it had been a gentle lob. "Good shot, that, Joe," he would say to the man who had cracked it in. No matter who was captain there was only one boss in Swifty's goalmouth. It went without saying, though he said it often enough: "If I shout, get out of my way. If you don't I'll knock you out of the way." He was the first goalkeeper I saw who threw the ball out, accurately and over great distances, to a colleague, instead of merely punting it up the pitch and giving the other team an equal chance of getting it. He would pick it up one-handed and throw it like a cricket ball.

For a big man, Swifty was phenomenally agile. He narrowed the angle for an opponent to shoot in as if he had made a science of it. His showmanship was not exhibitionism. He wanted to demonstrate that football could include a bit of fun, a quality sadly missing from the game today. He was immensely popular everywhere he played, as popular with opposition and opposition supporters as with his own team and his own team's supporters. If any footballer could be termed lovable, Big Swifty was the man.' (*Soccer at the Top*, 1973)

Fortunately Manchester City's stay in Division Two in the 1950s was brief and, with new man Les McDowall in charge, promotion behind Preston North End was achieved in 1950-51. Four seasons later Manchester City were back at Wembley in their first FA Cup Final since 1934. By now Frank Swift was writing for the *News of the World* and he covered the match with Newcastle United, who were seeking to capture the trophy for the third time in five seasons.

Manchester City had sought to utilise the Don Revie-plan that was modelled on the Hungarian tactics of employing a deep-lying centre-forward. In 1953 the Magyars had used this to devastating effect to beat England 6-3 at Wembley before triumphing 7-1 in Budapest when the sides met again the following year.

City's chances were dealt a devastating blow when England international Jimmy Meadows tore the ligaments in his right knee after 20 minutes. Despite going in at half-time level at 1-1, the 1934 winners were overrun in the first 15 minutes of the second and the two goals conceded during this time saw Newcastle win the game 3-1. In his match report Swift praised the winners and offered consoling words to the gallant losers.

City and Swift were back at Wembley the following season. The former 'keeper had reported on City's 1-0 defeat of Spurs in the semi-final for the *News of the World*. The victory had been a deserved one but Swift felt 'City never approached their sparkle of the past few weeks or cleared the last hurdle with brilliant football'. Facing Manchester City in the Final were Birmingham City.

The match on 5 May 1956 was the North's very first weekend of commercial television after Granada had begun their weekday service two days earlier. The FA Cup Final was shown live and in an attempt to persuade viewers to forsake the BBC coverage of the same event Frank Swift and England captain Billy Wright joined commentator Peter Lloyd at Wembley.

The following morning Frank Swift's *News of the World* column reported that 'the boil that kept Bill Spurdie out of the Cup Final turned out to be a blessing in disguise' for his former club as it allowed them to play both Bobby Johnstone, scorer of City's goal against Newcastle the previous season, and Don Revie. Johnstone became the first player to score in consecutive Wembley Finals when he netted his side's third in a 3-1 win.

The last time Manchester City had won the FA Cup their 'keeper had fainted at the end of the game. This time, the collapse of Bert Trautmann was much more serious as it was later discovered he had played on with a broken neck following a collision with Peter Murphy. Two vertebrae had wedged together, narrowly saving his life.

Chapter 20
Munich 1958

Frank Swift was one of nine journalists who joined the Manchester United squad to fly from Ringway Airport, Manchester to Belgrade on the morning of Monday 3 February 1958.

Ringway had seen its first aeroplane land there in May 1937 and had quickly expanded such that by 1958 half a million passengers were using it. Swirling fog meant there were grave doubts about whether the Elizabethan airliner would ever be allowed to take off for Yugoslavia, a country that later disintegrated during the Balkan Wars of the 1990s.

Despite the cold, damp weather the atmosphere was a good one. Manchester United had just played one of the greatest games ever seen in England, beating Arsenal 5-4 at Highbury to maintain the pressure on League leaders Wolverhampton Wanderers at the top of the table. The Black Country side were threatening to stop Matt Busby's team from winning the League in three consecutive seasons; a feat last achieved by Arsenal in the 1930s. The Championship rivals were due to meet at Old Trafford just two days after Manchester United were due to arrive back from their trip to play Red Star Belgrade in the quarter-finals of the European Cup.

The competition was in its third season. The previous season, Manchester United had become the first English side to take up UEFA's entry invitation. In 1955-56 the Football League had persuaded the Division One champions Chelsea not to enter the competition, as it was feared that European Football would eventually become as important as domestic football.

Busby though wanted to take on the very best and so when Manchester United won the League in 1955-56 he was never going to miss out on the chance of playing Europe's elite. In the first season Manchester United had reached the last four but were beaten by holders and eventual winners Real Madrid.

Manchester United had beaten Shamrock Rovers and Dukla Prague in the first two rounds of the 1957-58 competition and with the likes of Tommy Taylor, Duncan Edwards, Dennis Viollet and Eddie Colman showing increasing maturity there was genuine confidence that the side would go on to become European Champions in 1958.

Following the second leg away to Dukla Prague, heavy fog over England had prevented the Manchester United party from returning on the day after the game. It was this re-routing that led to Matt Busby and club secretary, Walter Crickmer chartering a plane for the trip to Belgrade as they did not want to be unable to fulfil their fixture against Wolves. A failure to do so would undoubtedly have resulted in a heavy fine and possibly a point's deduction.

When the mists did clear at 8am on 3 February the British European Airways Elizabethan class Airspeed AS-57 Ambassador, used to ferry Her Majesty the Queen, was quickly on its way to Belgrade, stopping en route to refuel in Munich.

Having won the first leg 2-1 at Old Trafford then a draw would be good enough to take the away side through. Against Arsenal, Manchester United had taken a three-goal lead only to be pulled back to 3-3 before eventually winning a nine-goal thriller. At half-time in Belgrade, United with goals from Viollet and two from Bobby Charlton again led 3-0 and Frank Swift was reported by fellow journalist Frank Taylor as telling his fellow journalists that 'if the lads don't get too cocky and take it too easily' then the tie was over.

In the second half the home side poured forward and after reducing the arrears to 3-2, Kostic from a free-kick just outside the box pulled the scores level on 88 minutes. Frank Swift thought the United 'keeper Harry Gregg had made a mistake and said to Frank Taylor: 'What a shame, Harry has had a wonderful game. But he should have stood at the near post and let Kostic shoot for the far post. The ball has longer to travel – and Harry would have longer to see it in its flight.'

This would not have been the first time Swift had criticised the Irishman following his December 1957 transfer from Doncaster Rovers to Manchester United for a world record fee for a goalkeeper of £23,000.

In January Workington Town had at one point led Manchester 1-0 in the third round FA Cup before a Dennis Viollet hat-trick had seen Matt Busby's side past the plucky Third Division North side.

'He wrote that I had spent too much time off my goalline' says Harry Gregg 'so when I say Frank was a wonderful character it is not because he always wrote nice things about me. It is easy to be a character and not have the ability, but Big Swiftie had ability and character. Put these two things together, what more could you want?'

The day before the match in Belgrade Frank Swift told the Manchester United 'keeper about where he had purchased his goalkeeping gloves during his long career. As a mark of respect Gregg later made the trip to the Ashton-under-Lyne shop to buy a pair.

Despite the Yugoslavian champion's late equaliser it was the away side that advanced on a 5-4 aggregate to face Italian champions AC Milan in the semi-finals of the competition. Next morning the party of players, club officials and journalists flew to Munich for a refuelling stop.

Frank Swift along with seven of his journalist colleagues sat in the back, telling Taylor that the 'tail is the safest place', a view he had formed from the experiences of the war in which many tail gunners had been thrown safely clear when their bomber planes had crash-landed. Taylor, having read that in a terrible air crash the only survivor had been a person facing the rear of the plane, had refused the offer and thus spent the trip to Germany regretting doing so as he looked back down the plane to see his colleagues laughing and carrying on among themselves.

There was a good atmosphere among journalists covering the European matches, although that didn't prevent all of them trying to obtain an exclusive at each other's expense. Journalism, then and now, is a highly competitive world and newspaper editors want good copy in order to sell their papers.

The trip back to Manchester was over 2,000 miles and would take over 10 hours. The stop in Munich was brief; although still long enough to have journalists worrying that their colleagues had picked up some exclusives since departure from Belgrade and were now phoning the news back to their sports desks. When the plane did begin take off at 14.31 Captain Kenneth Rayment was forced to abort it after Captain James Thain noticed a fluctuation in boost pressures in the engine of the aircraft.

When a second attempt was made at 14.34 this was also called off without the aircraft having left the ground after the engines over-accelerated. All passengers were asked to disembark and Bobby Charlton later recalled in his autobiography that this resulted in the 'mood dipping not in a dramatic way but quite perceptibly and people became less chatty and the card players became less absorbed by their game.

Frank Swift, the former Manchester City and England 'keeper demanded to know what was going on and was told there was a small technical problem that was being sorted out.

'I just assumed there was just a shortage of power and it was something they were working on in an attempt to get everything right before we took off.' Charlton disliked travelling abroad before the days of jet engines and particularly disliked the Elizabethan aircraft as he felt it was too heavy and took too long to climb into its flight path.

When the travelling party returned to the airport lounge Duncan Edwards took the chance to wire a telegram to his Manchester landlady that read: 'All flights cancelled, flying tomorrow. Duncan.'

Back in Manchester the *Evening News* and *Evening Chronicle* were both able to sell a few more of their early edition newspapers by reporting the team had been held up in Munich. Aware of the big game looming on the Saturday it would be the sort of story that would attract United fans' attention.

Edwards was wrong, and within minutes the party was asked to reboard for the fateful flight. Harry Gregg recalls, 'Frank had taken Donnny Davies coat and was acting the clown in trying to get it on'. Davies was just 5ft 2in.

At 14.56 clearance was sought to fly home and just after three o'clock permission was granted. The plane quickly gained speed before according to Thain the needle dropped back from 117 knots an hour to 105. Both pilots realised they were running out of runway and in the back Taylor later recalled seeing the perimeter fence rushing towards the plane. On it hurtled before hitting a nearby house, home to a family of six. The mother and three children inside narrowly escaped with their lives.

Not so lucky were many of those in the aircraft, which by now was in two and divided by a gap of 100 yards. Twenty were dead. Seven were Manchester United players Geoff Bent, Roger Byrne, Eddie Colman, Mark Jones, David Pegg, Tommy Taylor, Liam Whelan. Three members of the Manchester United staff had perished – Walter Crickmer, Tom Curry and Bert Whalley. Travel agent Bela Miklos and Willie Satinoff, racecourse owner and close friend of Matt Busby, had been killed. So too had cabin steward Tom Cable.

Seven journalists had perished – Alf Clarke (who for many years after the war provided the opposition player's profiles in the City programme), Donny Davies, George Follows, Henry Rose, Eric Thompson, Tom Jackson – the man who had first coined the phrase 'The Busby Babes' and Henry Rose. Frank Swift had survived the crash but like his very good friend Matt Busby he was in a critical condition.

The United manager, like a number of those who survived, benefitted from some tremendous acts of bravery – especially by Captain James Thain, Harry Gregg and *Daily Mail* photographer Peter Howard and his colleague Ted Ellyard – who ignoring burning fuel that threatened to blow up the remainder of the aircraft, pulled people to safety.

German inefficiency

Help though was slow in arriving, and in what is easily the best (some might say only accurate) account of the tragedy, Harry Gregg recalls in his autobiography *Harry's Game* that it was 'ordinary folk, not firemen or ambulance crews' who were first on the scene. Gregg himself helped Jackie Blanchflower and Matt Busby into the back of a coal truck and along with Berry, Viollet, Charlton, Bill Foulkes and Maria Miklos, the wife of Bela, the driver set off at record pace.

At the Rechts der Isar hospital in Munich, staff battled to cope with the scale of the crash. Among the medical specialists was Professor Franz Kessel, head of the neuro-surgical department. When Germany had invaded his home country of Austria in 1938 he had left his native Vienna for Manchester where he worked for many years. He was an avid sportsman and he quickly recognised Frank Swift and then when he saw Matt Busby he told his colleagues that the injured and dying were an English football team.

According to Frank Taylor, Kessel told him that initially he did not believe the former Manchester City 'keeper was too badly injured, but the 44-year-old Blackpool larger-than-life character died as he was carried into the hospital. Later a post mortem examination revealed his aorta artery carrying blood to the heart had been severed, probably by his seat belt. Whether Frank Swift would have survived if the rescue services had been quicker to the scene after the aircraft had crashed no one can say for certain but his chances would surely have been greater. He was the 21st person to die and later Duncan Edwards and Captain Rayment became the 22nd and 23rd victims of the Munich air crash.

No wonder therefore that the following day the *Daily Mirror* reported 'THIS WAS THE BLACKEST DAY IN BRITISH SPORT' as Peter Wilson wrote of his 'old friend and colleague, Archie Ledbrooke, the man who lived for Soccer'. His body, and that of the 20 other crash victims, including Frank Swift, were returned to England on the following Monday. When 10 of the coffins were subsequently transported from Manchester airport to Old Trafford a crowd in excess of 100,000 people lined the streets to pay their respects.

Frank Swift's young half-brother Alf was working for John C. Lowes, builders' merchants on Collingwood Avenue, Blackpool, on the day of the tragedy. His transport manager told him there had been a crash involving Manchester United players and it was very serious and that there would be a news bulletin at 6pm. Interviewed in 2008 Alf said: 'That's how I found out our Frank was dead – by watching the news. The next few days were rough.

All the family was very upset – my sister and my two brothers. We went to Manchester and because the coffin had come from abroad it was sealed, so we never really got the chance to say goodbye.

The last time I saw him was the Sunday before he went to Munich. Me and the wife took one of our children for a visit and that was the last time we spoke.'

Frank Swift's wife Doris and daughter Jean had first become aware of the tragedy through the latter's work at Granada Television newsroom. Jean was pregnant at the time with daughter Kari who was the first born to her and husband Carl Robert on 31 July 1958. After meeting at work, the pair had wed the previous year. Working in television and radio later took them all over the world.

'It came through on a Telex from Reuters that the United side had crashed, and that evening Doris and Jean walked from their home on Wyverne Road to the Busby's house, where they were regular visitors, to await news. There was a lot of confusion about who was injured and who had been killed,' says Kari Dodson, whose three children Mark, Ben and Andrew are all very proud of their great-granddad.

Reuters telex said 'Manchester United aircraft crashed on take-off …heavy loss of life feared.'

Later Jean had two more children. Rolf was born on 6 September 1959 and as a teenager was good enough to be taken on Fulham and Manchester United's books as a goalkeeper.

Jane was born on St George's Day 1964. Her three children Tom, Alice and Jim are proud of their great-granddad's achievements.

Funeral

The funeral of Frank Swift was held at St Margaret's Church, Whalley Range, Manchester, on Wednesday 12 February 1958. The same day Roger Byrne, who like his England colleague had played 33 times for his country, was also laid to rest.

There were 50 wreaths, including those from the Football Association and Football League plus the various clubs and organisations with whom the 'keeper had been associated.

Two hours before the service started at 3.30pm 80 people had gathered and the Church was full by 3pm with over 300 people outside in the Church gardens.

The principal mourners were Mrs Doris Swift, widow, her daughter Jean and son-in-law Carl, two brothers and a sister, Mrs Alice Barker.

Among those present were former Manchester City colleagues, Jack Bray, Fred Tilson, Alec Herd, Eric Brook, Bert Sproston and Eric Westwood, some of whom acted as pallbearers. Frank's former captain at Manchester City, Sam Cowan, remembered him by saying:

'Big man, big hands, big heart. At six feet three inches tall and weighing 14 stone, he treated a football with the same contemptuous ease that a fast bowler treated a cricket ball – he had the heart of a lion, both on and off the field. He was simply special.

There may have been a few goalkeepers as good, but there will never be another "Big Swifty". He was just a great 'keeper with a superb sense of anticipation, boundless physical fitness, loads of confidence and, of course, an enormous pair of hands. He would pick a ball out of the air as easy as a fielder would gobble up a catch at slip. What a man.'

Later in 1958, Basil Easterbrook, London football correspondent of *Thomson Newspapers* wrote: 'Try to picture Frank in his early days in thigh boots, rough blue jersey, and large competent hands hauling in the nets at Fleetwood. It was almost worth a chorus of the famous old ballad *The Fishermen of England*. When he put on his sou'wester and went out with the local lifeboat, Frank made the perfect subject for a portrait of a lifeboatman to be shown on posters on National Flag Day.'

On 23 February 1958 the people of Blackpool were given their chance to say their final farewells to a local hero. Many hundreds packed out the Central Working Men's Club for a Memorial Service conducted by the Reverend R. Kirkham and Councillor Clifford Cross, the Deputy Mayor of Blackpool.

There was a third service conducted two days later at St Bride's Church, Fleet Street, London when the lives of all eight journalists killed at Munich were remembered in a service conducted by the Reverend Cyril M. Armitage and the Reverend Canon C.B. Mortlock.

Just under two months later it was reported that Frank Swift left £3,592 in his will. This would be the equivalent of £68,000 today.

In memoriam
Since Frank Swift was killed at Munich a number of events have been held that mark his passing. The first saw a charity concert at the Central Workingmen's Club in Blackpool raise funds for a magnificent trophy, the lid of which was in the shape of the goalkeeper. This was presented to the Blackpool and District Schools' FA, who decided to award the trophy to the winners of a new under-15s competition.

The first winners in 1958 were Highfield School and the competition ran until 2010.

In 1960 Frank Swift's colleague Frank Taylor unveiled a bronze plaque at Old Trafford to his eight fallen journalist colleagues. This original was stolen in 1980 but a replica is now located behind the counter in the press entrance. There are also two memorials in Germany in which all 23 victims of the tragedy are remembered, including one in the vicinity of the old Munich airport. It states in both English and German, 'In memory of all those who lost their lives here in the Munich air disaster on 6 February 1958.'

Meanwhile in 1977 a street near to Manchester City's Maine Road ground was named in Frank Swift's honour.

Twenty-one years later when the Football League, in celebration of its 100th season, selected their 100 legends, Frank Swift was one of 11 'keepers to be on the hallowed list.

Then in 2004 Frank Swift was among the first group of former Manchester City players to be inducted into the Manchester City Hall of Fame. Joining him were two members of the 1936-37 Championship winning side, Peter Doherty and Eric Brook.

On 6 February 2008, 50 years to the day of the Munich tragedy, a memorial service was held at Old Trafford. Frank Swift's daughter Jean and granddaughter Kari, accompanied by her three sons, attended.

'It was very enjoyable and Manchester United were superb. We had gone with this great sense of anticipation, certainly my sons had and they were looking forward to meeting famous people such as Sir Bobby Charlton and Sir Alex Ferguson.

'When we entered Old Trafford, people were falling over themselves to come and meet my boys. They were going "You're Frank Swift's great-grandson". They were blown away by these very famous people showing such an interest – people like Harry Gregg, Bobby Charlton and Sandy Busby. They loved Harry Gregg to bits. It was extraordinary and the plaque that was unveiled in the tunnel was very good and everything was done with great dignity,' says Kari Dodson.

Four days later Kari's sister Jane, and Frank Swift's six great-grandchildren were guests of Manchester United when they played Manchester City in the local derby match. They were again warmly welcomed by Manchester United, who all agree have done more to keep alive the memory of Frank Swift than Manchester City.

As Jane explains though watching the match proved an unpleasant experience: 'After enjoying some lovely food we were ushered into the VIP areas but when we cheered for a City goal people screamed at us. They did not know who we were and the stewards said "don't get up or clap". It is lovely that my granddad is remembered, and there is a connection with both Manchester clubs, but he wouldn't have wanted us to endure such hostility.'

In 2009 Frank Swift was also inducted into the National Football Museum Hall of Fame and in the same year the website goal.com selected the 'keeper at number 25 in the list of all time English greats, one place ahead of Manchester City's next highest placed player, Colin Bell.

If he had still been around, Frank Swift would no doubt have been delighted. At the same time he would have been at least as happy with knowing that his talent had been recognised by children from St Annes, near Blackpool. Hove Road Park, near the Young Men's Christian Association (YMCA), was transformed by the 'Shaping the Place' regeneration project in 2008-09.

It had been used as a dumping ground and the playground was a sight for sore eyes. Fylde Borough Council aimed to do it up and asked children from three local primary schools, Heyhouses, St Thomas' and Our Lady of the Star to help them. To go alongside the new multi-use games area, artist Shane Johnstone worked with them on an intricate mosaic portrait of Frank Swift, who according to Christine Miller, head of partnerships at the council 'was chosen by the children themselves after they read a YMCA booklet from 1972. This referred to Frank playing on Hove Road Park as a youngster for Revoe YMCA in the end of season YM Medal Competition tournament that drew teams from across the area and which attracted crowds of up to a few thousand.

I think they were mesmerised by his hand span as in their presentation to the community that is what they mentioned. They also saw him as a local boy who had gone from a less than charmed background to make good. Someone who played for England, who had then become a journalist and who then tragically died in the air disaster.'

In a ceremony undertaken by Blackpool legend Jimmy Armfield and Mayor of Fylde Councillor Susan Fazackerley a large crowd helped celebrate the park's official opening on 5 April 2009. Following which the new facilities have been widely used by the local community.

In summary, how good was Frank Swift?

Frank Swift was by any standards an exceptional 'keeper. If you had to select an England World Cup squad from all the ages then along with Peter Shilton and Gordon Banks he would be one of the three 'keepers selected. The author of this book never saw him play, but many who did rate him better than the latter two. For Manchester City it would be a straight choice between the Blackpool lad and Bert Trautmann as to who is the club's finest.

Frank Swift statistics

Fleetwood reserves
13 League, 5 Cup
Manchester City
1933-34 – 22 League, 8 FA Cup
1934-35 – 42 League, 1 FA Cup, 1 Charity Shield
1935-36 – 42 League, 3 FA Cup
1936-37 – 42 League, 4 FA Cup
1937-38 – 42 League, 5 FA Cup, 1 Charity Shield
1938-39 – 41 League (Division Two), 2 FA Cup
1945-46 – 4 FA Cup
1946-47 – 35 League (Division Two), 4 FA Cup
1947-48 – 33 League, 3 FA Cup
1948-49 – 35 League, 1 FA Cup
1949-50 – 4 League

Frank Swift also played in the first three matches of 1939-40, before war brought the League season to an end. He also made 102 League War appearances for Manchester City plus 31 War Cup appearances.

Wartime appearances with other clubs
Aldershot 12, Hamilton Academical 11, Fulham 5, Reading 4, Liverpool 2, Charlton 1

England caps
19 full, 14 wartime

Football League appearances
4

Bibliography

Football in the Goalmouth Frank Swift and Roy Peskett, 1948

Spotlight on Football Peter Doherty, 1947

Stanley Matthews – My Autobiography The Way it Was Stanley Matthews

Football is my Game Stanley Mortensen, 1948

The Clown Prince of Soccer Len Shackleton, 1956

Sir Matt Busby: A Tribute – The Official Authorised Biography Rick Glanvill

Joe Fagan – Reluctant Champion Andrew Fagan and Mark Platt

The Day a Team Died Frank Taylor

Harry's Game: An Autobiography Harry Gregg and Roger Anderson

Purnell's Encyclopedia of Association Football 1972

The Hamlyn Book of World Soccer Peter Arnold and Christopher Davis, 1973

Football Legend: The Authorised Biography of Tom Finney Paul Agnew

Golden Boy: A Biography of Wilf Mannion Nick Varley

League Football and the Men Who Made it Simon Inglis

Yesterday's Britain: The Illustrated Story of How We Lived, Worked and Played in this Century Reader's Digest

Manchester the Greatest City Gary James

Farewell to Maine Road Gary James

"Get in There!": Tommy Lawton – My Friend, My Father Barrie Williams and Tom Lawton Junior

Charlie Hurley: 'The Greatest Centre Half the World has Ever Seen' Mark Metcalf

Golden Boot: Football's Top Scorers Tony Matthews and Mark Metcalf

Raich Carter - The Biography Frank Garrick

Stan Cullis: The Iron Manager Jim Holden

Football Nation Andrew Ward and John Williams

Soccer at War 1939-1945 Jack Rollins

Jackie Milburn: A Man of Two Halves Jack Milburn

Viollet: the Life of a Legendary Goalscorer Roy Cavanagh and Brian Hughes

My Manchester United Years Bobby Charlton

Dixie Dean: The Inside Story of a Football Icon John Keith

Billy Liddell: The Legend Who Carried the Kop John Keith

Manchester United's First Championship 1907-08 Mark Metcalf

Total Football: Sunderland AFC 1935-37 Paul Days and Mark Metcalf

Lytham St Anne's and Fylde YMCA Golden Jubilee Commemorative Brochure 1922-1972 Harry Yules and Ian Patterson

The Who's Who of:
　Arsenal – Tony Matthews
　Aston Villa – Tony Matthews
　Barnsley – Grenville Firth and Cath Speight
　Chelsea – Tony Matthews
　Derby County – Gerald Mortimer
　England – Dean Hayes
　Everton – Tony Matthews
　Liverpool – Tony Matthews
　Manchester United – Garth Dykes
　Newcastle – Paul Joannou
　Stoke City – Tony Matthews
　Sunderland – Garth Dykes and Doug Lamming

The Complete Record of:
　Birmingham City – Tony Matthews
　Blackburn Rovers – Mike Jackman
　Blackpool – Roy Calley
　Bolton Wanderers – Simon Marland
　Middlesbrough – Harry Glasper
　Millwall – Richard Lindsay and Eddie Tarrant
　Wolverhampton Wanderers – Tony Matthews

The FA Cup – Mike Collett
The History of Sunderland 1979-1986 Bill Simmons and Bob Graham

Acknowledgements

Special thanks to:

Robert Boyling
David Wood
Jim Fox
Gerry Wolstenholme
Staff at Manchester, Bolton, Blackpool and Liverpool Local Studies Libraries
King of the Kippax fanzine
Peter Holme
Steve Caron
Tony Collier and Phil Brown at Fleetwood Town
Graeme Brown at Hamilton Accies Trust
Jim Watson at Hamilton Academical
Malcolm Finlayson
Tony Matthews
Andrea Wood
Iris Swift
Bryan Douglas
Jane Wilkin
Kari Dodson
Walter Allison
Geoff Ireland
Mary Donsworth
Ian Niven
Arthur Bower
Eddie Humphrys
Michael Duffy
Steve Gordos
Harry Gregg
Rolf Robert
Bryn Owen
Christine Miller
Arnold Sumner
Roger Booth
Alwynne Cains